I0832780

J. W. De FOREST,

(*Author of "Overland," etc.*)

OVERLAND.

A NOVEL.

BY

J. W. DE FOREST,

AUTHOR OF "KATE BEAUMONT," "MISS RAVENEL'S CONVERSION," &c.

NEW YORK:

SHELDON AND COMPANY,

677 BROADWAY, AND 214 & 216 MERCER ST.

Entered according to Act of Congress, in the year 1871, by
SHELDON AND COMPANY,
In the Office of the Librarian of Congress, at Washington.

Steretoyped by SMITH & McDOUGAL, 82 Beekman Street, New York.

OVERLAND.

By J. W. De Forest, Author of "Kate Beaumont," etc.

CHAPTER I.

IN those days, Santa Fé, New Mexico, was an undergrown, decrepit, out-at-elbows ancient hidalgo of a town, with not a scintillation of prosperity or grandeur about it, except the name of capital.

It was two hundred and seventy years old; and it had less than five thousand inhabitants. It was the metropolis of a vast extent of country, not destitute of natural wealth; and it consisted of a few narrow, irregular streets, lined by one-story houses built of sun-baked bricks. Owing to the fine climate, it was difficult to die there; but owing to many things not fine, it was almost equally difficult to live.

Even the fact that Santa Fé had been for a period under the fostering wings of the American eagle did not make it grow much. Westward-ho emigrants halted there to refit and buy cattle and provisions; but always started resolutely on again, westward-hoing across the continent. Nobody seemed to want to stay in Santa Fé, except the aforesaid less than five thousand inhabitants, who were able to endure the place because they had never seen any other, and who had become a part of its gray, dirty, lazy lifelessness and despondency.

For a wonder, this old atom of a metropolis had lately had an increase of population, which was nearly as great a wonder as Sarah having a son when she was "well stricken in years." A couple of new-comers—not a man nor woman less than a couple—now stood on the flat roof of one of the largest of the sun-baked brick houses. By great good luck, moreover, these two were, I humbly trust, worthy of attention. The one was interesting because she was the handsomest girl in Santa Fé, and would have been considered a handsome girl anywhere; the other was interesting because she was a remarkable woman, and even, as Mr. Jefferson Brick might have phrased it, "one of the most remarkable women in our country, sir." At least so she judged, and judged it too with very considerable confidence, being one of those persons who say, "If I know myself, and I think I do."

The beauty was of a mixed type. She combined the blonde and the brunette fashions of loveliness. You might guess at the first glance that she had in her the blood of both the Teutonic and the Latin races. While her skin was clear and rosy, and her curling hair was of a light and bright chestnut, her long, shadowy eyelashes were almost black, and her eyes were of a deep hazel, nearly allied to blackness. Her form had the height of the usual American girl, and the round plumpness of the usual Spanish girl. Even in her bearing and expression you could discover more or less of this union of different races. There was shyness and frankness; there was mistrust and confidence; there was sentimentality and gayety. In short, Clara Muñoz Garcia Van Diemen was a handsome and interesting young lady.

Now for the remarkable woman. Sturdy and prominent old character, obviously. Forty-seven years old, or thereabouts; lots of curling iron-gray hair twisted about her round forehead; a few wrinkles, and not all of the newest. Round face, round and earnest eyes, short, self-confident nose, chin sticking out in search of its own way, mouth trembling with unuttered ideas. Good figure—what Lord Dundreary would call "dem robust," but not so sumptuous as to be merely ornamental; tolerably convenient figure to get about in. Walks up and down, man-fashion, with her hands behind her back—also man-fashion. Such is Mrs. Maria Stanley, the sister of Clara Van Diemen's father, and best known to Clara as Aunt Maria.

"And so this is Santa Fé?" said Aunt Maria, rolling her spectacles over the little wilted city. "Founded in 1581; two hundred and seventy years old. Well, if this is all that man can do in that time, he had better leave colonization to woman."

Clara smiled with an innocent air of half wonder and half amusement, such as you may see on the face of a child when it is shown some new and rather awe-striking marvel of the universe, whether a jack-in-a-box or a comet. She had only known Aunt Maria for the last four years, and she had not yet got used to her rough-and-ready mannish ways, nor learned to see any sense in her philosophizings. Looking upon her as a comical character, and supposing that she talked mainly for the fun of the thing, she was disposed to laugh at her doings and sayings, though mostly meant in solemn earnest.

"But about your affairs, my child," continued Aunt Maria, suddenly gripping a fresh subject after her quick and startling fashion. "I don't understand them. How is it possible? Here is a great fortune gone; gone in a moment; gone incomprehensibly. What does it mean? Some rascality here. Some man at the bottom of this."

"I presume my relative, Garcia, must be right," commenced Clara.

"No, he isn't," interrupted Aunt Maria. "He is wrong. Of course he's wrong. I never knew a man yet but what he was wrong."

"You make me laugh in spite of my troubles," said Clara, laughing, however, only through her eyes, which had great faculties for sparkling out meanings. "But see here," she added, turning grave again, and putting up her hand to ask attention. "Mr. Garcia tells a straight story, and gives reasons enough. There was the war," and here she began to count on her fingers. "That destroyed a great deal. I know when my father could scarcely send on money to pay my bills in New York. And then there was the signature for Señor Pedraez. And then there were the Apaches who burnt the hacienda and drove off the cattle. And then he——"

Her voice faltered and she stopped; she could not say, "He died."

"My poor, dear child!" sighed Aunt Maria, walking up to the girl and caressing her with a tenderness which was all womanly.

"That seems enough," continued Clara, when she could speak again. "I suppose that what Garcia and the lawyers tell us is true. I suppose I am not worth a thousand dollars."

"Will a thousand dollars support you here?"

"I don't know. I don't think it will."

"Then if I can't set this thing straight, if I can't make somebody disgorge your property, I must take you back with me."

"Oh! if you would!" implored Clara, all the tender helplessness of Spanish girlhood appealing from her eyes.

"Of course I will," said Aunt Maria, with a benevolent energy which was almost terrific.

"I would try to do something. I don't know. Couldn't I teach Spanish?"

"You *shan't*," decided Aunt Maria. "Yes, you *shall*. You shall be professor of foreign languages in a Female College which I mean to have founded."

Clara stared with astonishment, and then burst into a hearty fit of laughter, the two finishing the drying of her tears. She was so far from wishing to be a strong-minded person of either gender, that she did not comprehend that her aunt could wish it for her, or could herself seriously claim to be one. The talk about a professorship was in her estimation the wayward, humorous whim of an eccentric who was fond of solemn joking. Mrs. Stanley, meanwhile, could not see why her utterance should not be taken in earnest, and opened her eyes at Clara's merriment.

We must say a word or two concerning the past of this young lady. Twenty-five years previous a New Yorker named Augustus Van Diemen, the brother of that Maria Jane Van Diemen now known to the world as Mrs. Stanley, had migrated to California, set up in the hide business, and married by stealth the daughter of a wealthy Mexican named Pedro Muñoz. Muñoz got into a Spanish Catholic rage at having a Yankee Protestant son-in-law, disowned and formally disinherited his child, and worried her husband into quitting the country. Van Diemen returned to the United States, but his wife soon became homesick for her native land, and, like a good husband as he was, he went once more to Mexico. This time he settled in Santa Fé, where he accumulated a handsome fortune, lived in the best house in the city, and owned haciendas.

Clara's mother dying when the girl was fourteen years old, Van Diemen felt free to give her, his only child, an American education, and sent her to New York, where she went through four years of schooling. During this period came the war between the United States and Mexico. Foreign residents were ill-treated; Van Diemen was sometimes a prisoner, sometimes a fugitive; in one way or another his fortune went to pieces. Four months previous to the opening of this story he died in a state little better than insolvency. Clara, returning to Santa Fé under the care of her energetic and affectionate relative, found that the deluge of debt would cover town house and haciendas, leaving her barely a thousand dollars. She was handsome and accomplished, but she was an orphan and poor. The main chance with her seemed to lie in the likelihood that she would find a mother (or a father) in Aunt Maria.

Yes, there was another sustaining possibility, and of a more poetic nature. There was a young American officer named Thurstane, a second lieutenant acting as quartermaster of the department, who had met her heretofore in New York, who had seemed delighted to welcome her to Santa Fé, and who now called on her nearly every day. Might it not be that Lieutenant Thurstane would want to make her Mrs. Thurstane, and would have power granted him to induce her to consent to the arrangement? Clara was sufficiently a woman, and sufficiently a Spanish woman especially, to believe in marriage. She did not mean particularly to be Mrs. Thurstane, but she did mean generally to be Mrs. Somebody. And why not Thurstane? Well, that was for him to decide, at least to a considerable extent. In the mean time she did not love him; she only disliked the thought of leaving him.

While these two women had been talking and thinking, a lazy Indian servant had been lounging up the stairway. Arrived on the roof, he advanced to La Señorita Clara, and handed her a letter. The girl opened it, glanced through it with a flushing face, and cried out delightedly, "It is from my grandfather. How wonderful! O holy Maria, thanks! His heart has been softened. He invites me to come and live with him in San Francisco. *O Madre de Dios!*"

Although Clara spoke English perfectly, and although she was in faith quite as much of a Protestant as a Catholic, yet in her moments of strong excitement she sometimes fell back into the language and ideas of her childhood.

"Child, what are you jabbering about?" asked Aunt Maria.

"There it is. See! Pedro Muñoz! It is his own signature. I have seen letters of his. Pedro Muñoz! Read it. Oh! you don't read Spanish."

Then she translated the letter aloud. Aunt Maria listened with a firm and almost stern aspect, like one who sees some justice done, but not enough.

"He doesn't beg your pardon," she said at the close of the reading.

Clara, supposing that she was expected to laugh, and not seeing the point of the joke, stared in amazement.

"But probably he is in a meeker mood now," continued Aunt Maria. "By this time it is to be hoped that he sees his past conduct in a proper light. The letter was written three months ago."

"Three months ago," repeated Clara. "Yes, it has taken all that time to come. How long will it take me to go there? How shall I go?"

"We will see," said Aunt Maria, with the air of one who holds the fates in her hand, and doesn't mean to open it till she gets ready. She was by no means satisfied as yet that this grandfather Muñoz was a proper person to be intrusted with the destinies of a young lady. In refusing to let his daughter select her own husband, he had shown a very squinting and incomplete perception of the rights of woman.

"Old reprobate!" thought Aunt Maria. "Probably he has got gouty with his vices, and wants to be nursed. I fancy I see him getting Clara without going on his sore marrow-bones and begging pardon of gods and women."

"Of course I must go," continued Clara, unsuspicious of her aunt's reflections. "At all events he will support me. Besides, he is now the head of my family."

"Head of the family!" frowned Aunt Maria. "Because he is a man? So much the more reason for his being the tail of it. My dear, you are your own head."

"Ah—well. What is the use of all *that?*" asked Clara, smiling away those views. "I have no money, and he has."

"Well, we will see," persisted Aunt Maria. "I just told you so. We will see."

The two women had scarcely left the roof of the house and got themselves down to the large, breezy, sparsely furnished parlor, ere the lazy, dawdling Indian servant announced Lieutenant Thurstane.

Lieutenant Ralph Thurstane was a tall, full-chested, finely-limbed gladiator of perhaps four and twenty. Broad forehead; nose straight and high enough; lower part of the face oval; on the whole a good physiognomy. Cheek bones rather strongly marked ; a hint of Scandinavian ancestry supported by his name. Thurstane is evidently Thor's stone or altar ; forefathers priests of the god of thunder. His complexion was so reddened and darkened by sunburn that his untanned forehead looked unnaturally white and delicate. His yellow, one might almost call it golden hair, was wavy enough to be handsome. Eyes quite remarkable ; blue, but of a very dark blue, like the coloring which is sometimes given to steel ; so dark indeed that one's first impression was that they were black. Their natural expression seemed to be gentle, pathetic, and almost imploring ; but authority, responsibility, hardship, and danger had given them an ability to be stern. In his whole face, young as he was, there was already the look of the veteran, that calm reminiscence of trials endured, that preparedness for trials to come. In fine, taking figure, physiognomy, and demeanor together, he was attractive.

He saluted the ladies as if they were his superior officers. It was a kindly address, but ceremonious ; it was almost humble, and yet it was self-respectful.

"I have some great news," he presently said, in the full masculine tone of one who has done much drilling. "That is, it is great to me. I change station."

"How is that?" asked Clara eagerly. She was not troubled at the thought of losing a beau ; we must not be so hard upon her as to make that supposition ; but here was a trustworthy friend going away just when she wanted counsel and perhaps aid.

"I have been promoted first lieutenant of Company I, Fifth Regiment, and I must join my company."

"Promoted! I am glad," said Clara.

"You ought to be pleased," put in Aunt Maria, staring at the grave face of the young man with no approving expression. "I thought men were always pleased with such things."

"So I am," returned Thurstane. "Of course I am pleased with the step. But I must leave Santa Fé. And I have found Santa Fé very pleasant."

There was so much meaning obvious in these last words that Clara's face colored like a sunset.

"I thought soldiers never indulged in such feelings," continued the unmollified Aunt Maria.

"Soldiers are but men," observed Thurstane, flushing through his sunburn.

"And men are weak creatures."

Thurstane grew still redder. This old lady (old in his young eyes) was always at him about his manship, as if it were a crime and disgrace. He wanted to give her one, but out of respect for Clara he did not, and merely moved uneasily in his seat, as men are apt to do when they are set down hard.

"How soon must you go? Where?" demanded Clara.

"As soon as I can close my accounts here and turn over my stores to my successor. Company I is at Fort Yuma on the Colorado. It is the first post in California."

"California!" And Clara could not help brightening up in cheeks and eyes with fine tints and flashes. "Why, I am going to California."

"We will see," said Aunt Maria, still holding the fates in her fist.

Then came the story of Grandfather Muñoz's letter, with a hint or two concerning the decay of the Van Diemen fortune, for Clara was not worldly wise enough to hide her poverty.

Thurstane's face turned as red with pleasure as if it had been dipped in the sun. If this young lady was going to California, he might perhaps be her knight-errant across the desert, guard her from privations and hardships, and crown himself with her smiles. If she was poor, he might—well, he would not speculate upon that; it was too dizzying.

We must say a word as to his history in order to show why he was so shy and sensitive. He had been through West Point, confined himself while there closely to his studies, gone very soon into active service, and so seen little society. The discipline of the Academy and three years in the regular army had ground into him the soldier's respect for superiors. He revered his field officers; he received a communication from the War Department as a sort of superhuman revelation; he would have blown himself sky-high at the command of General Scott. This habit of subordination, coupled with a natural fund of reverence, led him to feel that many persons were better than himself, and to be humble in their presence. All women were his superior officers, and the highest in rank was Clara Van Diemen.

Well, hurrah! he was to march under her to California! and the thought made him half wild. He would protect her; he would kill all the Indians in the desert for her sake; he would feed her on his own blood, if necessary.

As he considered these proper and feasible projects, the audacious thought which he had just tried to expel from his mind forced its way back into it. If the Van Diemen estate were insolvent, if this semi-divine Clara were as poor as himself, there was a call on him to double his devotion to her, and there was a hope that his worship might some day be rewarded.

How he would slave and serve for her; how he would earn promotion for her sake; how he would fight her battle in life! But would she let him do it? Ah, it seemed too much to hope. Poor though she was, she was still a heaven or so above him; she was so beautiful and had so many perfections!

Oh, the purity, the self-abnegation, the humility of love! It makes a man scarcely lower than the angels, and quite superior to not a few reverenced saints.

CHAPTER II.

"I MUST say," observed Thurstane—"I beg your pardon for advising—but I think you had better accept your grandfather's invitation."

He said it with a pang at his heart, for if this adorable girl went to her grandfather, the old fellow would be sure to love her and leave her his property, in which case there would be no chance for a proud and poor lieutenant. He gave his advice under a grim sense that it was his duty to give it, because the following of it would be best for Miss Van Diemen.

"So I think," nodded Clara, fortified by this opinion to resist Aunt Maria, and the more fortified because it was the opinion of a man.

After a certain amount of discussion the elder lady was persuaded to loosen her mighty grip and give the destinies a little liberty.

"Well, it *may* be best," she said, pursing her mouth as if she tasted the bitter of some half-suspected and disagreeable future. "I don't know. I won't undertake positively to decide. But, if you do go," and here she became authentic and despotic—"if you do go, I shall go with you and see you safe there."

"Oh! *will* you?" exclaimed Clara, all Spanish and all emotion in an instant. "How sweet and good and beautiful of you! You are my guardian angel. Do you know? I thought you would offer to go. I said to myself, She came on to Santa Fé for my sake, and she will go to California. But oh, it is too much for me to ask. How shall I ever pay you?"

"I will pay myself," returned Aunt Maria. "I have plans for California."

It was as if she had said, "Go to, we will make California in our own image."

The young lady was satisfied. Her strong-minded relative was a mighty mystery to her, just as men were mighty mysteries. Whatever she or they said could be done and should be done, why of course it would be done, and that shortly.

By the time that Aunt Maria had announced her decision, another visitor was on the point of entrance. Carlos Maria Muñoz Garcia de Coronado was a nephew of Manuel Garcia, who was a cousin of Clara's grandfather; only, as Garcia was merely his uncle by marriage, Coronado and Clara were not related by blood, though calling each other cousin. He was a man of medium stature, slender in build, agile and graceful in movement, complexion very dark, features high and aristocratic, short black hair and small black moustache, eyes black also, but veiled and dusky. He was about twenty-eight, but he seemed at least four years older, partly because of a deep wrinkle which slashed down each cheek, and partly because he was so perfectly self-possessed and elaborately courteous. His intellect was apparently as alert and adroit as his physical action. A few words from Clara enabled him to seize the situation.

"Go at once," he decided without a moment's hesitation. "My dear cousin, it will be the happy turning point of your fortunes. I fancy you already inheriting the hoards, city lots, haciendas, mines, and cattle of our excellent relative Muñoz—long may he live to enjoy them! Certainly. Don't whisper an objection. Muñoz owes you that reparation. His conduct has been—we will not describe it—we will hope that he means to make amends for it. Unquestionably he will. My dear cousin, nothing can resist you. You will enchant your grandfather. It will all end, like the tales of the Arabian Nights, in your living in a palace. How delightful to think of this long family quarrel at last coming to a close! But how do you go?"

"If Miss Van Diemen goes overland, I can do something toward protecting her and making her comfortable," suggested Thurstane. "I am ordered to Fort Yuma."

Coronado glanced at the young officer, noted the guilty blush which peeped out of his tanned cheek, and came to a decision on the instant.

"Overland!" he exclaimed, lifting both his hands. "Take her overland! My God! my God!"

Thurstane reddened at the insinuation that he had given bad advice to Miss Van Diemen; but though he wanted to fight the Mexican, he controlled himself, and did not even argue. Like all sensitive and at the same time self-respectful persons, he was exceedingly considerate of the feelings of others, and was a very lamb in conversation.

"It is a desert," continued Coronado in a kind of scream of horror. "It is a waterless desert, without a blade of grass, and haunted from end to end by Apaches. My little cousin would die of thirst and hunger. She would be hunted and scalped. O my God! overland!"

"Emigrant parties are going all the while," ventured Thurstane, very angry at such extravagant opposition, but merely looking a little stiff.

"Certainly. You are right, Lieutenant," bowed Coronado. "They do go. But how many perish on the way? They march between the unburied and withered corpses of their predecessors. And what a journey for a woman—for a lady accustomed to luxury—for my little cousin! I beg your pardon, my dear Lieutenant Thurstane, for disagreeing with you. My advice is—the isthmus."

"I have, of course, nothing to say," admitted the officer, returning Coronado's bow. "The family must decide."

"Certainly, the isthmus, the steamers," went on the fluent Mexican. "You sail to Panama. You have an easy and safe land trip of a few days. Then steamers again. Poff! you are there. By all means, the isthmus."

We must allot a few more words of description to this Don Carlos Coronado. Let no one expect a stage Spaniard, with the air of a matador or a guerrillero, who wears only picturesque and outlandish costumes, and speaks only magniloquent Castilian. Coronado was dressed, on this spring morning, precisely as American dandies then dressed for summer promenades on Broadway. His hat was a fine panama with a broad black ribbon; his frock-coat was of thin cloth, plain, dark, and altogether civilized; his light trousers were cut gaiter-fashion, and strapped under the instep; his small boots were patent-leather, and of the ordinary type. There was nothing poetic about his attire except a reasonably wide Byron collar and a rather dashing crimson neck-tie, well suited to his dark complexion.

His manner was sometimes excitable, as we have seen above; but usually he was like what gentlemen with us desire to be. Perhaps he bowed lower and smiled oftener and gestured more gracefully than Americans are apt to do. But there was in general nothing Oriental about him, no assumption of barbaric pompousness, no extravagance of bearing. His prevailing deportment was calm, grave, and deliciously courteous. If you had met him, no matter how or where, you would probably have been pleased with him. He would have made conversation for you, and put you at ease in a moment; you would have believed that he liked you, and you would therefore have been disposed to like him. In short, he was agreeable to most people, and to some people fascinating.

And then his English! It was wonderful to hear him talk it. No American could say that he spoke better English than Coronado, and no American surely ever spoke it so fluently. It rolled off his lips in a torrent, undefiled by a mispronunciation or a foreign idiom. And yet he had begun to learn the language after reaching the age of manhood, and had acquired it mainly during three years of exile and teaching of Spanish in the United States. His linguistic cleverness was a fair specimen of his general quickness of intellect.

Mrs. Stanley had liked him at first sight—that is, liked him for a man. He knew it; he had seen that she was a person worth conciliating; he had addressed himself to her, let off his bows at her, made her the centre of conversation. In ten minutes from the entrance of Coronado Mrs. Stanley was of opinion that Clara ought to go to California by way of the isthmus, although she had previously taken the overland route for granted. In another ten minutes the matter was settled: the ladies were to go by way of New Orleans, Panama, and the Pacific.

Shortly afterward, Coronado and Thurstane took their leave; the Mexican affable, sociable, smiling, smoking; the American civil, but taciturn and grave.

"Aha! I have disappointed the young gentleman," thought Coronado as they parted, the one going to his quartermaster's office and the other to Garcia's house.

Coronado, although he had spent great part of his life in courting women, was a bachelor. He had been engaged once in New Mexico and two or three times in New York, but had always, as he could tell you with a smile, been disappointed. He now lived with his uncle, that Señor Manuel Garcia whom Clara has mentioned, a trader with California, an owner of vast estates and much cattle, and reputed to be one of the richest men in New Mexico. The two often quarrelled, and the elder had once turned the younger out of doors, so lively were their dispositions. But as Garcia had lost one by one all his children, he had at last taken his nephew into permanent favor, and would, it was said, leave him his property.

The house, a hollow square built of *adobe* bricks in one story, covered a vast deal of ground, had spacious rooms and a court big enough to bivouac a regiment. It was, in fact, not only a dwelling, but a magazine where Garcia stored his merchandise, and a caravansary where he parked his wagons. As Coronado lounged into the main doorway he was run against by a short, pursy old gentleman who was rushing out.

"Ah! there you are!" exclaimed the old gentleman, in Spanish. "O you pig! you dog! you never are here. O Madre de Dios! how I have needed you! There is no time to lose. Enter at once."

A dyspeptic, worn with work and anxieties, his nervous system shattered, Garcia was subject to fits of petulance which were ludicrous. In these rages he called everybody who would bear it pigs, dogs, and other more unsavory nicknames. Coronado bore it because thus he got his living, and got it without much labor.

"I want you," gasped Garcia, seizing the young man by the arm and dragging him into a private room. "I want to speak to you in confidence—in confidence, mind you, in confidence—about Muñoz."

"I have heard of it," said Coronado, as the old man stopped to catch his breath.

"Heard of it!" exclaimed Garcia, in such consternation that he turned yellow, which was his way of turning pale. "Has the news got here? O Madre de Dios!"

"Yes, I was at our little cousin's this evening. It is an ugly affair."

"And *she* knows it?" groaned the old man. "O Madre de Dios!"

"She told me of it. She is going there. I did the best I could, She was about to go overland, in charge of the American, Thurstane. I broke that up. I persuaded her to go by the isthmus."

"It is of little use," said Garcia, his eyes filmy with despair, as if he were dying. "She will get there. The property will be hers."

"Not necessarily. He has simply invited her to live with him. She may not suit."

"How?" demanded Garcia, open-eyed and open-mouthed with anxiety.

"He has simply invited her to live with him," repeated Coronado. "I saw the letter."

"What! you don't know, then?"

"Know what?"

"Muñoz is dead."

Coronado threw out, first a stare of surprise, and then a shout of laughter.

"And here they have just got a letter from him," he said presently; "and I have been persuading her to go to him by the isthmus!"

"May the journey take her to him!" muttered Garcia. "How old was this letter?"

"Nearly three months. It came by sea, first to New York, and then here."

"My news is a month later. It came overland by special messenger. Listen to me, Carlos. This affair is worse than you know. Do you know what

Muñoz has done? Oh, the pig! the dog! the villainous pig! He has left everything to his granddaughter."

Coronado, dumb with astonishment and dismay, mechanically slapped his boot with his cane and stared at Garcia.

"I am ruined," cried the old man. "The pig of hell has ruined me. He has left me, his cousin, his only male relative, to ruin. Not a doubloon to save me.'

"Is there *no* chance?" asked Coronado, after a long silence.

"None! Oh—yes—one. A little one, a miserable little one. If she dies without issue and without a will, I am heir. And you, Carlos" (changing here to a wheedling tone), "you are mine."

The look which accompanied these last words was a terrible mingling of cunning, cruelty, hope, and despair.

Coronado glanced at Garcia with a shocking comprehension, and immediately dropped his dusky eyes upon the floor.

"You know I have made my will," resumed the old man, "and left you everything."

"Which is nothing," returned Coronado, aware that his uncle was insolvent in reality, and that his estate when settled would not show the residuum of a dollar.

"If the fortune of Muñoz comes to me, I shall be very rich."

"When you get it."

"Listen to me, Carlos. Is there no way of getting it?"

As the two men stared at each other they were horrible. The uncle was always horrible; he was one of the very ugliest of Spaniards; he was a brutal caricature of the national type. He had a low forehead, round face, bulbous nose, shaking fat cheeks, insignificant chin, and only one eye, a black and sleepy orb, which seemed to crawl like a snake. His exceedingly dark skin was made darker by a singular bluish tinge which resulted from heavy doses of nitrate of silver, taken as a remedy for epilepsy. His face was, moreover, mottled with dusky spots, so that he reminded the spectator of a frog or a toad. Just now he looked nothing less than poisonous; the hungriest of cannibals would not have dared eat him.

"I am ruined," he went on groaning. "The war, the Yankees, the Apaches, the devil—I am completely ruined. In another year I shall be sold out. Then, my dear Carlos, you will have no home."

"*Sangre de Dios!*" growled Coronado. "Do you want to drive me to the devil?

"O God! to force an old man to such an extremity!" continued Garcia. "It is more than an old man is fitted to strive with. An old man—an old, sick, worn-out man!"

"You are sure about the will?" demanded the nephew.

"I have a copy of it," said Garcia, eagerly. "Here it is. Read it. O Madre de Dios! there is no doubt about it. I can trust my lawyer. It all goes to her. It only comes to me if she dies childless and intestate."

"This is a horrible dilemma to force us into," observed Coronado, after he had read the paper.

"So it is," assented Garcia, looking at him with indescribable anxiety. "So it is; so it is. What is to be done?"

"Suppose I should marry her?"

The old man's countenance fell; he wanted to call his nephew a pig, a dog, and everything else that is villainous; but he restrained himself and merely whimpered, "It would be better than nothing. You could help me."

"There is little chance of it," said Coronado, seeing that the proposition was not approved. "She likes the American lieutenant much, and does not like me at all."

"Then——" began Garcia, and stopped there, trembling all over.

"Then what?"

The venomous old toad made a supreme effort and whispered, "Suppose she should die?"

Coronado wheeled about, walked two or three times up and down the room, returned to where Garcia sat quivering, and murmured, "It must be done quickly."

"Yes, yes," gasped the old man. "She must—it must be childless and intestate."

"She must go off in some natural way," continued the nephew.

The uncle looked up with a vague hope in his one dusky and filmy eye.

"Perhaps the isthmus will do it for her."

Again the old man turned to an image of despair, as he mumbled, "O Madre de Dios! no, no. The isthmus is nothing."

"Is the overland route more dangerous?" asked Coronado.

"It might be made more dangerous. One gets lost in the desert. There are Apaches."

"It is a horrible business," growled Coronado, shaking his head and biting his lips.

"Oh, horrible, horrible!" groaned Garcia. "Muñoz was a pig, and a dog, and a toad, and a snake."

"You old coward! can't you speak out?" hissed Coronado, losing his patience. "Do you want me both to devise and execute, while you take the purses? Tell me at once what your plan is."

"The overland route," whispered Garcia, shaking from head to foot. "You go with her. I pay—I pay everything. You shall have men, horses, mules, wagons, all you want."

"I shall want money, too. I shall need, perhaps, two thousand dollars. Apaches."

"Yes, yes," assented Garcia. "The Apaches make an attack. You shall have money. I can raise it; I will."

"How soon will you have a train ready?"

"Immediately. Any day you want. You must start at once. She must not know of the will. She might remain here, and let the estate be settled for her, and draw on it. She might go back to New York. Anybody would lend her money."

"Yes, events hurry us," muttered Coronado. "Well, get your cursed train ready. I will induce her to take it. I must unsay now all that I said in favor of the isthmus."

"Do be judicious," implored Garcia. "With judgment, with judgment. Lost on the plains. Stolen by Apaches. No killing. No scandals. O my God, how I hate scandals and uproars! I am an old man, Carlos. With judgment, with judgment."

"I comprehend," responded Coronado, adding a long string of Spanish curses, most of them meant for his uncle.

CHAPTER III.

THAT very day Coronado made a second call on Clara and her Aunt Maria, to retract, contradict, and disprove all that he had said in favor of the isthmus and against the overland route.

Although his visit was timed early in the evening, he found Lieutenant Thurstane already with the ladies. Instead of scowling at him, or crouching in conscious guilt before him, he made a cordial rush for his hand, smiled sweetly in his face, and offered him incense of gratitude.

"My dear Lieutenant, you are perfectly right," he said, in his fluent English. "The journey by the isthmus is not to be thought of. I have just seen a friend who has made it. Poisonous serpents in myriads. The most deadly climate in the world. Nearly everybody had the *vomito;* one-fifth died of it. You eat a little fruit; down you go on your back—dead in four hours. Then there are constant fights between the emigrants and the sullen, ferocious Indians of the isthmus. My poor friend never slept with his revolver out of his hand. I said to him, "My dear fellow, it is cruel to rejoice in your misfortunes, but I am heartily glad that I have heard of them. You have saved the life of the most remarkable woman that I ever knew, and of a cousin of mine who is the star of her sex."

Here Coronado made one bow to Mrs. Stanley and another to Clara, at the same time kissing his sallow hand enthusiastically to all creation. Aunt Maria tried to look stern at the compliment, but eventually thawed into a smile over it. Clara acknowledged it with a little wave of the hand, as if, coming from Coronado, it meant nothing more than good-morning, which indeed was just about his measure of it.

"Moreover," continued the Mexican, "overland route? Why, it is overland route both ways. If you go by the isthmus, you must traverse all Texas and Louisiana, at the very least. You might as well go at once to San Diego. In short, the route by the isthmus is not to be thought of."

"And what of the overland route?" asked Mrs. Stanley.

"The overland route is the *other*," laughed Coronado.

"Yes, I know. We must take it, I suppose. But what is the last news about it? You spoke this morning of Indians, I believe. Not that I suppose they are very formidable."

"The overland route does not lead directly through paradise, my dear Mrs. Stanley," admitted Coronado with insinuating candor. "But it is not as bad as has been represented. I have never tried it. I must rely upon the report of others. Well, on learning that the isthmus would not do for you, I rushed off immediately to inquire about the overland. I questioned Garcia's teamsters. I catechized some newly-arrived travellers. I pumped dry every source of information. The result is that the overland route will do. No suffering; absolutely none; not a bit. And no danger worth mentioning. The Apaches are under a cloud. Our American conquerors and fellow-citizens" (here he gently patted Thurstane on the shoulder-strap), "our Romans of the nineteenth century, they tranquillize the Apaches. A child might walk from here to Fort Yuma without risking its little scalp."

All this was said in the most light-hearted and airy manner conceivable. Coronado waved and floated on zephyrs of fancy and fluency. A butterfly or a humming-bird could not have talked more cheerily about flying over a parterre of flowers than he about traversing the North American desert. And, with all this frivolous, imponderable grace, what an accent of verity he had! He spoke of the teamsters as if he had actually conversed with them, and of the overland route as if he had been studiously gathering information concerning it.

"I believe that what you say about the Apaches is true," observed Thurstane, a bit awkwardly.

Coronado smiled, tossed him a little bow, and murmured in the most cordial, genial way, "And the rest?"

"I beg pardon," said the Lieutenant, reddening. "I didn't mean to cast doubt upon any of your statements, sir."

Thurstane had the army tone; he meant to be punctiliously polite; perhaps he was a little stiff in his politeness. But he was young, had had small practice in society, was somewhat hampered by modesty, and so sometimes made a blunder. Such things annoyed him excessively; a breach of etiquette seemed something like a breach of orders; hadn't meant to charge Coronado with drawing the long bow; couldn't help coloring about it. Didn't think much of Coronado, but stood somewhat in awe of him, as being four years older in time and a dozen years older in the ways of the world.

"I only meant to say," he continued, "that I have information concerning the Apaches which coincides with yours, sir. They are quiet, at least for the present. Indeed, I understand that Red Sleeve, or Manga Colorada, as you call him, is coming in with his band to make a treaty."

"Admirable!" cried Coronado. "Why not hire him to guarantee our safety? Set a thief to catch a thief. Why does not your Government do that sort of thing? Let the Apaches protect the emigrants, and the United States pay the Apaches. They would be the cheapest military force possible. That is the way the Turks manage the desert Arabs."

"Mr. Coronado, you ought to be Governor of New Mexico," said Aunt Maria, stricken with admiration at this project.

Thurstane looked at the two as if he considered them a couple of fools, each bigger than the other. Coronado advanced to Mrs. Stanley, took her hand, bowed over it, and murmured, "Let me have your influence at Washington, my dear Madame." The remarkable woman squirmed a little, fearing lest he should kiss her fingers, but nevertheless gave him a gracious smile.

"It strikes me, however," she said, "that the isthmus route is better. We know by experience that the journey from here to Bent's Fort is safe and easy. From there down the Arkansas and Missouri to St. Louis it is mostly water carriage; and from St. Louis you can sail anywhere."

Coronado was alarmed. He must put a stopper on this project. He called up all his resources.

"My dear Mrs. Stanley, allow me. Remember that emigrants move westward, and not eastward. Coming from Bent's Fort you had protection and company; but going towards it would be different. And then think what you would lose. The great American desert, as it is absurdly styled, is one of the most interesting regions on earth. Mrs. Stanley, did you ever hear of the Casas Grandes, the Casas de Montezuma, the ruined cities of New Mexico? In this so-called desert there was once an immense population. There was a civilization which rose, flourished, decayed, and disappeared without a historian. Nothing remains of it but the walls of its fortresses and palaces. Those you will see. They are wonderful. They are worth ten times the labor and danger which we shall encounter. Buildings eight hundred feet long by two hundred and fifty feet deep, Mrs. Stanley. The resting-places and wayside strongholds of the Aztecs on their route from the frozen North to found the Empire of the Montezumas! This whole region is strewn, and cumbered, and glorified with ruins. If we should go by the way of the San Juan——"

"The San Juan!" protested Thurstane. "Nobody goes by the way of the San Juan."

Coronado stopped, bowed, smiled, waited to see if Thurstane had finished, and then proceeded.

"Along the San Juan every hilltop is crowned with these monuments of antiquity. It is like the castled Rhine. Ruins looking in the faces of ruins. It is a tragedy in stone. It is like Niobe and her daughters. Moreover, if we take this route we shall pass the Moquis. The independent Moquis are a fragment of the ancient ruling race of New Mexico. They live in stone-built cities on lofty eminences. They weave blankets of exquisite patterns and colors, and produce a species of pottery which almost deserves the name of porcelain."

"Really, you ought to write all this," exclaimed Aunt Maria, her imagination fired to a white heat.

"I ought," said Coronado, impressively. "I owe it to these people to celebrate them in history. I owe them that much because of the name I bear. Did you ever hear of Coronado, the conqueror of New Mexico, the stormer of the seven cities of Cibola? It was he who gave the final shock to this antique civilization. He was the Cortes of this portion of the continent. I bear his name, and his blood runs in my veins."

He held down his head as if he were painfully oppressed by the sense of his crimes and responsibilities as a descendant of the waster of aboriginal New Mexico. Mrs. Stanley, delighted with his emotion, slily grasped and pressed his hand.

"Oh, man! man!" she groaned. "What evils has that creature man wrought in this beautiful world! Ah, Mr. Coronado, it would have been a very different planet had woman had her rightful share in the management of its affairs."

"Undoubtedly," sighed Coronado. He had already obtained an insight into this remarkable person's views on the woman question, the superiority of her own sex, the stolidity and infamy of the other. It was worth his while to humor her on this point, for the sake of gaining an influence over her, and so over Clara. Cheered by the success of his history, he now launched into pure poetry.

"Woman has done something," he said. "There is every reason to believe that the cities of the San Juan were ruled by queens, and that some of them were inhabited by a race of Amazons."

"Is it possible?" exclaimed Aunt Maria, flushing and rustling with interest.

"It is the opinion of the best antiquarians. It is my opinion. Nothing else can account for the exquisite earthenware which is found there. Women, you are aware, far surpass men in the arts of beauty. Moreover, the inscriptions on hieroglyphic rocks in these abandoned cities evidently refer to Amazons. There you see them doing the work of men—carrying on war, ruling conquered regions, founding cities. It is a picture of a golden age, Mrs. Stanley."

Aunt Maria meant to go by way of the San Juan, if she had to scalp Apaches herself in doing it.

"Lieutenant Thurstane, what do you say?" she asked, turning her sparkling eyes upon the officer.

"I must confess that I never heard of all these things," replied Thurstane, with an air which added, "And I don't believe in most of them."

"As for the San Juan route," he continued, "it is two hundred miles at least out of our way. The country is a desert and almost unexplored. I don't fancy the plan—I beg your pardon, Mr. Coronado—but I don't fancy it at all."

Aunt Maria despised him and almost hated him for his stupid, practical, unpoetic common sense.

"I must say that I quite fancy the San Juan route," she responded, with proper firmness.

"I venture to agree with you," said Coronado, as meekly as if her fancy were not of his own making. "Only a hundred miles off the straight line (begging your pardon, my dear Lieutenant), and through a country which is naturally fertile—witness the immense population which it once supported. As for its being unexplored, I have explored it myself; and I shall go with you."

"Shall you!" cried Aunt Maria, as if that made all safe and delightful.

"Yes. My excellent Uncle Garcia (good, kind-hearted old man) takes the strongest interest in this affair. He is resolved that his charming little relative here, La Señorita Clara, shall cross the continent in safety and comfort. He offers a special wagon train for the purpose, and insists that I shall accompany it. Of course I am only too delighted to obey him."

"Garcia is very good, and so are you, Coronado," said Clara, very thankful and profoundly astonished. "How can I ever repay you both? I shall always be your debtor."

"My dear cousin!" protested Coronado, bowing and smiling. "Well, it is settled. We will start as soon as may be. The train will be ready in a day or two."

"I have no money," stammered Clara. "The estate is not settled."

"Our good old Garcia has thought of everything. He will advance you what you want, and take your draft on the executors."

"Your uncle is one of nature's noblemen," affirmed Aunt Maria. "I must call on him and thank him for his goodness and generosity."

"Oh, never!" said Coronado. "He only waits your permission to visit you and pay you his humble respects. Absence has prevented him from attending to that delightful duty heretofore. He has but just returned from Albuquerque."

"Tell him I shall be glad to see him," smiled Aunt Maria. "But what does he say of the San Juan route?"

"He advises it. He has been in the overland trade for thirty years. He is tenderly interested in his relative Clara; and he advises her to go by way of the San Juan."

"Then so it shall be," declared Aunt Maria.

"And how do you go, Lieutenant?" asked Coronado, turning to Thurstane.

"I had thought of travelling with you," was the answer, delivered with a grave and troubled air, as if now he must give up his project.

Coronado was delighted. He had urged the northern and circuitous route mainly to get rid of the officer, taking it for granted that the latter must join his new command as soon as possible. He did not want him courting Clara all across the continent; and he did not want him saving her from being lost, if it should become necessary to lose her.

"I earnestly hope that we shall not be deprived of your company," he said.

Thurstane, in profound thought, simply bowed his acknowledgments. A few minutes later, as he rose to return to his quarters, he said, with an air of solemn resolution, "If I can possibly go with you, I *will*."

All the next day and evening Coronado was in and out of the Van Diemen house. Had there been a mail for the ladies, he would have brought it to them; had it contained a letter from California, he would have abstracted and burnt it. He helped them pack for the journey; he made an inventory of the furniture and found storeroom for it; he was a valet and a spy in one. Meantime Garcia hurried up his train, and hired suitable muleteers for the animals and suitable assassins for the travellers. Thurstane was also busy, working all day and half of the night over his government accounts, so that he might if possible get off with Clara.

Coronado thought of making interest with the post-commandant to have Thurstane kept a few days in Santa Fé. But the post-commandant was a grim and taciturn old major, who looked him through and through with a pair of icy gray eyes, and returned brief answers to his musical commonplaces. Coronado did not see how he could humbug him, and concluded not to try it. The attempt might excite suspicion; the major might say, "How is this your business?" So, after a little unimportant tattle, Coronado made his best bow to the old fellow, and hurried off to oversee his so-called cousin.

In the evening he brought Garcia to call on the ladies. Aunt Maria was rather surprised and shocked to see such an excellent man look so much like an infamous scoundrel. "But good people are always plain," she reasoned; and so she was as cordial to him as one can be in English to a saint who understands nothing but Spanish. Garcia, instructed by Coronado, could not bow low enough nor smile greasily enough at Aunt Maria. His dull commonplaces, moreover, were translated by his nephew into flowering compliments for the lady herself, and enthusiastic professions of faith in the superior intelligence and moral worth of all women. So the two got along famously, although neither ever knew what the other had really said.

When Clara appeared, Garcia bowed humbly without lifting his eyes to her face, and received her kiss without returning it, as one might receive the kiss of a corpse.

"Contemptible coward!" thought Coronado. Then, turning to Mrs. Stanley, he whispered, "My uncle is almost broken down with this parting."

"Excellent creature!" murmured Aunt Maria, surveying the old toad with warm sympathy. "What a pity he has lost one eye! It quite injures the benevolent expression of his face."

Although Garcia was very distantly connected with Clara, she gave him the title of uncle.

"How is this, my uncle?" she said, gaily. "You send your merchandise trains through Bernalillo, and you send me through Santa Anna and Rio Arriba."

Garcia, cowed and confounded, made no reply that was comprehensible.

"It is a newly discovered route," put in Coronado, "lately found to be easier and safer than the old one. Two hundred and fifty years in learning the fact, Mrs. Stanley! Just as we were two hundred and fifty years without discovering the gold of California."

"Ah!" said Clara. Absent since her childhood from New Mexico, she knew little about its geography, and could be easily deceived.

After a while Thurstane entered, out of breath and red with haste. He had stolen ten minutes from his accounts and stores to bring Miss Van Diemen a piece of information which was to him important and distressing.

"I fear that I shall not be able to go with you," he said. "I have received orders to wait for a sergeant and three recruits who have been assigned to my company. The messenger reports that they are on the march from Fort Bent with an emigrant train, and will not be here for a week. It annoys me horribly, Miss Van Diemen. I thought I saw my way clear to be of your party. I assure you I earnestly desired it. This route—I am afraid of it—I wanted to be with you."

"To protect me?" queried Clara, her face lighting up with a grateful smile, so innocent and frank was she. Then she turned grave again, and added, "I am sorry."

Thankful for these last words, but nevertheless quite miserable, the youngster worshipped her and trembled for her.

This conversation had been carried on in a quiet tone, so that the others of the party had not overheard it, not even the watchful Coronado.

"It is too unfortunate," said Clara, turning to them. "Lieutenant Thurstane cannot go with us."

Garcia and Coronado exchanged a look which said, "Thank—the devil!"

CHAPTER IV.

THE next day brought news of an obstacle to the march of the wagon train through Santa Anna and Rio Arriba.

It was reported that the audacious and savage Apache chieftain, Manga Colorada, or Red Sleeve, under pretence of wanting to make a treaty with the Americans, had approached within sixty miles of Santa Fé to the west, and camped there, on the route to the San Juan country, not making treaties at all, but simply making hot beefsteaks out of Mexican cattle and cold carcasses out of Mexican rancheros.

"We shall have to get those fellows off that trail and put them across the Bernalillo route," said Coronado to Garcia.

"The pigs! the dogs! the wicked beasts! the devils!" barked the old man, dancing about the room in a rage. After a while he dropped breathless into a chair and looked eagerly at his nephew for help.

"It will cost at least another thousand," observed the younger man.

"You have had two thousand," shuddered Garcia. "You were to do the whole accursed job with that."

"I did not count on Manga Colorada. Besides, I have given a thousand to our little cousin. I must keep a thousand to meet the chances that may come. There are men to be bribed."

Garcia groaned, hesitated, decided, went to some hoard which he had put aside for great needs, counted out a hundred American eagles, toyed with them, wept over them, and brought them to Coronado.

"Will that do?" he asked. "It must do. There is no more."

"I will try with that," said the nephew. "Now let me have a few good men and your best horses. I want to see them all before I trust myself with them."

Coronado felt himself in a position to dictate, and it was curious to see how quick he put on magisterial airs; he was one of those who enjoy authority, though little and brief.

"Accursed beast!" thought Garcia, who did not dare just now to break out with his "pig, dog," etc. "He wants me to pay everything. The thousand ought to be enough for men and horses and all. Why not poison the girl at once, and save all this money? If he had the spirit of a man! O Madre de Dios! Madre de Dios! What extremities! what extremities!"

But Garcia was like a good many of us; his thoughts were worse than his deeds and words. While he was cogitating thus savagely, he was saying aloud, "My son, my dear Carlos, come and choose for yourself."

Turning into the court of the house, they strolled through a medley of wagons, mules, horses, merchandise, muleteers, teamsters, idlers, white men and Indians. Coronado soon picked out a couple of rancheros whom he knew as capital riders, fair marksmen, faithful and intelligent. Next his eye fell upon a man in Mexican clothing, almost as dark and dirty too as the ordinary Mexican, but whose height, size, insolence of carriage, and ferocity of expression marked him as of another and more pugnacious, more imperial race.

"You are an American," said Coronado, in his civil manner, for he had two manners as opposite as the poles.

"I be," replied the stranger, staring at Coronado as a Lombard or Frankish warrior might have stared at an effeminate and diminutive Roman.

"May I ask what your name is?"

"Some folks call me Texas Smith."

Coronado shifted uneasily on his feet, as a man might shift in presence of a tiger, who, as he feared, was insufficiently chained. He was face to face with a fellow who was as much the terror of the table-land, from the borders of Texas to California, as if he had been an Apache chief.

This noted desperado, although not more than twenty-six or seven years old, had the horrible fame of a score of murders. His appearance mated well with his frightful history and reputation. His intensely black eyes, blacker even than the eyes of Coronado, had a stare of absolutely indescribable ferocity. It was more ferocious than the merely brutal glare of a tiger; it was an intentional malignity, super-beastly and sub-human. They were eyes which no other man ever looked into and afterward forgot. His sunburnt, sallow, haggard, ghastly face, stained early and for life with the corpse-like coloring of malarious fevers, was a fit setting for such optics. Although it was nearly oval in contour, and although the features were or had been fairly regular, yet it was so marked by hard, and one might almost say fleshless muscles, and so brutalized by long indulgence in savage passions, that it struck you as frightfully ugly. A large dull-red scar on the right jaw and another across the left cheek added the final touches to this countenance of a cougar.

"He is my man," whispered Garcia to Coronado. "I have hired him for the great adventure. Sixty piastres a month. Why not take him with you to-day?"

Coronado gave another glance at the gladiator and meditated. Should he trust this beast of a Texan to guard him against those other beasts, the Apaches? Well, he could die but once; this whole affair was detestably risky; he must not lose time in shuddering over the first steps.

"Mr. Smith," he said, "very glad to know that you are with us. Can you start in an hour for the camp of Manga Colorada? Sixty miles there. We must be back by to-morrow night. It would be best not to say where we are going."

Texas Smith nodded, turned abruptly on the huge heels of his Mexican boots, stalked to where his horse was fastened, and began to saddle him.

"My dear uncle, why didn't you hire the devil?" whispered Coronado as he stared after the cutthroat.

"Get yourself ready, my nephew," was Garcia's reply. "I will see to the men and horses.'

In an hour the expedition was off at full gallop. Coronado had laid aside his American dandy raiment, and was in the fnll costume of a Mexican of the provinces—broad-brimmed hat of white straw, blue broadcloth jacket adorned with numerous small silver buttons, velvet vest of similar splendor, blue trousers slashed from the knee downwards and gay with buttons, high, loose embroidered boots of crimson leather, long steel spurs jingling and shining. The change became him; he seemed a larger and handsomer man for it; he looked the caballero and almost the hidalgo.

Three hours took the party thirty miles to a hacienda of Garcia's, where they changed horses, leaving their first mounting for the return. After half an hour for dinner, they pushed on again, always at a gallop, the hoofs clattering over the hard, yellow, sunbaked earth, or dashing recklessly along smooth sheets of rock, or through fields of loose, slippery stones. Rare halts to breathe the animals; then the steady, tearing gallop again; no walking or other leisurely gait. Coronado led the way and hastened the pace. There was no tiring him; his thin, sinewy, sun-hardened frame could bear enormous fatigue; moreover, the saddle was so familiar to him that he almost reposed in it. If he had needed physical support, he would have found it in his mental energy. He was capable of that executive furor, that intense passion of exertion, which the man of Latin race can exhibit when he has once fairly set himself to an enterprise. He was of the breed which in nobler days had produced Gonsalvo, Cortes, Pizarro, and Darien.

These riders had set out at ten o'clock in the morning; at five in the afternoon they drew bridle in sight of the Apache encampment. They were on the brow of a stony hill: a pile of bare, gray, glaring, treeless, herbless layers of rock; a pyramid truncated near its base, but still of majestic altitude; one of the pyramids of nature in that region; in short, a butte. Below them lay a valley of six or eight miles in length by one or two in breadth, through the centre of which a rivulet had drawn a paradise of verdure. In the middle of the valley, at the head of a bend in the rivulet, was a camp of human brutes. It was a bivouac rather than a camp. The large tents of bison hide used by the northern Indians are unknown to the Apaches; they have not the bison, and they have less need of shelter in winter. What Coronado saw at this distance was, a few huts of branches, a strolling of many horses, and some scattered riders.

Texas Smith gave him a glance of inquiry which said, "Shall we go ahead—or fire?"

Coronado spurred his horse down the rough, disjointed, slippery declivity, and the others followed. They were soon perceived; the Apache swarm was instantly in a buzz; horses were saddled and mounted, or mounted without saddling; there was a consultation, and then a wild dash toward the travellers. As the two parties neared each other at a gallop, Coronado rode to the front of his squad, waving his sombrero. An Indian who wore the dress of a Mexican caballero, jacket, loose trousers, hat, and boots, spurred in like manner to the front, gestured to his followers to halt, brought his horse to a walk, and slowly approached the white man. Coronado made a sign to show that his pistols were in his holsters; and the Apache responded by dropping his lance and slinging his bow over his shoulder. The two met midway between the two squads of staring, silent horsemen.

"Is it Manga Colorada?" asked the Mexican, in Spanish.

"Manga Colorada," replied the Apache, his long, dark, haggard, savage face lighting up for a moment with a smile of gratified vanity.

"I come in peace, then," said Coronado. "I want your help; I will pay for it."

In our account of this interview we shall translate the broken Spanish of the Indian into ordinary English.

"Manga Colorada will help," he said, "if the pay is good."

Even during this short dialogue the Apaches had with difficulty restrained their curiosity; and their little wiry horses were now caracoling, rearing, and plunging in close proximity to the two speakers.

"We will talk of this by ourselves," said Coronado. "Let us go to your camp."

The conjoint movement of the leaders toward the Indian bivouac was a signal for their followers to mingle and exchange greetings. The adventurers were enveloped and very nearly ridden down by over two hundred prancing, screaming horsemen, shouting to their visitors in their own guttural tongue or in broken Spanish, and enforcing their wild speech with vehement gestures. It was a pandemonium which horribly frightened the Mexican rancheros, and made Coronado's dark cheek turn to an ashy yellow.

The civilized imagination can hardly conceive such a tableau of savagery as that presented by these Arabs of the great American desert. Arabs! The similitude is a calumny on the descendants of Ishmael; the fiercest Bedouin are refined and mild compared with the Apaches. Even the brutal and criminal classes of civilization, the pugilists, roughs, burglars, and pickpockets of our large cities, the men whose daily life is rebellion against conscience, commandment, and justice, offer a gentler and nobler type of character and expression than these "children of nature." There was hardly a face among that gang of wild riders which did not outdo the face of Texas Smith in degraded ferocity. Almost every man and boy was obviously a liar, a thief, and a murderer. The air of beastly cruelty was made even more hateful by an air of beastly cunning. Taking color, brutality, grotesqueness, and filth together, it seemed as if here were a mob of those malignant and ill-favored devils whom Dante has described and the art of his age has painted and sculptured.

It is possible, by the way, that this appearance of moral ugliness was due in part to the physical ugliness of features, which were nearly without exception coarse, irregular, exaggerated, grotesque, and in some cases more like hideous masks than like faces.

Ferocity of expression was further enhanced by poverty and squalor. The mass of this fierce cavalry was wretchedly clothed and disgustingly dirty. Even the showy Mexican costume of Manga Colorada was ripped, frayed, stained with grease and perspiration, and not free from sombre spots which looked like blood. Every one wore the breech-cloth, in some cases nicely fitted and sewed, in others nothing but a shapeless piece of deerskin tied on anyhow. There were a few, either minor chiefs, or leading braves, or professional dandies (for this class exists among the Indians), who sported something like a full Apache costume, consisting of a helmet-shaped cap with a plume of feathers, a blanket or *serape* flying loose from the shoulders, a shirt and breech-cloth, and a pair of long boots, made large and loose in the Mexican style and showy with dyeing and embroidery. These boots, very necessary to men who must ride through thorns and bushes, were either drawn up so as to cover the thighs or turned over from the knee downward, like the leg-covering of Rupert's cavaliers. Many heads were bare, or merely shielded by wreaths of grasses and leaves, the greenery contrasting fantastically with the unkempt hair and fierce faces, but producing at a distance an effect which was not without sylvan grace.

The only weapons were iron-tipped lances eight or nine feet long, thick and strong bows of three or three and a half feet, and quivers of arrows slung across the thigh or over the shoulder. The Apaches make little use of firearms, being too lazy or too stupid to keep them in order, and finding it difficult to get ammunition. But so long as they have to fight only the unwarlike Mexicans, they are none the worse for this lack. The Mexicans fly at the first yell; the Apaches ride after them and lance them in the back; clumsy *escopetos* drop loaded from the hands of dying cowards. Such are the battles of New Mexico. It is only when these red-skinned Tartars meet Americans or such high-spirited Indians as the Opates that they have to recoil before gunpowder.*

The fact that Coronado dared ride into this camp of thieving assassins shows what risks he could force himself to run when he thought it necessary. He was not physically a very brave man; he had no pugnacity and no adventurous love of danger for its own sake; but when he was resolved on an enterprise, he could go through with it.

There was a rest of several hours. The rancheros fed the horses on corn which they had brought in small sacks. Texas Smith kept watch, suffered no Apache to touch him, had his pistols always cocked, and stood ready to sell life at the highest price. Coronado walked deliberately to a retired spot with Manga Colorada, Delgadito, and two other chiefs, and made known his propositions. What he desired was that the Apaches should quit their present post immediately, perform a forced march of a hundred and forty miles or so to the southwest, place themselves across the overland trail through Bernalillo, and do something to alarm people. No great harm; he did not want men murdered nor houses burned; they might eat a few cattle, if they were hungry: there were plenty of cattle, and Apaches must live. And if they should yell at a train or so and stampede the loose mules, he had no objection. But no slaughtering; he wanted them to be merciful: just make a pretence of harrying in Bernalillo; nothing more.

The chiefs turned their ill-favored countenances on each other, and talked for a while in their own language. Then, looking at Coronado, they grunted, nodded, and sat in silence, waiting for his terms.

"Send that boy away," said the Mexican, pointing to a youth of twelve or fourteen, better dressed than most Apache urchins, who had joined the little circle.

"It is my son," replied Manga Colorada. "He is learning to be a chief."

The boy stood upright, facing the group with dignity, a handsomer youth than is often seen among his people. Coronado, who had something of the artist in him, was so interested in noting the lad's regular features and tragic firmness of expression, that for a moment he forgot his projects. Manga Colorada, mistaking the cause of his silence, encouraged him to proceed.

"My son does not speak Spanish," he said. "He will not understand."

"You know what money is?" inquired the Mexican.

"Yes, we know," grunted the chief.

"You can buy clothes and arms with it in the villages, and aguardiente.'

Another grunt of assent and satisfaction.

"Three hundred piastres," said Coronado.

The chiefs consulted in their own tongue, and then replied, "The way is long.

"How much?"

Manga Colorada held up five fingers.

"Five hundred?'

A unanimous grunt.

"It is all I have," said Coronado.

The chiefs made no reply.

* Since those times the Apaches have learned to use firearms.

Coronado rose, walked to his horse, took two small packages out of his saddle-bags and slipped them slily into his boots, and then carried the bags to where the chiefs sat in council. There he held them up and rolled out five *rouleaux*, each containing a hundred Mexican dollars. The Indians tore open the envelopes, stared at the broad pieces, fingered them, jingled them together, and uttered grunts of amazement and joy. Probably they had never before seen so much money, at least not in their own possession. Coronado was hardly less content; for while he had received a thousand dollars to bring about this understanding, he had risked but seven hundred with him, and of these he had saved two hundred.

Four hours later the camp had vanished, and the Indians were on their way toward the southwest, the moonlight showing their irregular column of march, and glinting faintly from the heads of their lances.

At nine or ten in the evening, when every Apache had disappeared, and the clatter of ponies had gone far away into the quiet night, Coronado lay down to rest. He would have started homeward, but the country was a complete desert, the trail led here and there over vast sheets of trackless rock, and he feared that he might lose his way. Texas Smith and one of the rancheros had ridden after the Apaches to see whether they kept the direction which had been agreed upon. One ranchero was slumbering already, and the third crouched as sentinel.

Coronado could not sleep at once. He thought over his enterprise, cross-examined his chances of success, studied the invisible courses of the future. Leave Clara on the plains, to be butchered by Indians, or to die of starvation? He hardly considered the idea; it was horrible and repulsive; better marry her. If necessary, force her into a marriage; he could bring it about somehow; she would be much in his power. Well, he had got rid of Thurstane; that was a great obstacle removed. Probably, that fellow being out of sight, he, Coronado, could soon eclipse him in the girl's estimation. There would be no need of violence; all would go easily and end in prosperity. Garcia would be furious at the marriage, but Garcia was a fool to expect any other result.

However, here he was, just at the beginning of things, and by no means safe from danger. He had two hundred dollars in his boot-legs. Had his rancheros suspected it? Would they murder him for the money? He hoped not; he just faintly hoped not; for he was becoming very sleepy; he was asleep.

He was awakened by a noise, or perhaps it was a touch, he scarcely knew what. He struggled as fiercely and vainly as one who fights against a nightmare. A dark form was over him, a hard knee was on his breast, hard knuckles were at his throat, an arm was raised to strike, a weapon was gleaming.

On the threshold of his enterprise, after he had taken its first hazardous step with safety and success, Coronado found himself at the point of death.

CHAPTER V.

WHEN Coronado regained a portion of the senses which had been throttled out of him, he discovered Texas Smith standing by his side, and two dead men lying near, all rather vaguely seen at first through his dizziness and the moonlight.

"What does this mean?" he gasped, getting on his hands and knees, and then on his feet. "Who has been assassinating?"

The borderer, who, instead of helping his employer to rise, was coolly reloading his rifle, did not immediately reply. As the shaken and somewhat unmanned Coronado looked at him, he was afraid of him. The moonlight made Smith's sallow, disfigured face so much more ghastly than usual, that he had the air of a ghoul or vampyre. And when, after carefully capping his piece, he drawled forth the word "Patchies," his harsh, croaking voice had an unwholesome, unhuman sound, as if it were indeed the utterance of a feeder upon corpses.

"Apaches!" said Coronado. "What! after I had made a treaty with them?"

"This un is a 'Patchie," remarked Texas, giving the nearest body a shove with his boot. "Thar was two of 'em. They knifed one of your men. T'other cleared, he did. I was comin' in afoot. I had a notion of suthin' goin' on, 'n' left the critters out thar, with the rancheros, 'n' stole in. Got in just in time to pop the cuss that had you. T'other un vamosed."

"Oh, the villains!" shrieked Coronado, excited at the thought of his narrow escape. "This is the way they keep their treaties."

"Mought be these a'n't the same," observed Texas. "Some 'Patchies is wild, 'n' live separate, like bachelor beavers."

Coronado stooped and examined the dead Indian. He was a miserable object, naked, except a ragged, filthy breech-clout, his figure gaunt, and his legs absolutely scaly with dirt, starvation, and hard living of all sorts. He might well be one of those outcasts who are in disfavor with their savage brethren, lead a precarious existence outside of the tribal organization, and are to the Apaches what the Texas Smiths are to decent Americans.

"One of the bachelor-beaver sort, you bet," continued Texas. "Don't run with the rest of the crowd."

"And there's that infernal coward of a ranchero," cried Coronado, as the runaway sentry sneaked back to the group. "You cursed poltroon, why didn't you give the alarm? Why didn't you fight?"

He struck the man, pulled his long hair, threw him down, kicked him, and spat on him. Texas Smith looked on with an approving grin, and suggested, "Better shute the dam cuss."

But Coronado was not bloodthirsty; having vented his spite, he let the fellow go. "You saved my life," he said to Texas. "When we get back you shall be paid for it."

At the moment he intended to present him with the two hundred dollars which were cumbering his boots. But by the time they had reached Garcia's hacienda on the way back to Sante Fé, his gratitude had fallen off seventy-five per cent., and he thought fifty enough. Even that diminished his profits on the expedition to four hundred and fifty dollars. And Coronado, although extravagant, was not generous; he liked to spend money, but he hated to give it or pay it.

During the four days which immediately followed his safe return to Santa Fé, he and Garcia were in a worry of anxiety. Would Manga Colorada fulfil his contract and cast a shadow of peril over the Bernalillo route? Would letters or messengers arrive from California, informing Clara of the death and will of Muñoz? Everything happened as they wished; reports came that the Apaches were raiding in Bernalillo; the girl received no news concerning her grandfather. Coronado, smiling with success and hope, met Thurstane at the Van Diemen house, in the presence of Clara and Aunt Maria, and blandly triumphed over him.

"How now about your safe road through the southern counties?" he said, "Apaches!"

"So I hear," replied the young officer soberly. "It is horribly unlucky."

"We start to-morrow," added Coronado.

"To-morrow!" replied Thurstane, with a look of dismay.

"I hope you will be with us," said Coronado.

"Everything goes wrong," exclaimed the annoyed lieutenant. "Here are some of my stores damaged, and I have had to ask for a board of survey. I couldn't possibly leave for two days yet, even if my recruits should arrive."

"How very unfortunate!" groaned Coronado. "My dear fellow, we had counted on you."

"Lieutenant Thurstane, can't you overtake us?" inquired Clara.

Thurstane wanted to kneel down and thank her, while Coronado wanted to throw something at her.

"I will try," promised the officer, his fine, frank, manly face brightening with pleasure. "If the thing can be done, it will be done."

Coronado, while hoping that he would be ordered by the southern route, or that he would somehow break his neck, had the superfine brass to say, "Don't fail us, Lieutenant."

In spite of the managements of the Mexican to keep Clara and Thurstane apart, the latter succeeded in getting an aside with the young lady.

"So you take the northern trail?" he said, with a seriousness which gave his blue-black eyes an expression of almost painful pathos. Those eyes were traitors; however discreet the rest of his face might be, they revealed his feelings; they were altogether too pathetic to be in the head of a man and an officer.

"But you will overtake us," Clara replied, out of a charming faith that with men all things are possible.

"Yes," he said, almost fiercely.

"Besides, Coronado knows," she added, still trusting in the male being. "He says this is the surest road."

Thurstane did not believe it, but he did not want to alarm her when alarm was useless, and he made no comment.

"I have a great mind to resign," he presently broke out.

Clara colored; she did not fully understand him, but she guessed that all this emotion was somehow on her account; and a surprised, warm Spanish heart beat at once its alarm.

"It would be of no use," he immediately added. "I couldn't get away until my resignation had been accepted. I must bear this as well as I can."

The young lady began to like him better than ever before, and yet she began to draw gently away from him, frightened by a consciousness of her liking.

"I beg your pardon, Miss Van Diemen," said Thurstane, in an inexplicable confusion.

"There is no need," replied Clara, equally confused.

"Well," he resumed, after a struggle to regain his self-control, "I will do my utmost to overtake you."

"We shall be very glad," returned Clara, with a singular mixture of consciousness and artlessness.

There was an exquisite innocence and almost childish simplicity in this girl of eighteen. It was, so to speak, not quite civilized; it was not in the style of American young ladies; our officer had never, at home, observed anything like it; and, of course—O yes, of course, it fascinated him. The truth is, he was so far gone in loving her that he would have been charmed by her ways no matter what they might have been.

On the very morning after the above dialogue Garcia's train started for Rio

Arriba, taking with it a girl who had been singled out for a marriage which she did not guess, or for a death whose horrors were beyond her wildest fears.

The train consisted of six long and heavy covered vehicles, not dissimilar in size, strength, and build to army wagons. Garcia had thought that two would suffice; six wagons, with their mules, etc., were a small fortune: what if the Apaches should take them? But Coronado had replied: "Nobody sends a train ot two wagons; do you want to rouse suspicion?"

So there were six; and each had a driver and a muleteer, making twelve hired men thus far. On horseback, there were six Mexicans, nominally cattle-drivers going to California, but really guards for the expedition—the most courageous bullies that could be picked up in Santa Fé, each armed with pistols and a rifle. Finally, there were Coronado and his terrible henchman, Texas Smith, with their rifles and revolvers. Old Garcia perspired with anguish as he looked over his caravan, and figured up the cost in his head.

Thurstane, wretched at heart, but with a cheering smile on his lips, came to bid the ladies farewell.

"What do you think of this?" Aunt Maria called to him from her seat in one of the covered wagons. "We are going a thousand miles through deserts and savages. You men suppose that women have no courage. I call this heroism."

"Certainly," nodded the young fellow, not thinking of her at all, unless it was that she was next door to an idiot.

Although his mind was so full of Clara that it did not seem as if he could receive an impression from any other human being, his attention was for a moment arrested by a countenance which struck him as being more ferocious than he had ever seen before except on the shoulders of an Apache. A tall man in Mexican costume, with a scar on his chin and another on his cheek, was glaring at him with two intensely black and savage eyes. It was Texas Smith, taking the measure of Thurstane's fighting power and disposition. A hint from Coronado had warned the borderer that here was a person whom it might be necessary some day to get rid of. The officer responded to this ferocious gaze with a grim, imperious stare, such as one is apt to acquire amid the responsibilities and dangers of army life. It was like a wolf and a mastiff surveying each other.

Thurstanc advanced to Clara, helped her into her saddle, and held her hand while he urged her to be careful of herself, never to wander from the train, never to be alone, etc. The girl turned a little pale; it was not exactly because of his anxious manner; it was because of the eloquence that there is in a word of parting. At the moment she felt so alone in the world, in such womanish need of sympathy, that had he whispered to her, "Be my wife," she might have reached out her hands to him. But Thurstane was far from guessing that an angel could have such weak impulses; and he no more thought of proposing to her thus abruptly than of ascending off-hand into heaven.

Coronado observed the scene, and guessing how perilous the moment was, pushed forward his uncle to say good-by to Clara. The old scoundrel kissed her hand; he did not dare to lift his one eye to her face; he kissed her hand and bowed himself out of reach.

"Farewell, Mr. Garcia," called Aunt Maria. "Poor, excellent old creature! What a pity he can't understand English! I should so like to say something nice to him. Farewell, Mr. Garcia."

Garcia kissed his fat fingers to her, took off his sombrero, waved it, bowed a dozen times, and smiled like a scared devil. Then, with other good-bys, delivered right and left, from everybody to everybody, the train rumbled away.

Thurstane was about to accompany it out of the town when his clerk came to tell him that the board of survey required his immediate presence. Cursing his hard fate, and wishing himself anything but an officer in the army, he waved a last farewell to Clara, and turned his back on her, perhaps forever.

Santa Fé is situated on the great central plateau of North America, seven thousand feet above the level of the sea. Around it spreads an arid plain, sloping slightly where it approaches the Rio Grande, and bordered by mountains which toward the south are of moderate height, while toward the north they rise into fine peaks, glorious with eternal snow. Although the city is in the latitude of Albemarle Sound, North Carolina, its elevation and its neighborhood to Alpine ranges give it a climate which is in the main cool, equable, and healthy.

The expedition moved across the plain in a southwesterly direction. Coronado's intention was to cross the Rio Grande at Peña Blanca, skirt the southern edge of the Jemez Mountains, reach San Isidoro, and then march northward toward the San Juan region. The wagons were well fitted out with mules, and as Garcia had not chosen to send much merchandise by this risky route, they were light, so that the rate of progress was unusually rapid. We cannot trouble ourselves with the minor incidents of the journey. Taking it for granted that the Rio Grande was passed, that halts were made, meals cooked and eaten, nights passed in sleep, days in pleasant and picturesque travelling, we will leap into the desert land beyond San Isidoro.

The train was now seventy-five miles from Santa Fé. Coronado had so pushed the pace that he had made this distance in the rather remarkable time of three days. Of course his object in thus hurrying was to get so far ahead of Thurstane that the latter would not try to overtake him, or would get lost in attempting it.

Meanwhile he had not forgotten Garcia's little plan, and he had even better remembered his own. The time might come when he would be driven to *lose* Clara; it was very shocking to think of, however, and so for the present he did not think of it; on the contrary, he worked hard (much as he hated work) at courting her.

It is strange that so many men who are morally in a state of decomposition should be, or at least can be, sweet and charming in manner. During these three days Coronado was delightful; and not merely in this, that he watched over Clara's comfort, rode a great deal by her side, gathered wild flowers for her, talked much and agreeably; but also in that he poured oil over his whole conduct, and was good to everybody. Although his natural disposition was to be domineering to inferiors and irascible under the small provocations of life, he now gave his orders in a gentle tone, never stormed at the drivers for their blunders, made light of the bad cooking, and was in short a model for travellers, lovers, and husbands. Few human beings have so much self-control as Coronado, and so little. So long as it was policy to be sweet, he could generally be a very honeycomb; but once a certain limit of patience passed, he was like a swarm of angry bees; he became blind, mad, and poisonous with passion.

"Mr. Coronado, you are a wonder," proclaimed the admiring Aunt Maria. "You are the only man I ever knew that was patient."

"I catch a grace from those who have it abundantly and to spare," said Coronado, taking off his hat and waving it at the two ladies.

"Ah, yes, we women know how to be patient," smiled Aunt Maria. "I think we are born so. But, more than that, we learn it. Moreover, our physical nature teaches us. We have lessons of pain and weakness that men know nothing of. The great, healthy savages! If they had our troubles, they might have some of our virtues."

"I refuse to believe it," cried Coronado. "Man acquire woman's worth? Never! The nature of the beast is inferior. He is not fashioned to become an angel."

"How charmingly candid and humble!" thought Aunt Maria. "How different from that sulky, proud Thurstane, who never says anything of the sort, and never thinks it either, I'll be bound."

All this sort of talk passed over Clara as a desert wind passes over an oasis, bringing no pleasant songs of birds, and sowing no fruitful seed. She had her born ideas as to men and women, and she was seemingly incapable of receiving any others. In her mind men were strong and brave, and women weak and timorous; she believed that the first were good to hold on to, and that the last were good to hold on; all this she held by birthright, without ever reasoning upon it or caring to prove it.

Coronado, on his part, hooted in his soul at Mrs. Stanley's whimsies, and half supposed her to be of unsound mind. Nor would he have said what he did about the vast superiority of the female sex, had he supposed that Clara would attach the least weight to it. He knew that the girl looked upon his extravagant declarations as merely so many compliments paid to her eccentric relative, equivalent to bowings and scrapings and flourishes of the sombrero. Both Spaniards, they instinctively comprehended each other, at least in the surface matters of intercourse. Meanwhile the American strong-minded female understood herself, it is to be charitably hoped, but understood herself alone.

Coronado did not hurry his courtship, for he believed that he had a clear field before him, and he was too sagacious to startle Clara by overmuch energy. Meantime he began to be conscious that an influence from her was reaching his spirit. He had hitherto considered her a child; one day he suddenly recognized her as a woman. Now a woman, a beautiful woman especially, alone with one in the desert, is very mighty. Matches are made in trains overland as easily and quickly as on sea voyages or at quiet summer resorts. Coronado began—only moderately as yet—to fall in love.

But an ugly incident came to disturb his opening dream of affection, happiness, wealth, and success. Toward the close of his fourth day's march, after he had got well into the unsettled region beyond San Isidoro, he discovered, several miles behind the train, a party of five horsemen. He was on one summit and they on another, with a deep, stony valley intervening. Without a moment's hesitation, he galloped down a long slope, rejoined the creeping wagons, hurried them forward a mile or so, and turned into a ravine for the night's halt.

Whether the cavaliers were Indians or Thurstane and his four recruits he had been unable to make out. They had not seen the train; the nature of the ground had prevented that. It was now past sundown, and darkness coming on rapidly. Whispering something about Apaches, he gave orders to lie close and light no fires for a while, trusting that the pursuers would pass his hiding place.

For a moment he thought of sending Texas Smith to ambush the party, and shoot Thurstane if he should be in it, pleading afterwards that the men looked, in the darkness, like Apaches. But no; this was an extreme measure; he revolted against it a little. Moreover, there was danger of retribution: settlements not so far off; soldiers still nearer.

So he lay quiet, chewing a bit of grass to allay his nervousness, and talking stronger love to Clara than he had yet thought needful or wise.

CHAPTER VI.

LIEUTENANT THURSTANE passed the mouth of the ravine in the dusk of twilight, without guessing that it contained Clara Van Diemen and her perils.

He had with him Sergeant Weber of his own company, just returned from recruiting service at St. Louis, and three recruits for the company, Kelly, Shubert, and Sweeny.

Weber, a sunburnt German, with sandy eyelashes, blue eyes, and a scar on his cheek, had been a soldier from his eighteenth to his thirtieth year, and wore the serious, patient, much-enduring air peculiar to veterans. Kelly, an Irishman, also about thirty, slender in form and somewhat haggard in face, with the same quiet, contained, seasoned look to him, the same reminiscence of unavoidable sufferings silently borne, was also an old infantry man, having served in both the British and American armies. Shubert was an American lad, who had got tired of clerking it in an apothecary's shop, and had enlisted from a desire for adventure, as you might guess from his larkish countenance. Sweeny was a diminutive Paddy, hardly regulation height for the army, as light and lively as a monkey, and with much the air of one.

Thurstane had obtained orders from the post commandant to lead his party by the northern route, on condition that he would investigate and report as to its practicability for military and other transit. He had also been allowed to draw by requisition fifty days' rations, a box of ammunition, and four mules. Starting thirty-six hours after Coronado, he made in two days and a half the distance which the train had accomplished in four. Now he had overtaken his quarry, and in the obscurity had passed it.

But Sergeant Weber was an old hand on the Plains, and notwithstanding the darkness and the generally stony nature of the ground, he presently discovered that the fresh trail of the wagons was missing. Thurstane tried to retrace his steps, but starless night had already fallen thick around him, and before long he had to come to a halt. He was opposite the mouth of the ravine; he was within five hundred yards of Clara, and raging because he could not find her. Suddenly Coronado's cooking fires flickered through the gloom; in five minutes the two parties were together.

It was a joyous meeting to Thurstane and a disgusting one to Coronado. Nevertheless the latter rushed at the officer, grasped him by both hands, and shouted, "All hail, Lieutenant! So, there you are at last! My dear fellow, what a pleasure!"

"Yes, indeed, by Jove!" returned the young fellow, unusually boisterous in his joy, and shaking hands with everybody, not rejecting even muleteers. And then what throbbing, what adoration, what supernal delight, in the moment when he faced Clara

In the morning the journey recommenced. As neither Thurstane nor Coronado had now any cause for hurry, the pace was moderate. The soldiers marched on foot, in order to leave the government mules no other load than the rations and ammunition, and so enable them to recover from their sharp push of over eighty miles. The party now consisted of twenty-five men, for the most part pretty well armed. Of the other sex there were, besides Mrs. Stanley and Clara, a half-breed girl named Pépita, who served as lady's maid, and two Indian women from Garcia's hacienda, whose specialties were cooking and washing. In all thirty persons, a nomadic village.

At the first halt Sergeant Weber approached Thurstane with a timorous air, saluted, and asked, "Leftenant, can we leafe our knabsacks in the vagons? The gentleman has gifen us bermission."

"The men ought to learn to carry their knapsacks," said Thurstane. "They will have to do it in serious service."

"It is drue, Leftenant," replied Weber, saluting again and moving off without a sign of disappointment.

"Let that man come back here," called Aunt Maria, who had overheard the dialogue. "Certainly they can put their loads in the wagons. I told Mr. Coronado to tell them so."

Weber looked at her without moving a muscle, and without showing either wonder or amusement. Thurstane could not help grinning good-naturedly as he said, "I receive your orders, Mrs. Stanley. Weber, you can put the knapsacks in the wagons."

Weber saluted anew, gave Mrs. Stanley a glance of gratitude, and went about his pleasant business. An old soldier is not in general so strict a disciplinarian as a young one.

"What a brute that Lieutenant is!" thought Aunt Maria. "Make those poor fellows carry those monstrous packs? Nonsense and tyranny! How different from Mr. Coronado! *He* fairly jumped at my idea."

Thurstane stepped over to Coronado and said, "You are very kind to relieve my men at the expense of your animals. I am much obliged to you."

"It is nothing," replied the Mexican, waving his hand graciously. "I am delighted to be of service, and to show myself a good citizen."

In fact, he had been quite willing to favor the soldiers; why not, so long as he could not get rid of them? If the Apaches would lance them all, including Thurstane, he would rejoice; but while that could not be, he might as well show himself civil and gain popularity. It was not Coronado's style to bark when there was no chance of biting.

He was in serious thought the while. How should he rid himself of this rival, this obstacle in the way of his well-laid plans, this interloper into his caravan? Must he call upon Texas Smith to assassinate the fellow? It was a disagreeably brutal solution of the difficulty, and moreover it might lead to loud suspicion and scandal, and finally it might be downright dangerous. There was such a thing as trial for murder and for conspiracy to effect murder. As to causing a United States officer to vanish quietly, as might perhaps be done with an ordinary American emigrant, that was too good a thing to be hoped. He must wait; he must have patience; he must trust to the future; perhaps some precipice would favor him; perhaps the wild Indians. He offered his cigaritos to Thurstane, and they smoked tranquilly in company.

"What route do you take from here?" asked the officer.

"Pass Washington, as you call it. Then the Moqui country. Then the San Juan."

"There is no possible road down the San Juan and the Colorado."

"If we find that to be so, we will sweep southward. I am, in a measure, exploring. Garcia wants a route to Middle California."

"I also have a sort of exploring leave. I shall take the liberty to keep along with you. It may be best for both."

The announcement sounded like a threat of surveillance, and Coronado's dark cheek turned darker with angry blood. This stolid and intrusive brute was absolutely demanding his own death. After saying, with a forced smile, "You will be invaluable to us, Lieutenant," the Mexican lounged away to where Texas Smith was examining his firearms, and whispered, "Well, will you do it?"

"I ain't afeared of *him*," muttered the borderer. "It's his clothes. I don't like to shute at jackets with them buttons. I mought git into big trouble. The army is a big thing."

"Two hundred dollars," whispered Coronado.

"You said that befo'," croaked Texas. "Go it some better."

"Four hundred."

"Stranger," said Texas, after debating his chances, "it's a big thing. But I'll do it for that."

Coronado walked away, hurried up his muleteers, exchanged a word with Mrs. Stanley, and finally returned to Thurstane. His thin, dry, dusky fingers trembled a little, but he looked his man steadily in the face, while he tendered him another cigarito.

"Who is your hunter?" asked the officer. "I must say he is a devilish bad-looking fellow."

"He is one of the best hunters Garcia ever had," replied the Mexican. "He is one of your own people. You ought to like him."

Further journeying brought with it topographical adventures. The country into which they were penetrating is one of the most remarkable in the world for its physical peculiarities. Its scenery bears about the same relation to the scenery of earth in general, that a skeleton's head or a grotesque mask bears to the countenance of living humanity. In no other portion of our planet is nature so unnatural, so fanciful and extravagant, and seemingly the production of caprice, as on the great central plateau of North America.

They had left far behind the fertile valley of the Rio Grande, and had placed between it and them the barren, sullen piles of the Jemez mountains. No more long sweeps of grassy plain or slope; they were amid the débris of rocks which hedge in the upper heights of the great plateau; they were struggling through it like a forlorn hope through *chevaux-de-frise*. The morning sun came upon them over treeless ridges of sandstone, and disappeared at evening behind ridges equally naked and arid. The sides of these barren masses, seamed by the action of water in remote geologic ages, and never softened or smoothed by the gentle attrition of rain, were infinitely more wild and jagged in their details than ruins. It seemed as if the Titans had built here, and their works had been shattered by thunderbolts.

Many heights were truncated mounds of rock, resembling gigantic platforms with ruinous sides, such as are known in this Western land as *mesas* or *buttes*. They were Nature's enormous mockery of the most ambitious architecture of man, the pyramids of Egypt and the platform of Baalbek. Terrace above terrace of shattered wall; escarpments which had been displaced as if by the explosion of some incredible mine; ramparts which were here high and regular, and there gaping in mighty fissures, or suddenly altogether lacking; long sweeps of stairway, winding dizzily upwards, only to close in an impossible leap: there was no end to the fantastic outlines and the suggestions of destruction.

Nor were the open spaces between these rocky mounds less remarkable. In one valley, the course of a river which vanished ages ago, the power of fire had left its monuments amid those of the power of water. The sedimentary rock of sandstone, shales, and marl, not only showed veins of ignitible lignite, but it was pierced by the trap which had been shot up from earth's flaming recesses. Dikes of this volcanic stone crossed each other or ran in long parallels, presenting forms of fortifications, walls of buildings, ruined lines of aqueducts. The sandstone and marl had been worn away by the departed river, and by the delicately sweeping, incessant, tireless wings of the afreets of the air, leaving the iron-like trap in bold projection.

Some of these dikes stretched long distances, with a nearly uniform height of four or five feet, closely resembling old field-walls of the solidest masonry. Others, not so extensive, but higher and pierced with holes, seemed to be fragments of ruined edifices, with broken windows and shattered portals. As the trap is columnar, and the columns are horizontal in their direction, the joints of the polygons show along the surface of the ramparts, causing them to look like the work of Cyclopean builders. The Indians and Mexicans of the expedition, deceived by the similarity between these freaks of creation and the results of human workmanship, repeatedly called out, "Casas Grandes! Casas de Montezuma!"

It would seem, indeed, as if the ancient peoples of this country, in order to arrive at the idea of a large architecture, had only to copy the grotesque rock-work of nature. Who knows but that such might have been the germinal idea of their constructions? Mrs. Stanley was quite sure of it. In fact, she was disposed to maintain that the trap walls were really human masonry, and the production of Montezuma, or of the Amazons invented by Coronado.

"Those four-sided and six-sided stones look altogether too regular to be accidental," was her conclusion. Notwithstanding her belief in a superintending Deity, she had an idea that much of this world was made by hazard, or perhaps by the Old Harry.

In one valley the ancient demon of water-force had excelled himself in enchantments. The slopes of the alluvial soil were dotted with little buttes of mingled sandstone and shale, varying from five to twenty feet in height, many of them bearing a grotesque likeness to artificial objects. There were columns, there were haystacks, there were enormous bells, there were inverted jars, there were junk bottles, there were rustic seats. Most of these fantastic figures were surmounted by a flat capital, the remnant of a layer of stone harder than the rest of the mass, and therefore less worn by the water erosion

One fragment looked like a monstrous gymnastic club standing upright, with a broad button to secure the grip. Another was a mighty centre-table, fit for the halls of the Scandinavian gods, consisting of a solid prop or pedestal twelve feet high, swelling out at the top into a leaf fifteen feet across. Another was a stone hat, standing on its crown, with a brim two yards in diameter. Occasionally there was a figure which had lost its capital, and so looked like a broken pillar, a sugar loaf, a pear. Imbedded in these grotesques of sandstone were fossils of wood, of fresh-water shells, and of fishes.

It was a land of extravagances and of wonders. The marvellous adventures of the "Arabian Nights" would have seemed natural in it. It reminded you after a vague fashion of the scenery suggested to the imagination by some of its details or those of the "Pilgrim's Progress." Sindbad the Sailor carrying the Old Man of the Sea; Giant Despair scowling from a make-believe window in a fictitious castle of eroded sandstone; a roc with wings eighty feet long, poising on a giddy pinnacle to pounce upon an elephant; pilgrim Christian advancing with sword and buckler against a demon guarding some rocky portal, would have excited no astonishment here.

Of a sudden there came an adventure which gave opening for knight-errantry. As Thurstane, Coronado, and Texas Smith were riding a few hundred yards ahead of the caravan, and just emerging from what seemed an enormous court or public square, surrounded by ruined edifices of gigantic magnitude, they discovered a man running toward them in a style which reminded the Lieutenant of Timorous and Mistrust flying from the lions. Impossible to see what he was afraid of; there was a broad, yellow plain, dotted with monuments of sandstone; no living thing visible but this man running.

He was an American; at least he had the clothes of one. As he approached, he appeared to be a lean, lank, narrow-shouldered, yellow-faced, yellow-haired creature, such as you might expect to find on Cape Cod or thereabouts. Hollow-chested as he was, he had a yell in him which was quite surprising. From the time that he sighted the three horsemen he kept up a steady screech until he was safe under their noses. Then he fell flat and gasped for nearly a minute without speaking. His first words were, "That's pooty good sailin' for a man who ain't used to't."

"Did you run all the way from Down East?" asked Thurstane.

"All the way from that bewt there—the one that looks most like a haystack."

"Well, who the devil are you?"

"I'm Phineas Glover—Capm Phineas Glover—from Fair Haven, Connecticut. I'm goin' to Californy after gold. Got lost out of the caravan among the mountings. Was comin' along alone, 'n' run afoul of some Injuns. They're hidin' behind that bewt, 'n' they've got my mewl."

"Indians! How many are there?"

"Only three. 'N' I expect they a'nt the real wild kind, nuther. Sorter half Injun, half engineer, like what come round in the circuses. Didn't make much of 'n offer towards carvin' me. But I judged best to quit, the first boat that put off. Ah, they're there yit, 'n' the mewl tew."

"You'll find our train back there," said Thurstane. "You had better make for it. We'll recover your property."

He dashed off at a full run for the butte, closely followed by Texas Smith and Coronado. The Mexican had the best horse, and he would soon have led the other two; but his saddle-girth burst, and in spite of his skill in riding he was nearly thrown. Texas Smith pulled up to aid his employer, but only for an instant, as Coronado called, "Go on."

The borderer now spurred after Thurstane, who had got a dozen rods the lead of him. Coronado rapidly examined his saddle-bags and then his pockets without finding the cord or strap which he needed. He swore a little at this, but not with any poignant emotion, for in the first place fighting was not a thing that he yearned for, and in the second place he hardly anticipated a combat. The robbers, he felt certain, were only vagrant rancheros, or the cowardly Indians of some village, who would have neither the weapons nor the pluck to give battle.

But suddenly an alarming suspicion crossed his mind. Would Texas Smith seize this chance to send a bullet through Thurstane's head from behind? Knowing the cutthroat's recklessness and his almost insane thirst for blood, he feared that this might happen. And there was the train in view; the deed would probably be seen, and, if so, would be seen as murder; and then would come pursuit of the assassin, with possibly his seizure and confession. It would not do; no, it would not do here and now; he must dash forward and prevent it.

Swinging his saddle upon his horse's back, he vaulted into it without touching pommel or stirrup, and set off at full speed to arrest the blow which he desired. Over the plain flew the fiery animal, Coronado balancing himself in his unsteady seat with marvellous ease and grace, his dark eyes steadily watching every movement of the bushwhacker. There were sheets of bare rock here and there; there were loose slates and detached blocks of sandstone. The beast dashed across the first without slipping, and cleared the others without swerving; his rider bowed and swayed in the saddle without falling.

Texas Smith was now within a few yards of Thurstane, and it could be seen that he had drawn his revolver. Coronado asked himself in horror whether the man had understood the words "Go on" as a command for murder. He was thinking very fast; he was thinking as fast as he rode. Once a terrible temptation came upon him: he might let the fatal shot be fired; then he might fire another. Thus he would get rid of Thurstane, and at the same time have the air of avenging him, while ridding himself of his dangerous bravo. But he rejected this plan almost as soon as he thought of it. He did not feel sure of bringing down Texas at the first fire, and if he did not, his own life was not worth a second's purchase. As for the fact that he had been lately saved from death by the borderer, that would not have checked Coronado's hand, even had he remembered it. He must dash on at full speed, and prevent a crime which would be a blunder. But already it was nearly too late, for the Texan was close upon the officer. Nothing could save the doomed man but Coronado's magnificent horsemanship. He seemed a part of his steed; he shot like a bird over the sheets and bowlders of rock; he was a wonder of speed and grace.

Suddenly the outlaw's pistol rose to a level, and Coronado uttered a shout of anxiety and horror.

CHAPTER VII.

AT the shout which Coronado uttered on seeing Texas Smith's pistol aimed at Thurstane, the assassin turned his head, discovered the train, and, lowering his weapon, rode peacefully alongside of his intended victim.

Captain Phin Glover's mule was found grazing behind the butte, in the midst of the gallant Captain's dishevelled baggage, while the robbers had vanished by a magic which seemed quite natural in this scenery of grotesque marvels. They had unquestionably seen or heard their pursuers ; but how had they got into the bowels of the earth to escape them ?

Thurstane presently solved the mystery by pointing out three crouching figures on the flat cap of stone which surmounted the shales and marl of the butte. Bare feet and desperation of terror could alone explain how they had reached this impossible refuge. Texas Smith immediately consoled himself for his disappointment as to Thurstane by shooting two of these wretches before his hand could be stayed.

"They're nothin' but Injuns," he said, with a savage glare, when the Lieutenant struck aside his revolver and called him a murdering brute.

The third skulker took advantage of the cessation of firing to tumble down from his perch and fly for his life. The indefatigable Smith broke away from Thurstane, dashed after the pitiful fugitive, leaned over him as he ran, and shot him dead.

"I have a great mind to blow your brains out, you beast," roared the disgusted officer, who had followed closely. "I told you not to shoot that man." And here he swore heartily, for which we must endeavor to forgive him, seeing that he belonged to the army.

Coronado interfered. "My dear Lieutenant! after all, they were robbers. They deserved punishment." And so on.

Texas Smith looked less angry and more discomfited than might have been expected, considering his hardening life and ferocious nature.

"Didn't s'p'ose you really keered much for the cuss," he said, glancing respectfully at the imperious and angry face of the young officer.

"Well, never mind now," growled Thurstane. "It's done, and can't be undone. But, by Jove, I do hate useless massacre. Fighting is another thing."

Sheathing his fury, he rode off rapidly toward the wagons, followed in silence by the others. The three dead vagabonds (perhaps vagrants from the region of Abiquia) remained where they had fallen, one on the stony plain and two on the cap of the butte. The train, trending here toward the northwest, passed six hundred yards to the north of the scene of slaughter; and when Clara and Mrs. Stanley asked what had happened, Coronado told them with perfect glibness that the robbers had got away.

The rescued man, delighted at his escape and the recovery of his mule and luggage, returned thanks right and left, with a volubility which further acquaintance showed to be one of his characteristics. He was a profuse talker; ran a stream every time you looked at him; it was like turning on a mill-race.

"Yes, capm, out of Fair Haven," he said. "Been in the coastin' 'n' Wes' Injy trade. Had 'n unlucky time out las' few years. Had a schuner burnt in port, 'n' lost a brig at sea. Pooty much broke me up. Wife 'n' dahter gone into th' oyster-openin' business. Thought I'd try my han' at openin' gold mines in Californy. Jined a caravan at Fort Leavenworth, 'n' lost my reckonin's back here a ways."

We must return to love matters. However amazing it may be that a man who has no conscience should nevertheless have a heart, such appears to have been the case with that abnormal creature Coronado. The desert had made him take a strong liking to Clara, and now that he had a rival at hand he became impassioned for her. He began to want to marry her, not alone for the sake of her great fortune, but also for her own sake. Her beauty unfolded and blossomed wonderfully before his ardent eyes; for he was under that mighty glamour of the emotions which enables us to see beauty in its completeness; he was favored with the greatest earthly second-sight which is vouchsafed to mortals.

Only in a measure, however; the money still counted for much with him. He had already decided what he would do with the Muñoz fortune when he should get it. He would go to New York and lead a life of frugal extravagance, economical in comforts (as we understand them) and expensive in pleasures. New York, with its adjuncts of Saratoga and Newport, was to him what Paris is to many Americans. In his imagination it was the height of grandeur and happiness to have a box at the opera, to lounge in Broadway, and to dance at the hops of the Saratoga hotels. New Mexico! he would turn his back on it; he would never set eyes on its dull poverty again. As for Clara? Well, of course she would share in his gayeties; was not that enough for any reasonable woman?

But here was this stumbling-block of a Thurstane. In the presence of a handsome rival, who, moreover, had started first in the race, slow was far from being sure. Coronado had discovered, by long experience in flirtation and much intelligent meditation upon it, that, if a man wants to win a woman, he must get her head full of him. He decided, therefore, that at the first chance he would give Clara distinctly to understand how ardently he was in love with her, and so set her to thinking especially of him, and of him alone. Meantime, he looked at her adoringly, insinuated compliments, performed little services, walked his horse much by her side, did his best in conversation, and in all ways tried to outshine the Lieutenant.

He supposed that he did outshine him. A man of thirty always believes that he appears to better advantage than a man of twenty-three or four. He trusts that he has more ideas, that he commits fewer absurdities, that he carries more weight of character than his juvenile rival. Coronado was far more fluent than Thurstane; had a greater command over his moods and manners, and a larger fund of animal spirits; knew more about such social trifles as women like to hear of; and was, in short, a more amusing prattler of small talk. There was a steady seriousness about the young officer—something of the earnest sentimentality of the great Teutonic race—which the mercurial Mexican did not understand nor appreciate, and which he did not imagine could be fascinating to a woman. Knowing well how magnetic passion is in its guise of Southern fervor, he did not know that it is also potent under the cloak of Northern solemnity.

Unluckily for Coronado, Clara was half Teutonic, and could comprehend the tone of her father's race. Notwithstanding Thurstane's shyness and silences, she discovered his moral weight and gathered his unspoken meanings. There was more in this girl than appeared on the surface. Without any power of reasoning concerning character, and without even a disposition to analyze it, she had an instinctive perception of it. While her talk was usually as simple as a child's, and her meditations on men and things were not a bit systematic or logical, her decisions and actions were generally just what they should be.

Some one may wish to know whether she was clever enough to see through the character of Coronado. She was clever enough, but not corrupt enough. Very pure people cannot fully understand people who are very impure. It is probable that angels are considerably in the dark concerning the nature of the devil, and derive their disagreeable impression of him mainly from a consideration of his actions. Clara, limited to a narrow circle of good intentions and conduct, might not divine the wide regions of wickedness through which roved the soul of Coronado, and must wait to see his works before she could fairly bring him to judgment.

Of course she perceived that in various ways he was insincere. When he prattled compliments and expressions of devotion, whether to herself or to others, she made Spanish allowance. It was polite hyperbole; it was about the same as saying good-morning; it was a cheerful way of talking that they had in Mexico; she knew thus much from her social experience. But while she cared little for his adulations, she did not because of them consider him a scoundrel, nor necessarily a hypocrite.

Coronado found and improved opportunities to talk in asides with Clara. Thurstane, the modest, proud, manly youngster, who had no meannesses or trickeries by nature, and had learned none in his honorable profession, would not allow himself to break into these dialogues if they looked at all like confidences. The more he suspected that Coronado was courting Clara, the more resolutely and grimly he said to himself, "Stand back!" The girl should be perfectly free to choose between them; she should be influenced by no compulsions and no stratagems of his; was he not "an officer and a gentleman"?

"By Jove! I am miserable for life," he thought when he suspected, as he sometimes did, that they two were in love. "I'll get myself killed in my next fight. I can't bear it. But I won't interfere. I'll do my duty as an honorable man. Of course she understands me."

But just at this point Clara failed to understand him. It is asserted by some philosophers that women have less conscience about "cutting each other out," breaking up engagements, etc., than men have in such matters. Love-making and its results form such an all-important part of their existence, that they must occasionally allow success therein to overbear such vague, passionless ideas as principles, sentiments of honor, etc. It is, we fear, highly probable that if Clara had been in love with Ralph, and had seen her chance of empire threatened by a rival, she would have come out of that calm innocence which now seemed to enfold her whole nature, and would have done such things as girls may do to avert catastrophes of the affections. She now thought to herself, If he cares for me, how can he keep away from me when he sees Coronado making eyes at me? She was a little vexed with him for behaving so, and was consequently all the sweeter to his rival. This when Ralph would have risked his commission for a smile, and would have died to save her from a sorrow!

Presently this slightly coquettish, yet very good and lovely little being—this seraph from one of Fra Angelica's pictures, endowed with a frailty or two of humanity—found herself the heroine of a trying scene. Coronado hastened it; he judged her ready to fall into his net; he managed the time and place for the capture. The train had been ascending for some hours, and had at last reached a broad plateau, a nearly even floor of sandstone, covered with a carpet of thin earth, the whole noble level bare to the eye at once, without a tree or a thicket to give it detail. It was a scene of tranquillity and monotony; no rains ever disturbed or remoulded the tabulated surface of soil; there, as distinct as if made yesterday, were the tracks of a train which had passed a year before.

"Shall we take a gallop?" said Coronado. "No danger of ambushes here."

Clara's eyes sparkled with youth's love of excitement, and the two horses sprang off at speed toward the centre of the plateau. After a glorious flight of five minutes, enjoyed for the most part in silence, as such swift delights usually are, they dropped into a walk two miles ahead of the wagons.

"That was magnificent," Clara of course said, her face flushed with pleasure and exercise.

"You are wonderfully handsome," observed Coronado, with an air of thinking aloud, which disguised the coarse directness of the flattery. In fact, he was so dazzled by her brilliant color, the sunlight in her disordered curls, and the joyous sparkling of her hazel eyes, that he spoke with an ingratiating honesty.

Clara, who was in one of her unconscious and innocent moods, simply replied, "I suppose people are always handsome enough when they are happy."

"Then I ought to be lovely," said Coronado. "I am happier than I ever was before."

"Coronado, you look very well," observed Clara, turning her eyes on him with a grave expression which rather puzzled him. "This out-of-door life has done you good."

"Then I don't look very well indoors?" he smiled.

"You know what I mean, Coronado. Your health has improved, and your face shows it."

Fearing that she was not in an emotional condition to be bewildered and fascinated by a declaration of love, he queried whether he had not better put off his enterprise until a more susceptible moment. Certainly, if he were without a rival; but there was Thurstane, ready any and every day to propose; it would not do to let *him* have the first word, and cause the first heart-beat. Coronado believed that to make sure of winning the race he must take the lead at the start. Yes, he would offer himself now; he would begin by talking her into a receptive state of mind; that done, he would say with all his eloquence, "I love you."

We must not suppose that the declaration would be a pure fib, or anything like it. The man had no conscience, and he was almost incomparably selfish, but he was capable of loving, and he did love. That is to say, he was inflamed by this girl's beauty and longed to possess it. It is a low species of affection, but it is capable of great violence in a man whose physical nature is ardent, and Coronado's blood could take a heat like lava. Already, although he had not yet developed his full power of longing, he wanted Clara as he had never wanted any woman before. We can best describe his kind of sentiment by that hungry, carnal word *wanted*.

After riding in silent thought for a few rods, he said, "I have lost my good looks now, I suppose."

"What do you mean, Coronado?"

"They depend on my happiness, and that is gone."

"Coronado, you are playing riddles."

"This table-land reminds me of my own life. Do you see that it has no verdure? I have been just as barren of all true happiness. There has been no fruit or blossom of true affection for me to gather. You know that I lost my excellent father and my sainted mother when I was a child. I was too young to miss them; but for all that the bereavement was the same; there was the less love for me. It seems as if there had been none."

"Garcia has been good to you—of late," suggested Clara, rather puzzled to find consolation for a man whose misery was so new to her.

Remembering what a scoundrel Garcia was, and what a villainous business Garcia had sent him upon, Coronado felt like smiling. He knew that the old man had no sentiments beyond egotism, and a family pride which mainly, if not entirely, sprang from it. Such a heart as Garcia's, what a place to nestle in! Such a creature as Coronado seeking comfort in such a breast as his uncle's was very much like a rattlesnake warming himself in a hole of a rock.

"Ah, yes!" sighed Coronado. "Admirable old gentleman! I should not have forgotten him. However, he is a solace which comes rather late. It is only two years since he perceived that he had done me injustice, and received me into favor. And his affection is somewhat cold. Garcia is an old man laden with affairs. Moreover, men in general have little sympathy with men. When we are saddened, we do not look to our own sex for cheer. We look to yours."

Almost every woman responds promptly to a claim for pity.

"I am sorry for you, Coronado," said Clara, in her artless way. "I am, truly."

"You do not know, you cannot know, how you console me."

Satisfied with the results of his experiment in boring for sympathy, he tried another, a dangerous one, it would seem, but very potent when it succeeds.

"This lack of affection has had sad results. I have searched everywhere for it, only to meet with disappointment. In my desperation I have searched where I should not. I have demanded true love of people who had no true love to give. And for this error and wrong I have been terribly punished. The mere failure of hope and trust has been hard enough to bear. But that was not the half. Shame, self-contempt, remorse have been an infinitely heavier burden. If any man was ever cured of trusting for happiness to a wicked world, it is Coronado."

In spite of his words and his elaborately penitent expression, Clara only partially understood him. Some kind of evil life he was obviously confessing, but what kind she only guessed in the vaguest fashion. However, she comprehended enough to interest her warmly: here was a penitent sinner who had forsaken ways of wickedness; here was a struggling soul which needed encouragement and tenderness. A woman loves to believe that she can be potent over hearts, and especially that she can be potent for good. Clara fixed upon Coronado's face a gaze of compassion and benevolence which was almost superhuman. It should have shamed him into honesty; but he was capable of trying to deceive the saints and the Virgin; he merely decided that she was in a fit frame to accept him.

"At last I have a faint hope of a sure and pure happiness," he said. "I have found one who I know can strengthen me and comfort me, if she will. I am seeking to be worthy of her. I am worthy of her so far as adoration can make me. I am ready to surrender my whole life—all that I am and that I can be—to her."

Clara had begun to guess his meaning; the quick blood was already flooding her cheek; the light in her eyes was tremulous with agitation.

"Clara, you must know what I mean," continued Coronado, suddenly reaching his hand toward her, as if to take her captive. "You are the only person I ever loved. I love you with all my soul. Can your heart ever respond to mine? Can you ever bring yourself to be my wife?"

CHAPTER VIII.

WHEN Coronado proposed to Clara, she was for a moment stricken dumb with astonishment and with something like terror.

Her first idea was that she must take him; that the mere fact of a man asking for her gave him a species of right over her; that there was no such thing possible as answering, No. She sat looking at Coronado with a helpless, timorous air, very much as a child looks at his father, when the father, switching his rattan, says, "Come with me."

On recovering herself a little, her first words—uttered slowly, in a tone of surprise and of involuntary reproach—were, "Oh, Coronado! I did not expect this."

"Can't you answer me?" he asked in a voice which was honestly tremulous with emotion. "Can't you say yes?"

"Oh, Coronado!" repeated Clara, a good deal touched by his agitation.

"Can't you?" he pleaded. Repetitions, in such cases, are so natural and so potent.

"Let me think, Coronado," she implored. "I can't answer you now. You have taken me so by surprise!"

"Every moment that you take to think is torture to me," he pleaded, as he continued to press her.

Perhaps she was on the point of giving way before his insistence. Consider the advantages that he had over her in this struggle of wills for the mastery. He was older by ten years; he possessed both the adroitness of self-command and the energy of passion; he had a long experience in love matters, while she had none. He was the proclaimed heir of a man reputed wealthy, and could therefore, as she believed, support her handsomely. Since the death of her father she considered Garcia the head of her family in New Mexico; and Coronado had had the face to tell her that he made his offer with the approval of Garcia. Then she was under supposed obligations to him, and he was to be her protector across the desert.

She was as it were reeling in her saddle, when a truly Spanish idea saved her.

"Muñoz!" she exclaimed. "Coronado, you forget my grandfather. He should know of this."

Although the man was unaccustoned to start, he drew back as if a ghost had confronted him; and even when he recovered from his transitory emotion, he did not at first know how to answer her. It would not do to say, "Muñoz is dead," and much less to add, "You are his heir."

"We are Americans," he at last argued. "Spanish customs are dead and buried. Can't you speak for yourself on a matter which concerns you and me alone?"

"Coronado, I think it would not be right," she replied, holding firmly to her position. "It is probable that my grandfather would be better pleased to have this matter referred to him. I ought to consider him, and you must let me do so."

"I submit," he bowed, seeing that there was no help for it, and deciding to make a grace of necessity. "It pains me, but I submit. Let me hope that you will not let this pass from your mind. Some day, when it is proper, I shall speak again."

He was not wholly dissatisfied, for he trusted that henceforward her head would be full of him, and he had not much hoped to gain more in a first effort.

"I shall always be proud and gratified at the compliment you have paid me," was her reply to his last request.

"You deserve many such compliments," he said, gravely courteous and quite sincere.

Then they cantered back in silence to meet the advancing train.

Yes, Coronado was partly satisfied. He believed that he had gained a firmer footing among the girl's thoughts and emotions than had been gained by Thurstane. In a degree he was right. No sensitive, and pure, and good girl can receive her first offer without being much moved by it. The man who has placed himself at her feet will affect her strongly. She may begin to dread him, or begin to like him more than before; but she cannot remain utterly indifferent to him. The probability is that, unless subsequent events make him disagreeable to her, she will long accord him a measure of esteem and gratitude.

For two or three days, while Clara was thinking much of Coronado, he gave her less than usual of his society. Believing that her mind was occupied with him, that she was wondering whether he were angry, unhappy, etc., he remained a good deal apart, wrapped himself in sadness, and trusted that time would do much for him. Had there been no rival, the plan would have been a good one; but Ralph Thurstane being present, it was less successful.

Ralph had already become more of a favorite than any one knew, even the young lady herself; and now that he found chances for long talks and short gallops with her, he got on better than ever. He was just the kind of youngster a girl of eighteen would naturally like to have ride by her side. He was handsome; at any rate, he was the handsomest man she had seen in the desert, and the desert was just then her sphere of society. You could see in his figure how strong he was, and in his face how brave he was. He was a good fellow, too; "tendir and trew" as the Douglas of the ballad; sincere, frank, thoroughly truthful and honorable. Every way he seemed to be that being that a woman most wants, a potential and devoted protector. Whenever Clara looked in his face her eyes said, without her knowledge, "I trust you."

Now, as we have already stated, Thurstane's eyes were uncommonly fine and expressive. Of the very darkest blue that ever was seen in anybody's head, and shaded, moreover, by remarkably long chestnut lashes, they had the advantages of both blue eyes and black ones, being as gentle as the one and as fervent as the other. Accordingly, a sort of optical conversation commenced between the two young people. Every time that Clara's glance said, "I trust you," Thurstane's responded, "I will die for you." It was a perilous sort of dialogue, and liable to involve the two souls which looked out from these sparkling, transparent windows. Before long the Lieutenant's modest heart took courage, and his stammering tongue began to be loosed somewhat, so that he uttered things which frightened both him and Clara. Not that the remarks were audacious in themselves, but he was conscious of so much unexpressed meaning behind them, and she was so ready to guess that there might be such a meaning!

It seems ridiculous that a fellow who could hold his head straight up before a storm of cannon shot, should be positively bashful. Yet so it was. The boy had been through West Point, to be sure; but he had studied there, and not flirted; the Academy had not in any way demoralized him. On the whole, in spite of swearing under gross provocation, and an inclination toward strictness in discipline, he answered pretty well for a Bayard.

His bashfulness was such, at least in the presence of Clara, that he trembled to the tips of his fingers in merely making this remark: "Miss Van Diemen, this journey is the pleasantest thing in my whole life."

Clara blushed until she dazzled him and seemed to burn herself. Nevertheless she was favored with her usual childlike artlessness of speech, and answered, "I am glad you find it agreeable."

Nothing more from Ralph for a minute; he was recovering his breath and self-possession.

"You cannot think how much safer I feel because you and your men are with us," said Clara.

Thurstane unconsciously gripped the handle of his sabre, with a feeling that he could and would massacre all the Indians of the desert, if it were necessary to preserve her from harm.

"Yes, you may rely upon my men, too," he declared. "They have a sort of adoration for you."

"Have they?" asked Clara, with a frank smile of pleasure. "I wonder at it. I hardly notice them. I ought to, they seem so patient and trusty."

"Ah, a lady!" said Thurstane. "A good soldier will die any time for a lady."

Then he wondered how she could have failed to guess that she must be worshipped by these rough men for her beauty.

"I have overheard them talking about you," he went on, gratified at being able to praise her to her face, though in the speech of others. "Little Sweeny says, in his Irish brogue, 'I can march twic't as fur for the seein' av her!'"

"Oh! did he?" laughed Clara. "I must carry Sweeny's musket for him some time."

"Don't, if you please," said Thurstane, the disciplinarian rising in him. "You would spoil him for the service."

"Can't I send him a dish from our table?"

"That would just suit his case. He hasn't got broken to hard-tack yet."

"Miss Van Diemen," was his next remark, "do you know what you are to do, if we are attacked?"

"I am to get into a wagon."

"Into which wagon?"

"Into my aunt's."

"Why into that one?"

"So as to have all the ladies together."

"When you have got into the wagon, what next?"

"Lie down on the floor to protect myself from the arrows."

"Very good," laughed Thurstane. "You say your tactics well."

This catechism had been put and recited every day since he had joined the train. The putting of it was one of the Lieutenant's duties and pleasures; and, notwithstanding its prophecy of peril, Clara enjoyed it almost as much as he.

Well, we have heard these two talk, and much in their usual fashion. Not great souls as yet: they may indeed become such some day; but at present they are only mature in moral power and in capacity for mighty emotions. Information, mental development, and conversational ability hereafter.

In one way or another two or three of these tête-à-têtes were brought about every day. Thurstane wanted them all the time; would have been glad to make life one long dialogue with Miss Van Diemen; found an aching void in every moment spent away from her. Clara, too, in spite of maidenly struggles with herself, began to be of this way of feeling. Wonderful place the Great American Desert for falling in love!

Coronado soon guessed, and with good reason, that the seed which he had sown in the girl's mind was being replaced by other germs, and that he had blundered in trusting that she would think of him while she was talking with Thurstane. The fear of losing her increased his passion for her, and made him hate his rival with correlative fervor.

"Why don't you find a chance at that fellow?" he muttered to his bravo, Texas Smith.

"How the h—l kin I do it?" growled the bushwhacker, feeling that his intelligence and courage were unjustly called in question. "He's allays around the train, an' his sojers allays handy. I hain't had nary chance."

"Take him off on a hunt."

"He ain't a gwine. I reckon he knows himself. I'm afeard to praise huntin' much to him; he might get on my trail. Tell you these army chaps is resky. I never wanted to meddle with them kind o' close. You know I said so. I said so, fair an' square, I did."

"You might manage it somehow, if you had the pluck."

"Had the pluck!" repeated Texas Smith. His sallow, haggard face turned dusky with rage, and his singularly black eyes flamed as if with hell-fire. A Malay, crazed with opium and ready to run *amok*, could not present a more savage spectacle than this man did as he swayed in his saddle, grinding his teeth, clutching his rifle, and glaring at Coronado. What chiefly infuriated him was that the insult should come from one whom he considered a "greaser," a man of inferior race. He, Texas Smith, an American, a *white man*, was treated as if he were an "Injun" or a "nigger." Coronado was thoroughly alarmed, and smoothed his ruffled feathers at once.

"I beg your pardon," he said, promptly. "My dear Mr. Smith, I was entirely wrong. Of course I know that you have courage. Everybody knows it. Besides, I am under the greatest obligations to you. You saved my life. By heavens, I am horribly ashamed of my injustice."

A minute or so of this fluent apologizing calmed the bushwhacker's rage and soothed his injured feelings.

"But you oughter be keerful how you talk that way to a white man," he said. "No white man, if he's a gentleman, can stan' being told he hain't got no pluck."

"Certainly," assented Coronado. "Well, I have apologized. What more can I do?"

"Square, you're all right now," said the forgiving Texan, stretching out his bony, dirty hand and grasping Coronado's. "But don't say it agin. White men can't stan' sech talk. Well, about this feller—I'll see, I'll see. Square, I'll try to do what's right."

As Coronado rode away from this interview, he ground his teeth with rage and mortification, muttering, "A *white* man! a *white* man! So I am a black man. Yes, I am a greaser. Curse this whole race of English-speaking people!"

After a while he began to think to the purpose. He too must work; he must not trust altogether to Texas Smith; the scoundrel might flinch, or might fail. Something must be done to separate Clara and Thurstane. What should it be? Here we are almost ashamed of Coronado. The trick that he hit upon was the stalest, the most threadbare, the most commonplace and vulgar that one can imagine. It was altogether unworthy of such a clever and experienced conspirator. His idea was this: to get lost with Clara for one night; in the morning to rejoin the train. Thurstane would be disgusted, and would unquestionably give up the girl entirely when Coronado should say to him, "It was a very unlucky accident, but I have done what a gentleman should, and we are engaged."

This coarse, dastardly, and rather stupid stratagem he put into execution as quickly as possible. There were some dangers to be guarded against, as for instance Apaches, and the chance of getting lost in reality.

"Have an eye upon me to-day," he suggested to Texas. "If I leave the train with any one, follow me and keep a lookout for Indians. Only stay out of sight."

Now for an opportunity to lead Clara astray. The region was favorable; they were in an arid land of ragged sandstone spurs and buttes; it would be necessary to march until near sunset, in order to find water and pasturage. Consequently there was both time and scenery for his project. Late in the afternoon the train crossed a narrrow *mesa* or plateau, and approached a sublime terrace of rock which was the face of a second table-land. This terrace was cleft by several of those wonderful grooves which are known as cañons, and which were wrought by that mighty water-force, the sculpturer of the American desert. In one place two of these openings were neighbors: the larger was the route and the smaller led nowhere.

"Let the train pass on," suggested Coronado to Clara. "If you will ride with me up this little cañon, you will find some of the most exquisite scenery imaginable. It rejoins the large one further on. There is no danger."

Clara would have preferred not to go, or would have preferred to go with Thurstane.

"My dear child, what do you mean?" urged Aunt Maria, looking out of her wagon. "Mr. Coronado, I'll ride there with you myself."

The result of the dialogue which ensued was that, after the train had entered the gorge of the larger cañon, Coronado and Clara turned back and wandered up the smaller one, followed at a distance by Texas Smith. In twenty minutes they were separated from the wagons by a barrier of sandstone several hundred feet high, and culminating in a sharp ridge or frill of rocky points, not unlike the spiny back of a John Dory. The scenery, although nothing new to Clara, was such as would be considered in any other land amazing. Vast walls on either side, consisting mainly of yellow sandstone, were variegated with white, bluish, and green shales, with layers of gypsum of the party-colored marl series, with long lines of white limestone so soft as to be nearly earth, and with red and green foliated limestone mixed with blood-red shales. The two wanderers seemed to be amid the landscapes of a Christmas drama as they rode between these painted precipices toward a crimson sunset.

It was a perfect solitude. There was not a breath of life besides their own in this gorgeous valley of desolation. The ragged, crumbling battlements, and the loftier points of harder rock, would not have furnished subsistence for a goat or a mouse. Color was everywhere and life nowhere: it was such a region as one might look for in the moon; it did not seem to belong to an inhabited planet.

Before they had ridden half an hour the sun went down suddenly behind serrated steeps, and almost immediately night hastened in with his obscurities. Texas Smith, riding hundreds of yards in the rear and concealing himself behind the turning points of the cañon, was obliged to diminish his distance in order to keep them under his guard. Clara had repeatedly expressed her doubts as to the road, and Coronado had as often asserted that they would soon see the train. At last the ravine became a gully, winding up a breast of shadowy mountain cumbered with loose rocks, and impassable to horses.

"We are lost," confessed Coronado, and then proceeded to console her. The train could not be far off; their friends would undoubtedly seek them; at all events, would not go on without them. They must bivouac there as well as might be, and in the morning rejoin the caravan.

He had been forethoughted enough to bring two blankets on his saddle, and he now spread them out for her, insisting that she should try to sleep. Clara cried frankly and heartily, and begged him to lead her back through the cañon. No; it could not be traversed by night, he asserted; they would certainly break their necks among the bowlders. At last the girl suffered herself to be wrapped in the blankets, and made an endeavor to forget her wretchedness and vexation in slumber.

Meantime, a few hundred yards down the ravine, a tragedy was on the verge of action. Thurstane, missing Coronado and Clara, and learning what direction they had taken, started with two of his soldiers to find them, and was now picking his way on foot along the cañon. Behind a detached rock at the base of one of the sandstone walls Texas Smith lay in ambush, aiming his rifle first at one and then at another of this stumbling trio, and cursing the starlight because it was so dim that he could not positively distinguish which was the officer.

CHAPTER IX.

FOR the second time within a week, Texas Smith found himself upon the brink of opportunity, without being able (as he had phrased it to Coronado) to do what was right.

He levelled at Thurstane, and then it did not seem to be Thurstane; he had a dead sure sight at Kelly, and then perceived that that was an error; he drew a bead on Shubert, and still he hesitated. He could distinguish the Lieutenant's voice, but he could not fix upon the figure which uttered it.

It was exasperating. Never had an assassin been better ambuscaded. He was kneeling behind a little ridge of sandstone; about a foot below its edge was an orifice made by the rains and winds of bygone centuries; through this, as through an embrasure, he had thrust his rifle. Not a chance of being hit by a return shot. while after the enemy's fire had been drawn he could fly down the ravine, probably without discovery and certainly without recognition. His horse was tethered below, behind another rock; and he felt positive that these men had not come upon it. He could mount, drive their beasts before him into the plain, and then return to camp. No need of explaining his absence; he was the head hunter of the expedition; it was his business to wander.

All this was so easy to do, if he could only take the first step. But he dared not fire lest he should merely kill a soldier, and so make an uproar and rouse suspicions without the slightest profit. It was not probable that Coronado would pay him for shooting the wrong man, and setting on foot a dangerous investigation. So the desperado continued to peer through the dim night, cursing his stars and everybody's stars for not shining better, and seeing his opportunity slip rapidly away. After Thurstane and the others had passed, after the chance of murder had stalked by him like a ghost and vanished, he left his ambush, glided down the ravine to his horse, waked him up with a vindictive kick, leaped into the saddle, and hastened to camp. To inquiries about the lost couple he replied in his sullen, brief way that he had not seen them; and when urged to go to their rescue, he of course set off in the wrong direction and travelled but a short distance.

Meantime Ralph had found the captives of the cañon. Clara, wrapped in her blankets, was lying at the foot of a rock, and crying while she pretended to sleep. Coronado, unable to make her talk, irritated by the faint sobs which he overheard, but stubbornly resolved on carrying out his stupid plot, had retired in a state of ill-humor unusual with him to another ròck, and was consoling himself by smoking cigarito after cigarito. The two horses, tied together neck and crupper, were fasting near by. As Coronado had forgotten to bring food with him, Clara was also fasting.

Think of Apaches, and imagine the terror with which she caught the sounds of approach, the heavy, stumbling steps through the darkness. Then imagine the joy with which she recognized Thurstane's call and groped to meet him. In the dizziness of her delight, and amid the hiding veils of the obscurity, it did not seem wrong nor unnatural to fall against his arm and be supported by it for a moment. Ralph received this touch, this shock, as if it had been a ball; and his nature bore the impress of it as long as if it had made a scar. In his whole previous life he had not felt such a thrill of emotion; it was almost too powerful to be adequately described as a pleasure.

Next came Coronado, as happy as a disappointed burglar whose cue it is to congratulate the rescuing policeman. "My dear Lieutenant! You are heaven's own messenger. You have saved us from a horrible night. But it is prodigious; it is incredible. You must have come here by enchantment. How in God's name could you find your way up this fearful cañon?"

"The cañon is perfectly passable on foot," replied the young officer, stiffly and angrily. "By Jove, sir! I don't see why you didn't make a start to get out. This is a pretty place to lodge Miss Van Diemen."

Coronado took off his hat and made a bow of submission and regret, which was lost in the darkness.

"I must say," Thurstane went on grumbling, "that, for a man who claims to know this country, your management has been very singular."

Clara, fearful of a quarrel, slightly pressed his arm and checked this volcano with the weight of a feather.

"We are not all like you, my dear Lieutenant," said Coronado, in a tone which might have been either apologetical or ironical. "You must make allowance for ordinary human nature."

"I beg pardon," returned Thurstane, who was thinking now chiefly of that pressure on his arm. "The truth is, I was alarmed for your safety. I can't help feeling responsibility on this expedition, although it is your train. My military education runs me into it, I suppose. Well, excuse my excitement. Miss Van Diemen, may I help you back through the gully?"

In leaning on him, being guided by him, being saved by him, trusting in him, the girl found a pleasure which was irresistible, although it seemed audacious and almost sinful. Before the cañon was half traversed she felt as if she could go on with him through the great dark valley of life, confiding in his strength and wisdom to lead her aright and make her happy. It was a temporary wave of emotion, but she remembered it long after it had passed.

Around the fires, after a cup of hot coffee, amid the odors of a plentiful supper, recounting the evening's adventure to Mrs. Stanley, Coronado was at his best. How he rolled out the English language! Our mother tongue hardly knew itself, it ran so fluently and sounded so magniloquently and lied so naturally. He praised everybody but himself; he praised Clara, Thurstane, and the two soldiers and the horses; he even said a flattering word or two for Divine Providence. Clara especially, and the whole of her heroic, more than human sex, demanded his enthusiastic admiration. How she had borne the terrors of the night and the desert! "Ah, Mrs. Stanley! only you women are capable of such efforts."

Aunt Maria's Olympian head nodded, and her cheerful face, glowing with tea and the camp fires, confessed "Certainly!"

"What nonsense, Coronado!" said Clara. "I was horribly frightened, and you know it."

Aunt Maria frowned with surprise and denial. "Absurd, child! You were not frightened at all. Of course you were not. Why, even if you had been slightly timorous, you had your cousin to protect you."

"Ah, Mrs. Stanley, I am a poor knight-errant," said Coronado. "We Mexicans are no longer formidable. One man of your Anglo-Saxon blood is supposed to be a better defence than a dozen of us. We have been subdued; we must submit to depreciation. I must confess, in fact, that I had my fears. I was greatly relieved on my cousin's account when I heard the voice of our military chieftain here."

Then came more flattery for Ralph, with proper rations for the two privates. Those faithful soldiers—he must show his gratitude to them; he had forgotten them in the basest manner. "Here, Pedronillo, take these cigaritos to privates Kelly and Shubert, with my compliments. Begging *your* permission, Lieutenant. *Thank* you."

"Pooty tonguey man, that Seenor," observed Captain Phineas Glover to Mrs. Stanley, when the Mexican went off to his blankets.

"Yes; a very agreeable and eloquent gentleman," replied the lady, wishing to correct the skipper's statement while seeming to assent to it.

"Jess so," admitted Glover. "Ruther airy. Big talkin' man. Don't raise no sech our way."

Captain Glover was not fully aware that he himself had the fame of possessing an imagination which was almost too much for the facts of this world.

"S'pose it's in the breed," he continued. "Or likely the climate has suthin' to do with it: kinder thaws out the words 'n' sets the idees a-bilin'. Niggers is pooty much the same. Most niggers kin talk like a line runnin' out, 'n' tell lies 's fast 's our Fair Haven gals open oysters—a quart a minute."

"Captain Glover, what do you mean?" frowned Aunt Maria. "Mr. Coronado is a friend of mine."

"Oh, I was speakin' of niggers," returned the skipper promptly. "Forgot we begun about the Seenor. Sho! niggers was what I was talkin' of. B' th' way, that puts me in mind 'f one I had for cook once. Jiminy! how that man would cook! He'd cook a slice of halibut so you wouldn't know it from beefsteak."

"Dear me! how did he do it?" asked Aunt Maria, who had a fancy for kitchen mysteries.

"Never could find out," said Glover, stepping adroitly out of his difficulty. "Don't s'pose that nigger would a let on how he did it for ten dollars."

"I should think the receipt would be worth ten dollars," observed Aunt Maria thoughtfully.

"Not 'xactly here," returned the captain, with one of his dried smiles, which had the air of having been used a great many times before. "Halibut too skurce. Wal, I was goin' to tell ye 'bout this nigger. He come to be the cook he was because he was a big eater. We was wrecked once, 'n' had to live three days on old shoes 'n' that sort 'f truck. Wal, this nigger was so darned ravenous he ate up a pair o' long boots in the time it took me to git down one 'f the straps."

"Ate up a pair of boots!" exclaimed Aunt Maria, amazed and almost incredulous.

"Yes, by thunder!" insisted the captain, "grease, nails, 'n' all. An' then went at the patent leather forepiece 'f his cap."

"What privations!" said Aunt Maria, staring fit to burst her spectacles.

"Oh, that's nothin'," chuckled Glover. "I'll tell ye suthin' some time that 'll astonish ye. But jess now I'm sleepy, 'n' I guess I'll turn in."

"Mr. Cluvver, it is your durn on card do-night," interposed Meyer, the German sergeant, as the captain was about to roll himself in his blankets.

"So 'tis, returned Glover in well feigned astonishment. "Don't forgit a feller, do ye, Sergeant? How 'n the world do ye keep the 'count so straight? Oh, got a little book there, hey, with all our names down. Wal, that's shipshape. You'd make a pooty good mate, Sergeant. When does my watch begin?"

"Right away. You're always on the virst relief. You'll fall in down there at the gorner of the vagon bark."

"Wal—yes—s'pose I will," sighed the skipper, as he rolled up his blankets and prepared for two hours' sentry duty.

Let us look into the arrangements for the protection of the caravan. With Coronado's consent Thurstane had divided the eighteen Indians and Mexicans, four soldiers, Texas Smith, and Glover, twenty-four men in all, into three equal squads, each composed of a sergeant, corporal, and six privates. Meyer was sergeant of one squad, the Irish veteran Kelly had another, and Texas Smith the third. Every night a detachment went on duty in three reliefs, each relief consisting of two men, who stood sentry for two hours, at the end of which time they were relieved by two others.

The six wagons were always parked in an oblong square, one at each end and two on each side; but in order to make the central space large enough for camping purposes, they were placed several feet apart; the gaps being closed with lariats, tied from wheel to wheel, to pen in the animals and keep out charges of Apache cavalry. On either flank of this enclosure, and twenty yards or so distant from it, paced a sentry. Every two hours, as we have said, they were relieved, and in the alternate hours the posts were visited by the sergeant or corporal of the guard, who took turns in attending to this service. The squad that came off duty in the morning was allowed during the day to take naps in the wagons, and was not put upon the harder camp labor, such as gathering firewood, going for water, etc.

The two ladies and the Indian women slept at night in the wagons, not only because the canvas tops protected them from wind and dew, but also because the wooden sides would shield them from arrows. The men who were not on guard lay under the vehicles so as to form a cordon around the mules. Thurstane and Coronado, the two chiefs of this armed migration, had their alternate nights of command, each when off duty sleeping in a special wagon known as "headquarters," but holding himself ready to rise at once in case of an alarm.

The cooking fires were built away from the park, and outside the beats of the sentries. The object was twofold: first, to keep sparks from lighting on the wagon covers; second, to hide the sentries from prowling archers. At night you can see everything between yourself and a fire, but nothing beyond it. As long as the wood continued to blaze, the most adroit Indian skulker could not approach the camp without exposing himself, while the guards and the garrison were veiled from his sight by a wall of darkness behind a dazzle of light.

Such were the bivouac arrangements, intelligent, systematic, and military. Not only had our Lieutenant devised them, but he saw to it that they were kept in working order. He was zealously and faithfully seconded by his men, and especially by his two veterans. There is no human machine more accurate and trustworthy than an old soldier, who has had year on year of the discipline and drill of a regular service, and who has learned to carry out instructions to the letter.

The arrangements for the march were equally thorough and judicious. Texas Smith, as the Nimrod of the party, claimed the right of going where he pleased; but while he hunted, he of course served also as a scout to nose out danger. The six Mexicans, who were nominally cattle-drivers, but really Coronado's minor bravos, were never suffered to ride off in a body, and were expected to keep on both sides of the train, some in advance and some in rear. The drivers and muleteers remained steadily with their wagons and animals. The four soldiers were also at hand, trudging close in front or in rear, accoutrements always on and muskets always loaded.

In this fashion the expedition had already journeyed over two hundred and twenty miles. Following Colonel Washington's trail, it had crossed the ranges of mountains immediately west of Abiquia, and, striking the Rio de Chaco, had tracked its course for some distance with the hope of reaching the San Juan. Stopped by a cañon, a precipitous gully hundreds of feet deep, through which the Chaco ran like a chased devil, the wagons had turned westward, and then had been forced by impassable ridges and lack of water into a southwest direction, at last gaining and crossing Pass Washington.

It was now on the western side of the Sierra de Chusca, in the rude, barren country over which Fort Defiance stands sentry. Ever since the second day after leaving San Isidoro it had been on the great western slope of the continent, where every drop of water tends toward the Pacific. The pilgrims would have had cause to rejoice could they have travelled as easily as the drops of water, and been as certain of their goal. But the rivers had made roads for themselves, and man had not yet had time to do likewise.

The great central plateau of North America is a Mer de Glace in stone. It is a continent of rock, gullied by furious rivers ; plateau on plateau of sandstone, with sluiceways through which lakes have escaped ; the whole surface gigantically grotesque with the carvings of innumerable waters. What is remarkable in the scenery is, that its sublimity is an inversion of the sublimity of almost all other grand scenery. It is not so much the heights that are prodigious as the abysses. At certain points in the course of the Colorado of the West you can drop a plumb line six thousand feet before it will reach the bosom of the current ; and you can only gain the water level by turning backward for scores of miles and winding laboriously down some subsidiary cañon, itself a chasm of awful grandeur.

Our travellers were now amid wild labyrinths of ranges, and buttes, and cañons, which were not so much a portion of the great plateau as they were the *débris* that constituted its flanks. Although thousands of feet above the level of the sea, they still had thousands of feet to ascend before they could dominate the desert. Wild as the land was, it was thus far passable, while toward the north lay the untraversable. What course should be taken ? Coronado, who had crimes to commit and to conceal, did not yet feel that he was far enough from the haunts of man. As soon as possible he must again venture a push northward.

But not immediately. The mules were fagged with hard work, weak with want of sufficient pasture, and had suffered much from thirst. He resolved to continue westward to the pueblas of the Moquis, that interesting race of agricultural and partially civilized Indians, perhaps the representatives of the architects of the Casas Grandes if not also descended from the mound-builders of the

Mississippi valley. Having rested and refitted there, he might start anew for the San Juan.

Thus far they had seen no Indians except the vagrants who had robbed Phineas Glover. But they might now expect to meet them; they were in a region which was the raiding ground of four great tribes: the Utes on the north, the Navajos on the west, the Apaches on the south, and the Comanches on the east. The peaceful and industrious Moquis, with their gay and warm blankets, their fields of corn and beans, and their flocks of sheep, are the quarry which attracts this ferocious cavalry of the desert, these Tartars and Bedouin of America.

Thurstane took more pains than ever with the guard duty. Coronado, unmilitary though he was, and heartily as he abominated the Lieutenant, saw the wisdom of submitting to the latter's discipline, and made all his people submit. A practical-minded man, he preferred to owe the safety of his carcass to his rival rather than have it impaled on Apache lances. Occasionally, however, he made a suggestion.

"It is very well, this night-watching," he once observed, "but what we have most to fear is the open daylight. These mounted Indians seldom attack in the darkness."

Thurstane knew all this, but he did not say so; for he was a wise, considerate commander already, and he had learned not to chill an informant. He looked at Coronado inquiringly, as if to say, What do you propose?

"Every cañon ought to be explored before we enter it," continued the Mexican.

"It is a good hint," said Ralph. "Suppose I keep two of your cattle-drivers constantly in advance. You had better instruct them yourself. Tell them to fire the moment they discover an ambush. I don't suppose they will hit anybody, but we want the warning."

With two horsemen three or four hundred yards to the front, two more an equal distance in the rear, and, when the ground permitted, one on either flank, the train continued its journey. Every wagon-driver and muleteer had a weapon of some sort always at hand. The four soldiers marched a few rods in advance, for the ground behind had already been explored, while that ahead might contain enemies. The precautions were extraordinary; but Thurstane constantly trembled for Clara. He would have thought a regiment hardly sufficient to guard such a treasure.

"How timorous these men are," sniffed Aunt Maria, who, having seen no hostile Indians, did not believe there were any. "And it seems to me that soldiers are more easily scared than anybody else," she added, casting a depreciating glance at Thurstane, who was reconnoitring the landscape through his field glass.

Clara believed in men, and especially in soldiers, and more particularly in lieutenants. Accordingly she replied, "I suppose they know the dangers and we don't."

"Pshaw!" said Aunt Maria, an argument which carried great weight with her. "They don't know half what they claim to. It is a clever man who knows one-tenth of his own business." (She was right there.) "They don't know so much, I verily and solemnly believe, as the women whom they pretend to despise."

This peaceful and cheering conversation was interrupted by a shot ringing out of a cañon which opened into a range of rock some three hundred yards ahead of the caravan. Immediately on the shot came a yell as of a hundred demons, a furious trampling of the feet of many horses, and a cloud of the Tartars of the American desert.

In advance of the rush flew the two Mexican vedettes, screaming "Apaches! Apaches!

CHAPTER X.

WHEN the Apache tornado burst out of the cañon upon the train, Thurstane's first thought was, "Clara!"

"Get off!" he shouted to her, seizing and holding her startled horse. "Into the wagon, quick! Now lie down, both of you."

He thundered all this out as sternly as if he were commanding troops. Because he was a man, Clara obeyed him; and notwithstanding he was a man, Mrs. Stanley obeyed him. Both were so bewildered with surprise and terror as to be in a kind of animal condition of spirit, knowing just enough to submit at once to the impulse of an imperious voice. The riderless horse, equally frightened and equally subordinate, was hurried to the rear of the leading wagon and handed over to a muleteer.

By the time this work was done the foremost riders of the assailants were within two hundred yards of the head of the train, letting drive their arrows at the flying Mexican vedettes and uttering yells fit to raise the dead, while their comrades behind, whooping also, stormed along under a trembling and flickering of lances. The little, lean, wiry horses were going at full speed, regardless of smooth faces of rock and beds of loose stones. The blackguards were over a hundred in number, all lancers and archers of the first quality.

The vedettes never pulled up until they were in rear of the hindermost wagon, while their countrymen on the flanks and rear made for the same poor shelter. The drivers were crouching almost under their seats, and the muleteers were hiding behind their animals. Thus it was evident that the entire brunt of the opening struggle would fall upon Thurstane and his people; that, if there was to be any resistance at all, these five men must commence it, and, for a while at least, "go it alone."

The little squad of regulars, at this moment a few yards in front of the foremost wagon, was drawn up in line and standing steady, precisely as if it were a company or a regiment. Sergeant Meyer was on the right, veteran Kelly on the left, the two recruits in the centre, the pieces at a shoulder, the bayonets fixed. As Thurstane rode up to this diminutive line of battle, Meyer was shouting forth his sharp and decisive orders. They were just the right orders; excited as the young officer was, he comprehended that there was nothing to change; moreover, he had already learned how men are disconcerted in battle by a multiplicity of directions. So he sat quietly on his horse, revolver in hand, his blue-black eyes staring angrily at the coming storm.

"Kelly, reserfe your fire!" yelled Meyer. "Recruits, ready—bresent—aim—aim low—fire!"

Simultaneously with the report a horse in the leading group of charging savages pitched headlong on his nose and rolled over, sending his rider straight forward into a rubble of loose shales, both lying as they fell, without movement. Half a dozen other animals either dropped on their haunches or sheered violently to the right and left, going off in wild plunges and caracolings. By this one casualty the head of the attacking column was opened and its seemingly resistless impetus checked and dissipated, almost before Meyer could shout, "Recruits, load at will, load!"

A moment previous this fiery cavalry had looked irresistible. It seemed to have in it momentum, audacity, and dash enough to break a square of infantry or carry a battery of artillery. The horses fairly flew; the riders had the air of centaurs, so firm and graceful was their seat; the long lances were brandished as easily as if by the hands of footmen; the bows were managed and the arrows sent with dazzling dexterity. It was a show of brilliant equestrianism, surpassing the feats of circus riders. But a single effective shot into the centre of the column had cleft it as a rock divides a torrent. It was like the breaking of a water-spout.

The attack, however, had only commenced. The Indians who had swept off to right and left went scouring along the now motionless train, at a distance of sixty or eighty yards, rapidly enveloping it with their wild caperings, keeping in constant motion so as to evade gunshots, threatening with their lances or discharging arrows, and yelling incessantly. Their main object so far was undoubtedly to frighten the mules into a stampede and thus separate the wagons. They were not assaulting; they were watching for chances.

"Keep your men together, Sergeant," said Thurstane. "I must get those Mexicans to work."

He trotted deliberately to the other end of the train, ordering each driver as he passed to move up abreast of the leading wagon, directing the first to the right, the second to the left, and so on. The result of this movement would of course be to bring the train into a compact mass and render it more defensible. The Indians no sooner perceived the advance than they divined its object and made an effort to prevent it. Thurstane had scarcely reached the centre of the line of vehicles when a score or so of yelling horsemen made a caracoling, prancing charge upon him, accompanying it with a flight of arrows. Our young hero presented his revolver, but they apparently knew the short range of the weapon, and came plunging, curveting onward. Matters were growing serious, for an arrow already stuck in his saddle, and another had passed through his hat. Suddenly there was a bang, bang of firearms, and two of the savages went down.

Meyer had observed the danger of his officer, and had ordered Kelly to fire, blazing away too himself. There was a headlong, hasty scramble to carry off the fallen warriors, and then the assailants swept back to a point beyond accurate musket shot. Thurstane reached the rear of the train unhurt, and found the six Mexican cattle-drivers there in a group, pointing their rifles at such Indians as made a show of charging, but otherwise doing nothing which resembled fighting. They were obviously panic-stricken, one or two of them being of an ashy-yellow, their nearest possible approach to pallor. There, too, was Coronado, looking not exactly scared, but irresolute and helpless.

"What does this mean?" Thurstane stormed in Spanish. "Why don't you shoot the devils?"

"We are reserving our fire," stammered Coronado, half alarmed, half ashamed.

Thurstane swore briefly, energetically, and to the point. "Damned pretty fighting!" he went on. "If *we* had reserved our fire, we should all have been lanced by this time. Let drive!"

The cattle-drivers carried short rifles, of the then United States regulation pattern, which old Garcia had somehow contrived to pick up during the war perhaps buying them of drunken soldiers. Supported by Thurstane's pugnacious presence and hurried up by his vehement orders, they began to fire. They were shaky; didn't aim very well; hardly aimed at all, in fact; blazed away at extraordinary elevations; behaved as men do who have become demoralized. However, as the pieces had a range of several hundred yards, the small bullets hissed venomously over the heads of the Indians, and one of them, by pure accident, brought down a horse. There was an immediate scattering, a multitudinous glinting of hoofs through the light dust of the plain, and then a rally in prancing groups, at a safe distance.

"Hurrah!" shouted Thurstane, cheering the Mexicans. "That's very well. You see how easy it is. Now don't let them sneak up again; and at the same time don't waste powder."

Then turning to one who was near him, and who had just reloaded, he said in a calm, strong, encouraging tone—that voice of the thoroughly good officer which comes to the help of the shaken soldier like a reinforcement—"Now, my lad, steadily. Pick out your man; take your time and aim sure. Do you see him?"

"Si, señor," replied the herdsman. His coolness restored by this steady utterance and these plain, common-sense directions, he selected a warrior in helmet-shaped cap, blue shirt, and long boots, brought his rifle slowly to a level, took sight, and fired. The Indian bent forward, caught the mane of his plunging pony, hung there for a second or two, and then rolled to the ground, amid a yell of surprise and dismay from his comrades. There was a hasty rush to secure the body, and then another sweep backward of the loose array.

"Good!" called Thurstane, nodding and smiling at the successful marksman. "That is the way to do it. You are a match for half a dozen of them as long as you will keep cool."

The besieged travellers could now look about quietly and see how matters stood with them. The six wagons were by this time drawn up in two ranks of three each, so as to form a compact mass. As the one which contained the ladies had been the leader and the others had formed on it to right and left, it was in the centre of the first rank, and consequently pretty well protected by its neighbors. The drivers and muleteers had recovered their self-possession, and were all sitting or standing at their posts, with their miscellaneous arms ready for action. Not a human being had been hit as yet, and only three of the mules wounded, none of them seriously. The Apaches were all around the train, but none of them nearer than two hundred yards, and doing nothing but canter about and shout to each other.

"Where is Texas Smith?" demanded Thurstane, missing that mighty hunter, and wondering if he were a coward and had taken refuge in a wagon.

"He went off shutin' an hour ago," explained Phineas Glover. "Reckon he's astern somewhere."

Glover, by the way, had been useful. In the beginning of the affray he had brought his mule alongside of the headmost wagon, and there he had done really valuable service by blazing away alarmingly, though quite innocuously, at the gallopading enemy.

"It's a bad lookout for Texas," observed the Lieutenant. "I shouldn't want to bet high on his getting back to us."

Coronado looked gloomy, fearing lest his trusted assassin was lost, and not knowing where he could pick up such another.

"And how are the ladies?" asked Thurstane, turning to Glover.

"Safe 's a bug in a rug," was the reply. "Seen to that little job myself. Not a bugger in the hull crew been nigh 'em."

Thurstane cantered around to the front of the wagon which contained the two women, and called, "How are you?"

At the sound of his voice there was a rustle inside, and Clara showed her face over the shoulder of the driver.

"So you were not hurt?" laughed the young officer. "Ah! that's bully."

With a smile which was almost a boast, she answered, "And I was not very frightened."

At this, Aunt Maria struggled from between two rolls of bedding into a sitting posture and ejaculated, "Of course not!"

"Did they hit you?" asked Clara, looking eagerly at Thurstane.

"How brave you are!" he replied, admiring her so much that he did not notice her question.

"But I do hope it is over," added the girl, poking her head out of the wagon. "Ah! what is that?"

With this little cry of dismay she pointed at a group of savages who had gathered between the train and the mouth of the cañon ahead of it.

"They are the enemy," said Thurstane. "We may have another little tussle with them. Now lie down and keep close."

"Acquit yourselves like—men!" exhorted Aunt Maria, dropping back into her stronghold among the bedding.

Sergeant Meyer now approached Thurstane, touched his cap, and said, "Leftenant, here is brifate Sweeny who has not fired his beece once. I cannot make him fire."

"How is that, Sweeny?" demanded the officer, putting on the proper grimness. "Why haven't you fired when you were ordered?"

Sweeny was a little wizened shaving of an Irishman. He was not only quite short, but very slender and very lean. He had a curious teetering gait, and he took ridiculously short steps in marching, as if he were a monkey who had not learned to feel at ease on his hind legs. His small, wilted, wrinkled face, and his expression of mingled simplicity and shrewdness, were also monkey-like. At Thurstane's reprimand he trotted close up to him with exactly the air of a circus Jocko who expects a whipping, but who hopes to escape it by grinning.

"Why haven't you fired?" repeated his commander.

"Liftinint, I dasn't," answered Sweeny, in the rapid, jerking, almost inarticulate jabber which was his usual speech.

Now it is not an uncommon thing for recruits to dread to discharge their arms in battle. They have a vague idea that, if they bang away, they will attract the notice of some antagonist who will immediately single them out for retaliation.

"Are you afraid anybody will hit you?" asked Thurstane.

"No, I ain't, Liftinint," jabbered Sweeny. "I ain't afeard av them niggers a bit. They may shoot their bow arreys at me all day if they want to. I'm afeard of me gun, Liftinint. I fired it wonst, an' it kicked me to blazes."

"Come, come! That won't do. Level it now. Pick out your man. Aim. Fire."

Thus constrained, Sweeny brought his piece down to an inclination of forty-five degrees, shut his eyes, pulled trigger, and sent a ball clean over the most distant Apaches. The recoil staggered him, but he recovered himself without going over, and instantly roared out a horse-laugh.

"Ho! ho! ho!" he shouted. "That time I reckon I fetched won av 'em.

"Sweeny," said Thurstane, "you must have hit either the sun or the moon, I don't know which."

Sweeny looked discomfited; the next breath he bethought himself of a saving joke: "Liftinint, it 'ud sarve erry won av 'em right;" then another neigh of laughter.

"I ain't afeard av the ball," he hastened to asseverate; "it's the kick av it that murthers me. Liftinint, why don't they put the britch to the other end av the gun? They do in the owld counthry."

"Load your beece," ordered Sergeant Meyer, "and go to your bost again, to the left of Shupert."

The fact of Sweeny's opening fire did not cause a resumption of the close fighting. Quiet still continued, and the leaders of the expedition took advantage of it to discuss their situation, while the Indians gathered into little groups and seemed also to be holding council.

"There are over a hundred warriors," said Thurstane.

"Apaches," added one of the Mexican herdsmen.

"What band?"

"Manga Colorada or Delgadito."

"I supposed they were in Bernalillo."

"That was three weeks ago," put in Coronado.

He was in profound thought. These fellows, who had agreed to harry Bernalillo, and who had for a time carried out their bargain, why had they come to intercept him in the Moqui country, a hundred and twenty miles away? Did they want to extort more money, or were they ignorant that this was his train? And, supposing he should make himself known to them, would they spare him personally and such others as he might wish to save, while massacring the rest of the party? It would be a bold step; he could not at once decide upon it; he was pondering it.

We must do full justice to Coronado's coolness and readiness. This atrocious idea had occurred to him the instant he heard the charging yell of the Apaches; and it had done far more than any weakness of nerves to paralyze his fighting ability. He had thought, "Let them kill the Yankees; then I will proclaim myself and save *her;* then she will be mine." And because of these thoughts he had stood irresolute, aiming without firing, and bidding his Mexicans do the same. The result was that six good shots and superb horsemen, who were capable of making a gallant fight under worthy leadership, had become demoralized, and, but for the advent of Thurstane, might have been massacred like sheep.

Now that three or four Apaches had fallen, Coronado had less hope of making his arrangement. He considered the matter carefully and judiciously, but at last he decided that he could not trust the vindictive devils, and he turned his mind strenuously toward resistance. Although not pugnacious, he had plenty of the desperate courage of necessity, and his dusky black eyes were very resolute as he said to Thurstane, "Lieutenant, we trust to you."

The young veteran had already made up his mind as to what must be done.

"We will move on," he said. "We can't camp here, in an open plain, without grass or water. We must get into the cañon so as to have our flanks protected. I want the wagons to advance in double file so as to shorten the train. Two of my men in front and two in rear; three of your herdsmen on one flank and three on the other; Captain Glover alongside the ladies, and you and I everywhere; that's the programme. If we are all steady, we can do it, sure."

"They are collecting ahead to stop us," observed Coronado.

"Good!" said Thurstane. "All I want is to have them get in a heap. It is this attacking on all sides which is dangerous. Suppose you give your drivers and muleteers a sharp lecture. Tell them they must fight if the Indians charge, and not skulk inside and under the wagons. Tell them we are going to shoot the first man who skulks. Pitch into them heavy. It's a devilish shame that a dozen tolerably well-armed men should be so helpless. It's enough to justify the old woman's contempt for our sex.

Coronado rode from wagon to wagon, delivering his reproofs, threats, and instructions in the plainest kind of Spanish. At the signal to march, the drivers must file off two abreast, commencing on the right, and move at the fastest trot of the mules toward the cañon. If any scoundrel skulked, quitted his post, or failed to fight, he would be pistolled instanter by him, Coronado *sangre de Dios*, etc.!

While he was addressing Aunt Maria's coachman, that level-headed lady called out, "Mr. Coronado, your very voice is cheering."

"Mrs. Stanley, you are an example of heroism to our sex," replied the Mexican, with an ironical grin.

"What a brave, noble, intelligent man?" thought Aunt Maria. "If they were only all like him!"

This business took up five minutes. Coronado had just finished his round when a loud yell was raised by the Apaches, and twenty or thirty of them started at full speed down the trail by which the caravan had come. Looking for the cause of this stampede, the emigrants beheld, nearly half a mile away, a single horseman rushing to encounter a score. It was Texas Smith, making an apparently hopeless rush to burst through the environment of Parthians and reach the train.

"Shall we make a sally to save him?" demanded Coronado, glancing at Thurstane.

The officer hesitated; to divide his small army would be perilous; the Apaches would attack on all sides and with advantage.

But the sight of one man so overmatched was too much for him, and with a great throb of chivalrous blood in his heart, he shouted, "Charge!"

CHAPTER XI.

An hour before the attack Texas Smith had ridden off to stalk a deer; but the animal being in good racing condition in consequence of the thin fare of this sterile region, the hunting bout had miscarried; and our desperado was returning unladen toward the train when he heard the distant charging yell of the Apaches.

Scattered over the plateau which he was traversing, there were a few thickets of mesquite, with here and there a fantastic butte of sandstone. By dodging from one of these covers to another, he arrived undiscovered at a point whence he could see the caravan and the curveting mêlée which surrounded it. He was nearly half a mile from his comrades and over a quarter of a mile from his nearest enemies.

What should he do? If he made a rush, he would probably be overpowered and either killed instantly or carried off for torture. If he waited until night for a chance to sneak into camp, the wandering redskins would be pretty apt to surprise him in the darkness, and there would be small chance indeed of escaping with his hair. It was a nasty situation; but Texas, accustomed to perils, was as brave as he was wicked; and he looked his darkling fate in the face with admirable coolness and intelligence. His decision was to wait a favorable moment, and when it came, charge for life.

When he perceived that the mass of the Indians had gathered on the trail between the wagons and the cañon, he concluded that his chance had arrived; and with teeth grimly set, rifle balanced across his saddle-bow, revolver slung to his wrist, he started in silence and at full speed on his almost hopeless rush. If you will cease to consider the man as a modern bushwhacker, and invest him temporarily with the character, ennobled by time, of a borderer of the Scottish marches, you will be able to feel some sympathy for him in his audacious enterprise.

He was mounted on an American horse, a half-blood gray, large-boned and powerful, who could probably have traversed the half-mile in a minute had there been no impediment, and who was able to floor with a single shock two or three of the little animals of the Apaches. He was a fine spectacle as he thundered alone across the plain, upright and easy in his seat, balancing his heavy rifle as if it were a rattan, his dark and cruel face settled for fight and his fierce black eyes blazing.

Only a minute's ride, but that minute life or death. As he had expected, the Apaches discovered him almost as soon as he left the cover of his butte, and all the outlying members of the horde swarmed toward him with a yell, brandishing their spears and getting ready their bows as they rode. It would clearly be impossible for him to cut his way through thirty warriors unless he received assistance from the train. Would it come? His evil conscience told him, without the least reason, that Thurstane would not help. But from Coronado, whose life he had saved and whose evil work he had undertaken to do—from this man, "greaser" as he was, he did expect a sally. If it did not come, and if he should escape by some rare chance, he, Texas Smith, would murder the Mexican the first time he found him alone, so help him God!

While he thought and cursed he flew. But his goal was still five hundred yards away, and the nearest redskins were within two hundred yards, when he saw a rescuing charge shoot out from the wagons. Coronado led it. In this foxy nature the wolf was not wanting, and under strong impulse he could be somewhat of a Pizarro. He had no starts of humanity nor of real chivalry, but he had family pride and personal vanity, and he was capable of the fighting fury. When Thurstane had given the word to advance, Coronado had put himself forward gallantly.

"Stay here," he said to the officer; "guard the train with your infantry. I am a caballero, and I will do a caballero's work," he added, rising proudly in his stirrups. "Come on, you villains!" was his order to the six Mexicans.

All abreast, spread out like a skirmish line, the seven horsemen clattered over the plain, making for the point where Texas Smith was about to plunge among the whirling and caracoling Apaches.

Now came the crisis of the day. The moment the sixty or seventy Apaches near the mouth of the cañon saw Coronado set out on his charge, they raised a yell of joy over the error of the emigrants in dividing their forces, and plunged straight at the wagons. In half a minute two wild, irregular, and yet desperate combats were raging.

Texas Smith had begun his battle while Coronado was still a quarter of a mile away. Aiming his rifle at an Apache who was riding directly upon him, instead of dodging and wheeling in the usual fashion of these cautious fighters, he sent the audacious fellow out of his saddle with a bullet-hole through the lungs. But this was no salvation; the dreaded long-range firearm was now empty; the savages circled nearer and began to use their arrows. Texas let his rifle hang from the pommel and presented his revolver. But the bowshots were more than its match. It could not be trusted to do execution at forty yards, and at that distance the Indian shafts are deadly. Already several had hissed close by him, one had gashed the forehead of his horse, and another had pierced his clothing.

All that Texas wanted, however, was time. If he could pass a half minute without a disabling wound, he would have help. He retreated a little, or rather he edged away toward the right, wheeling and curveting after the manner of the Apaches, in order to present an unsteady mark for their archery. To keep them at a distance he fired one barrel of his revolver, though without effect. Meantime he dodged incessantly, now throwing himself forward and backward in the saddle, now hanging over the side of his horse and clinging to his neck. It was hard and perilous work, but he was gaining seconds, and every second was priceless. Notwithstanding his extreme peril, he calculated his chances with perfect coolness and with a sagacity which was admirable.

But this intelligent savage had to do with savages as clever as himself. The Apaches saw Coronado coming up on their rear, and they knew that they must make short work of the hunter, or must let him escape. While a score or so faced about to meet the Mexicans, a dozen charged with screeches and brandished lances upon the Texan. Now came a hand-to-hand struggle which looked as if it must end in the death of Smith and perhaps of several of his assailants. But cavalry fights are notoriously bloodless in comparison to their apparent fury; the violent and perpetual movement of the combatants deranges aim and renders most of the blows futile; shots are fired at a yard distance without hitting, and strokes are delivered which only wound the air.

One spear stuck in Smith's saddle; another pierced his jacket-sleeve and tore its way out; only one of the sharp, quickly-delivered points drew blood. He felt a slight pain in his side, and he found afterward that a lance-head had raked one of his ribs, tearing up the skin and scraping the bone for four or five inches. Meantime he shot a warrior through the head, sent another off with a hole in the shoulder, and fired one barrel without effect. He had but a single charge left (saving this for himself in the last extremity), when he burst through the prancing throng of screeching, thrusting ragamuffins, and reached the side of Coronado.

Here another hurly-burly of rearing and plunging combat awaited him. Coronado, charging as an old Castilian hidalgo might have charged upon the Moors, had plunged directly into the midst of the Apaches who awaited him, giving them little time to use their arrows, and at first receiving no damage. The six rifles of his Mexicans sent two Apaches out of their saddles, and then came a capering, plunging joust of lances, both parties using the same weapon. Coronado alone had sabre and revolver; and he handled them both with beautiful coolness and dexterity; he rode, too, as well as the best of all these other centaurs. His superb horse whirled and reared under the guidance of a touch of the knees, while the rider plied firearm with one hand and sharply-ground blade with the other. Thurstane, an infantryman, and only a fair equestrian, would not have been half so effective in this combat of caballeros.

Coronado's first bullet knocked a villainous-looking tatterdemalion clean into the happy hunting grounds. Then came a lance thrust; he parried it with his sabre and plunged within range of the point; there was a sharp, snake-like hiss of the light, curved blade; down went Apache number two. At this rate, providing there were no interruptions, he could finish the whole twenty. He went at his job with a handy adroitness which was almost scientific, it was so much like surgery, like dissection. His mind was bent, with a sort of preternatural calmness and cleverness, upon the business of parrying lance thrusts, aiming his revolver, and delivering sabre cuts. It was a species of fighting intellection, at once prudent and destructive. It was not the headlong, reckless, pugnacious rage of the old Anglo-Saxon and Scandinavian berserker. It was the practical, ready, rational furor of the Latin race.

Presently he saw that two of his rancheros had been lanced, and that there were but four left. A thrill of alarm, a commencement of panic, a desire to save himself at all hazards, crisped his heart and half paralyzed his energy. Remembering with perfect distinctness that four of his barrels were empty, he would perhaps have tried to retreat at the risk of being speared in the back, had he not at this critical moment been joined by Texas Smith.

That instinctive, ferocious, and tireless fighter, while seeming to be merely circling and curveting among his assailants, contrived to recharge two barrels of his revolver, and was once more ready for business, Down went one Apache; then the horse of another fell to reeling and crouching in a sickly way; then a charge of half a dozen broke to right and left in irresolute prancings. At sight of this friendly work Coronado drew a fresh breath of courage, and executed his greatest feat yet of horsemanship and swordsmanship. Spurring after and then past one of the wheeling braves, he swept his sabre across the fellow's bare throat with a drawing stroke, and half detached the scowling, furious, frightened head from the body.

There was a wide space of open ground before him immediately. The Apaches know nothing of sabre work; not one of those present had ever before seen such a blow or such an effect; they were not only panic-stricken, but horror-stricken. For one moment, right between the staring antagonists, a bloody corpse sat upright on a rearing horse, with its head fallen on one shoulder and hanging by a gory muscle. The next moment it wilted, rolled downward with outstreched arms, and collapsed upon the gravel, an inert mass.

Texas Smith uttered a loud scream of tigerish delight. He had never, in all his pugnacious and sanguinary life, looked upon anything so fascinating. It seemed to him as if *his* heaven—the savage Walhalla of his Saxon or Danish berserker race—were opened before him. In his ecstasy he waved his dirty, long fingers toward Coronado, and shouted, "Bully for you, old hoss!"

But he had self-possession enough, now that his hand was free for an instant from close battle, to reload his rifle and revolver. The four rancheros who still retained their saddles mechanically and hurriedly followed his example. The contest here was over; the Apaches knew that bullets would soon be humming about their ears, and they dreaded them; there was a retreat, and this retreat was a run of an eighth of a mile.

"Hurrah for the waggins!" shouted Texas, and dashed away toward the train. Coronado stared; his heart sank within him; the train was surrounded by a mob of prancing savages; there was more fighting to be done when he had already done his best. But not knowing where else to go, he followed his leader toward this new battle, loading his revolver as he rode, and wishing that he were in Santa Fé, or anywhere in peace.

We must go back a little. As already stated, the main body of the Apaches had perceived the error of the emigrants in separating, and had promptly availed themselves of it to charge upon the train. To attack it there were seventy ferocious and skilful warriors; to defend it there were twelve timorous muleteers and drivers, four soldiers, and Ralph.

"Fall back!" shouted the Lieutenant to his regulars when he saw the equestrian avalanche coming. "Each man take a wagon and hold it."

The order was obeyed in a hurry. The Apaches, heartened by what they supposed to be a panic, swarmed along at increased speed, and gave out their most diabolical screeches, hoping no doubt to scare men into helplessness, and beasts into a stampede. But the train was an immovable fortress, and the fortress was well garrisoned. Although the mules winced and plunged a good deal, the drivers succeeded in holding them to their places, and the double column of carriages, three in each rank, preserved its formation. In every vehicle there was a muleteer, with hands free for fighting, bearing something or other in the shape of a firelock, and inspired with what courage there is in desperation. The four flankers, necessarily the most exposed to assault, had each a United States regular, with musket, bayonet, and forty rounds of buck and ball. In front of the phalanx, directly before the wagon which contained the two ladies, sat as brave an officer as there was in the American army.

The Apaches had also committed their tactical blunder. They should all have followed Coronado, made sure of destroying him and his Mexicans, and then attacked the train. But either there was no sagacious military spirit among them, or the love of plunder was too much for judgment and authority, and so down they came on the wagons.

As the swarthy swarm approached, it spread out until it covered the front of the train and overlapped its flanks, ready to sweep completely around it and fasten upon any point which should seem feebly or timorously defended. The first man endangered was the lonely officer who sat his horse in front of the line of kicking and plunging mules. Fortunately for him, he now had a weapon of longer range than his revolver; he had remembered that in one of the wagons was stored a peculiar rifle belonging to Coronado; he had just had time to drag it out and strap its cartridge-box around his waist.

He levelled at the centre of the clattering, yelling column. It fluctuated; the warriors who were there did not like to be aimed at; they began to zigzag, caracole, and diverge to right or left; several halted and commenced using their bows. At one of these archers, whose arrow already trembled on the string, Thurstane let fly, sending him out of the saddle. Then he felt a quick, sharp pain in his left arm, and perceived that a shaft had passed clean through it.

There is this good thing about the arrow, that it has not weight enough to break bones, nor tearing power enough to necessarily paralyze muscle. Thurstane could still manage a revolver with his wounded arm, while his right was good for almost any amount of slashing work. Letting the rifle drop and swing from the pommel, he met the charge of two grinning and scowling lancers. One thrust he parried with his sabre; from the other he saved his neck by stooping; but it drove through his coat collar, and nearly unseated him. For a moment our bleeding and hampered young gladiator seemed to be in a bad way. But he was strong; he braced himself in his stirrups, and he made use of both his hands. The Indian whose spear was still free caught a bullet through the shoulder, dropped his weapon, and circled away yelling. Then Thurstane plunged at the other, reared his tall horse over him, broke the lance-shaft with a violent twist, and swung his long cavalry sabre. It was in vain that the Apache crouched, spurred, and skedaddled; he got away alive, but it was with a long bloody gash down his naked back; the last seen of him he was going at full speed, holding by his pony's mane. The Lieutenant remained master of the whole front of the caravan.

Meantime there was a busy popping along the flankers and through the hinder openings in the second line of wagons. The Indians skurried, wheeled, pranced, and yelled, let fly their arrows from a distance, dashed up here and there with their lances, and as quickly retreated before the threatening muzzles. The muleteers, encouraged by the presence of the soldiers, behaved with respectable firmness and blazed away rapidly, though not effectively. The regulars reserved their fire for close quarters, and then delivered it to bloody purpose.

Around Sweeney, who garrisoned the left-hand wagon of the rearmost line, the fight was particularly noisy. The Apaches saw that he was little, and perhaps they saw that he was afraid of his gun. They went for him; they were after him with their sharpest sticks; they counted on Sweeney. The speck of a man sat on the front seat of the wagon, outside of the driver, and fully exposed to the tribulation. He was in a state of the highest Paddy excitement. He grinned and bounced like a caravan of monkeys. But he was not much scared; he was mainly in a furious rage. Pointing his musket first at one and then at another, he returned yell for yell, and was in fact abusive.

"Oh, fire yer bow-arreys!" he screamed. "Ye can't hit the side av a waggin. Ah, ye bloody, murtherin' nagers! go 'way wid yer long poles. I'd fight a hundred av the loikes av ye wid ownly a shillelah."

One audacious thrust of a lance he parried very dexterously with his bayonet, at the same time screeching defiantly and scornfully in the face of his hideous assailant. But this fellow's impudent approach was too much to be endured, and Sweeney proceeded at once to teach him to keep at a more civil distance.

"Oh, ye pokin' blaggard!" he shouted, and actually let drive with his musket. The ball missed, but by pure blundering one of the buck-shot took effect.

and the brave retreated out of the mêlée with a sensation as if his head had been split. Some time later he was discovered sitting up doggedly on a rock, while a comrade was trying to dig the buckshot out of his thick skull with an arrow-point.

"I'll tache 'em to moind their bizniss," grinned Sweeney triumphantly, as he reloaded. "The nasty, hootin' nagers! They've no rights near a white man, anyhow."

On the whole, the attack lingered. The Apaches had done some damage. One driver had been lanced mortally. One muleteer had been shot through the heart with an arrow. Another arrow had scraped Shubert's ankle. Another, directed by the whimsical genius of accident, had gone clean through the drooping cartilage of Phineas Glover's long nose, as if to prepare him for the sporting of jewelled decorations. Two mules were dead, and several wounded. The sides of the wagons bristled with shafts, and their canvas tops were pierced with fine holes. But, on the other hand, the Apaches had lost a dozen horses, three or four warriors killed, and seven or eight wounded.

Such was the condition of affairs around the train when Coronado, Texas Smith, and the four surviving herdsmen came storming back to it.

CHAPTER XII.

THE Apaches were discouraged by the immovability of the train, and by the steady and deadly resistance of its defenders. From first to last some twenty-five or twenty-seven of their warriors had been hit, of whom probably one third were killed or mortally wounded.

At the approach of Coronado those who were around the wagons swept away in a panic, and never paused in their flight until they were a good half mile distant. They carried off, however, every man, whether dead or injured, except one alone. A few rods from the train lay a mere boy, certainly not over fifteen years old, his forehead gashed by a bullet, and life apparently extinct. There was nothing strange in the fact of so young a lad taking part in battle, for the military age among the Indians is from twelve to thirty-six, and one third of their fighters are children.

"What did they leave that fellow for?" said Coronado in surprise, riding up to the senseless figure.

"I'll fix him," volunteered Texas Smith, dismounting and drawing his hunting knife. "Reckon he hain't been squarely finished."

"Stop!" ordered Coronado. "He is not an Apache. He is some pueblo Indian. See how much he is hurt."

"Skull ain't broke," replied Texas, fingering the wound as roughly as if it had been in the flesh of a beast. "Reckon he'll flop round. May do mischief, if we don't fix him."

Anxious to stick his knife into the defenceless young throat, he nevertheless controlled his sentiments and looked up for instructions. Since the splendid decapitation which Coronado had performed, Texas respected him as he had never heretofore hoped to respect a "greaser."

"Perhaps we can get information out of him," said Coronado. "Suppose you lay him in a wagon."

Meanwhile preparations had been made for an advance. The four dead or badly wounded draft mules were disentangled from the harness, and their places supplied with the four army mules, whose packs were thrown into the wagons.

These animals, by the way, had escaped injury, partly because they had been tethered between the two lines of vehicles, and partly because they had been well covered by their loads, which were plentifully stuck with arrows.

"We are ready to march," said Thurstane to Coronado. "I am sorry we can't try to recover your men back there."

"No use," commented Texas Smith. "The Patchies have been at 'em. They're chuck full of spear holes by this time."

Coronado shouted to the drivers to start. Commencing on the right, the wagons filed off two by two toward the mouth of the cañon, while the Indians, gathered in a group half a mile away, looked on without a yell or a movement. The instant that the vehicle which contained the ladies had cleared itself of the others, Thurstane and Coronado rode alongside of it.

"So! you are safe!" said the former. "By Heavens, if they *had* hurt you!"

"And you?" asked Clara, very quickly and eagerly, while scanning him from head to foot.

Coronado saw that look, anxious for Thurstane alone; and, master of dissimulation though he was, his face showed both pain and anger.

"Ah—oh—oh dear!" groaned Mrs. Stanley, as she made her appearance in the front of the vehicle. "Well! this is rather more than I can bear. This is just as much as a woman can put up with. Dear me! what is the matter with your arm, Lieutenant?"

"Just a pin prick," said Thurstane.

Clara began to get out of the wagon, with the purpose of going to him, her eyes staring and her face pale.

"Don't!" he protested, motioning her back. "It is nothing."

And, although the lacerated arm hurt him and was not easy to manage, he raised it over his head to show that the damage was trifling.

"Do get in here and let us take care of you," begged Clara.

"Certainly!" echoed Aunt Maria, who was a compassionate woman at heart, and who only lacked somewhat in quickness of sympathy, perhaps by reason of her strong-minded notions.

"I will when I need it," said Ralph, flattered and gratified. "The arm will do without dressing till we reach camp. There are other wounded. Everybody has fought. Mr. Coronado here has done deeds worthy of his ancestors."

"Ah, Mr. Coronado!" smiled Aunt Maria, delighted that her favorite had distinguished himself.

"Captain Glover, what's the matter with your nose?" was the lady's next outcry.

"Wal, it's been bored," replied Glover, tenderly fingering his sore proboscis. "It's been, so to speak, eyelet-holed. I'm glad I hadn't but one. The more noses a feller kerries in battle, the wuss for him. I hope the darned rip 'll heal up. I've no 'casion to hev a line rove through it 'n' be towed, that I know of."

"How did it feel when it went through?" asked Aunt Maria, full of curiosity and awe.

"Felt 's though I'd got the dreadfullest influenzee thet ever snorted. Twitched 'n' tickled like all possessed."

"Was it an arrow?" inquired the still unsatisfied lady.

"Reckon 'twas. Never see it. But it kinder whished, 'n' I felt the feathers. Darn 'em! When I felt the feathers, tell ye I was 'bout half scairt. Hed 'n idee 'f th' angel 'f death, 'n' so on."

Of course Aunt Maria and Clara wanted to do much nursing immediately; but there were no conveniences and there was no time; and so benevolence was postponed.

"So you are hurt?" said Thurstane to Texas Smith, noticing his torn and bloody shirt.

"It's jest a scrape," grunted the bushwhacker. "Mought 'a' been worse."

"It was bad generalship trying to save you. We nearly paid high for it."

"That's so. Cost four greasers, as 'twas. Well, I'm worth four greasers."

"You're a devil of a fighter," continued the Lieutenant, surveying the ferocious face and sullen air of the cutthroat with a soldier's admiration for whatever expresses pugnacity.

"Bet yer pile on it," returned Texas, calmly conscious of his character. "So be you."

The savage black eyes and the imperious blue ones stared into each other without the least flinching and with something like friendliness.

Coronado rode up to the pair and asked, "Is that boy alive yet?"

"It's about time for him to flop round," replied Texas indifferently. "Reckon you'll find him in the off hind wagon. I shoved him in thar."

Coronado cantered to the off hind wagon, peeped through the rear opening of its canvas cover, discovered the youth lying on a pile of luggage, addressed him in Spanish, and learned his story. He belonged to a hacienda in Bernalillo, a hundred miles or more west of Santa Fé. The Apaches had surprised the hacienda and plundered it, carrying him off because, having formerly been a captive among them, he could speak their language, manage the bow, etc.

For all this Coronado cared nothing; he wanted to know why the band had left Bernalillo; also why it had attacked his train. The boy explained that the raiders had been driven off the southern route by a party of United States cavalry, and that, having lost a number of their braves in the fight, they had sworn vengeance on Americans.

"Did you hear them say whose train this was?" demanded Coronado.

"No, Señor."

"Do you think they knew?"

"Señor, I think not."

"Whose band was this?"

"Manga Colorada's."

"Where is Delgadito?"

"Delgadito went the other side of the mountain. They were both going to fight the Moquis."

"So we shall find Delgadito in the Moqui valley?"

"I think so, Señor."

After a moment of reflection Coronado added, "You will stay with us and take care of mules. I will do well by you."

"Thanks, Señor. Many thanks."

Coronado rejoined Thurstane and told his news. The officer looked grave; there might be another combat in store for the train; it might be an affair with both bands of the Apaches.

"Well," he said, "we must keep our eyes open. Every one of us must do his very utmost. On the whole, I can't believe they can beat us."

"Nombre de Dios!" thought Coronado. "How will this accursed job end? I wish I were out of it."

They were now traversing the cañon from which they had been so long debarred. It was a peaceful solitude; no life but their own stirred within its sandstone ramparts; and its windings soon carried them out of sight of their late assailants. For four hours they slowly threaded it, and when night came on they were still in it, miles away from their expected camping ground. No water and no grass; the animals were drooping with hunger, and all suffered with thirst; the worst was that the hurts of the wounded could not be properly dressed. But progress through this labyrinth of stones in the darkness was impossible, and the weary, anxious, fevered travellers bivouacked as well as might be.

Starting at dawn, they finished the cañon in about an hour, traversed an uneven plateau which stretched beyond its final sinuous branch gullies, and found themselves on the brow of a lofty terrace, overlooking a sublime panorama. There was an immense valley, not smooth and verdurous, but a gigantic nest of savage buttes and crags and hills, only to be called a valley because it was enclosed by what seemed a continuous line of eminences. On the north and east rose long ranges and elevated table-lands; on the west, the savage rolls and precipices of the Sierra del Carrizo; and on the south, a more distant bordering of hazy mountains, closing to the southwest, a hundred miles away, in the noble snowy peaks of Monte San Francisco.

With his field-glass, Thurstane examined one after another of the mesas and buttes which diversified this enormous depression. At last his attention settled on an isolated bluff or mound, with a flattened surface three or four miles in length, the whole mass of which seemed to be solid and barren rock. On this truncated pyramid he distinguished, or thought he distinguished, one or more of the pueblos of the Moquis. He could not be quite sure, because the distance was fifteen miles, and the walls of these villages are of the same stone with the buttes upon which they stand.

"There is our goal, if I am not mistaken," he said to Coronado. "When we get there we can rest."

The train pushed onward, slowly descending the terrace, or rather the succession of terraces. After reaching a more level region, and while winding between stony hills of a depressing sterility, it came suddenly, at the bottom of a ravine, upon fresh green turf and thickets of willows, the environment of a small spring of clear water. There was a halt; all hands fell to digging a trench across the gully; when it had filled, the animals were allowed to drink; in an hour more they had closely cropped all the grass. This was using up time perilously, but it had to be done, for the beasts were tottering.

Moving again; five miles more traversed; another spring and patch of turf discovered; a rough ravine through a low sandstone ridge threaded; at last they were on one of the levels of the valley. Three of the Moqui towns were now about eight miles distant, and with his glass Thurstane could distinguish the horizontal lines of building. The trail made straight for the pueblos, but it was almost impassable to wagons, and progress was very slow. It was all the slower because of the weakness of the mules, which throughout all this hair-brained journey had been severely worked, and of late had been poorly fed.

Presently the travellers turned the point of a naked ridge which projected laterally into the valley. There they came suddenly upon a wide-spread sweep of turf, contrasting so brilliantly with the bygone infertilities that it seemed to them a paradise, and stretching clear on to the bluff of the pueblos.

There, too, with equal suddenness, they came upon peril. Just beyond the nose of the sandstone promontory there was a bivouc of half-naked, dark-skinned horsemen, recognizable at a glance as Apaches. It was undoubtedly the band of Delgadito.

The camp was half a mile distant. The Indians, evidently surprised at the appearance of the train, were immediately in commotion. There was a rapid mounting, and in five minutes they were all on horseback, curveting in circles, and brandishing their lances, but without advancing.

"Manga Colorada hasn't reached here yet," observed Thurstane.

"That's so," assented Texas Smith. "They hain't heerd from the cuss, or they'd a bushwhacked us somewhar. Seein' he dasn't follow our trail, he had to make a big turn to git here. But he'll be droppin' along, an' then we'll hev a fight. I reckon we'll hev one anyway. Them cusses ain't friendly. If they was, they'd a piled in helter-skelter to hev a talk an' ask fur whiskey."

"We must keep them at a distance," said Thurstane.

"You bet! The first Injun that comes nigh us, I'll shute him. They mustn't be 'lowed to git among us. First you know you'd hear a yell, an' find yourself speared in the back. An' them that's speared right off is the lucky ones."

"Not one of us must fall into their hands," muttered the officer, thinking of Clara.

"Cap, that's so," returned Texas grimly. "When I fight Injuns, I never empty my revolver. I keep one barl for myself. You'd better do the same. Furthermore, thar oughter be somebody detailed to shute the women folks when it comes to the last pinch. I say this as a friend."

As a friend! It was the utmost stretch of Texas Smith's humanity and sympathy. Obviously the fellow had a soft side to him.

The fact is that he had taken a fancy to Thurstane since he had learned his fighting qualities, and would rather have done him a favor than murder him. At all events his hatred to "Injuns" was such that he wanted the lieutenant to kill a great many of them before his own turn came.

"So you think we'll have a tough job of it?" inferred Ralph.

"Cap, we ain't so many as we was. An' if Manga Colorada comes up, thar'll be a pile of red-skins. It may be they'll outlast us; an' so I say as a friend, save one shot; save it for yourself, Cap."

But the Apaches did not advance. They watched the train steadily; they held a long consultation which evidently referred to it; at last they seemed to decide that it was in too good order to fall an easy prey; there was some wild capering along its flanks, at a safe distance; and then, little by little, the gang re-settled in its bivouac. It was like a swarm of hornets, which should sally out to reconnoitre an enemy, buzz about threateningly for a while, and sail back to their nest.

The plain, usually dotted with flocks of sheep, was now a solitude. The Moquis had evidently withdrawn their woolly wealth either to the summit of the bluff, or to the partially sheltered pasturage around its base. The only objects which varied the verdant level were scattered white rocks, probably gypsum or oxide of manganese, which glistened surprisingly in the sunlight, reminding one of pearls sown on a mantel of green velvet. But already the travellers could see the peach orchards of the Moquis, and the sides of the lofty butte laid out in gardens supported by terrace-walls of dressed stone, the whole mass surmounted by the solid ramparts of the pueblos.

At this moment, while the train was still a little over two miles from the foot of the bluff, and the Apache camp more than three miles to the rear, Texas Smith shouted, "The cusses hev got the news."

It was true; the foremost riders, or perhaps only the messengers, of Manga Colorada had reached Delgadito; and a hundred warriors were swarming after the train to avenge their fallen comrades.

Now ensued a race for life, the last pull of the mules being lashed out of them, and the Indians riding at the topmost speed of their wiry ponies.

CHAPTER XIII.

WHEN the race for life and death commenced between the emigrants and the Apaches, it seemed as if the former would certainly be able to go two miles before the latter could cover six.

But the mules were weak, and the soil of the plain was a thin loam into which the wheels sank easily, so that the heavy wagons could not be hurried beyond a trot, and before long were reduced to a walk. Thus, while the caravan was still half a mile from its city of refuge, the foremost hornets of Delgadito's swarm were already circling around it.

The chief could not charge at once, however, for the warriors whom he had in hand numbered barely a score, and their horses, blown with a run of over five miles, were unfit for sharp fighting work. For a few minutes nothing happened, except that the caravan continued its silent, sullen retreat, while the pursuers cantered yelling around it at a safe distance. Not a shot was fired by the emigrants; not a brave dashed up to let fly his arrows. At last there were fifty Apaches; then there was a hurried council; then a furious rush. Evidently the savages were ashamed to let their enemies escape for lack of one audacious assault.

This charge was led by a child. A boy not more than fourteen years of age, screaming like a little demon and discharging his arrows at full speed with wicked dexterity, rode at the head of this savage *hourra* of the Cossacks of the American desert. As the fierce child came on, Coronado saw him and recognized him with a mixture of wonder, dread, and hate. Here was the son of the false-hearted savage who had accepted his money, agreed to do his work, and then turned against him. Should he kill him? It would open an account of blood between himself and the father. Never mind; vengeance is sweet; moreover, the youngster was dangerous.

Coronado raised his revolver, steadied it across his left arm, took a calm aim, and fired. The handsome, headlong, terrible boy swayed forward, rolled slowly over the pommel of his saddle, and fell to the ground motionless. In the next moment there was a general rattle of firearms from the train, and the mass of the charging column broke up into squads which went off in aimless caracolings. Barring a short struggle by half a dozen braves to recover the young chief's body, the contest was over; and in two minutes more the Apaches were half a mile distant, looking on in sulky silence while the train crawled toward the protecting bluff.

"Hurrah!" shouted Thurstane. "That was quick work. Delgadito doesn't take his punishment well."

"Reckon they see we had friends," observed Captain Glover. "Jest look at them critters pile down the mounting. Darned if they don't skip like nanny-goats."

Down the huge steep slope, springing along rocky, sinuous paths, or over the walls of the terraces, came a hundred or a hundred and fifty men, running with a speed which, considering the nature of the footing, was marvellous. Before many in the train were aware of their approach, they were already among the wagons, rushing up to the travellers with outstretched hands, the most cordial, cheerful, kindly-eyed people that Thurstane had seen in New Mexico. Good features, too; that is, they were handsomer than the usual Indian type; some even had physiognomies which reminded one of Italians. Their hair was fine and glossy for men of their race; and, stranger still, it bore an appearance of careful combing. Nearly all wore loose cotton trousers or drawers reaching to the knee, with a kind of blouse of woollen or cotton, and over the shoulders a gay woollen blanket tied around the waist. In view of their tidy raiment and their general air of cleanliness, it seemed a mistake to class them as Indians. These were the Moquis, a remnant of one of the semi-civilizations of America, perhaps a colony left behind by the Aztecs in their migrations, or possibly by the temple-builders of Yucatan.

Impossible to converse with them. Not a person in the caravan spoke the Moqui tongue, and not a Moqui spoke or understood a word of Spanish or English. But it was evident from their faces and gestures that they were enthusiastically friendly, and that they had rushed down from their fastness to aid the emigrants against the Apaches. There was even a little sally into the plain, the Moquis running a quarter of a mile with amazing agility, spreading out into a loose skirmishing line of battle, brandishing their bows and defying the enemy to battle. But this ended in nothing; the Apaches sullenly cantered away; the others soon checked their pursuit.

Now came the question of encampment. To get the wagons up the bluff, eight hundred feet or so in height, along a path which had been cut in the rock or built up with stone, was obviously impossible. Would there be safety where they were, just at the base of the noble slope? The Moquis assured them by signs that the plundering horse-Indians never came so near the pueblos. Camp then; the wagons were parked as usual in a hollow square; the half-starved animals were unharnessed and allowed to fly at the abundant grass; the cramped and wearied travellers threw themselves on the ground with delight.

"What a charming people these Monkeys are!" said Aunt Maria, surveying the neat and smiling villagers with approval.

"Moquis," Coronado corrected her, with a bow.

"Oh, Mo-kies," repeated Aunt Maria, this time catching the sound exactly. "Well, I propose to see as much of them as possible. Why shouldn't the women and the wounded sleep in the city?"

"It is an excellent idea," assented Coronado, although he thought with distaste that this would bring Clara and Thurstane together, while he would be at a distance.

"I suppose we shall get an idea from it of the ancient city of Mexico, as described by Prescott," continued the enthusiastic lady.

"You will discover a few deviations in the ground plan," returned Coronado, for once ironical.

Aunt Maria's suggestion with regard to the women and the wounded was adopted. The Moquis seemed to urge it; so at least they were understood. Within a couple of hours after the halt a procession of the feebler folk commenced climbing the bluff, accompanied by a crowd of the hospitable Indians. The winding and difficult path swarmed for a quarter of a mile with people in the gayest of blankets, some ascending with the strangers and some coming down to greet them.

"I should think we were going up to the Temple of the Sun to be sacrificed," said Clara, who had also read Prescott.

"To be worshipped," ventured Thurstane, giving her a look which made her blush, the boldest look that he had yet ventured.

The terraces, as we have stated, were faced with partially dressed stone. They were in many places quite broad, and were cultivated everywhere with admirable care, presenting long green lines of corn fields or of peach orchards. Half-way up the ascent was a platform of more than ordinary spaciousness which contained a large reservoir, built of chipped stone strongly cemented, and brimming with limpid water. From this cistern large earthen pipes led off in various directions to irrigate the terraces below.

"It seems to me that we are discovering America," exclaimed Aunt Maria, her face scarlet with exercise and enthusiasm.

Presently she asked, in full faith that she was approaching a metropolis, "What is the name of the city?"

"This must be Tegua," replied Thurstane. "Tegua is the most eastern of the Moqui pueblos. There are three on this bluff. Mooshaneh and two others are on a butte to the west. Oraybe is further north."

"What a powerful confederacy!" said Aunt Maria. "The United States of the Moquis!"

After a breathless ascent of at least eight hundred feet, they reached the undulated, barren, rocky surface of a plateau. Here the whole population of Tegua had collected; and for the first time the visitors saw Moqui women and children. Aunt Maria was particularly pleased with the specimens of her own sex; she went into ecstasies over their gentle physiognomies and their well-combed, carefully braided, glossy hair; she admired their long gowns of black woollen, each with a yellow stripe around the waist and a border of the same at the bottom.

"Such a sensible costume!" she said. "So much more rational and convenient than our fashionable fripperies!"

Another fact of great interest was that the Moquis were lighter complexioned than Indians in general. And when she discovered a woman with fair skin, blue eyes, and yellow hair—one of those albinos who are found among the inhabitants of the pueblos—she went into an excitement which was nothing less than ethnological.

"These are white people," she cried, losing sight of all the brown faces. "They are some European race which colonized America long before that modern upstart, Columbus. They are undoubtedly the descendants of the Northmen who built the old mill at Newport and sculptured the Dighton Rock."

"There is a belief," said Thurstane, "that some of these pueblo people, particularly those of Zuni, are Welsh. A Welsh prince named Madoc, flying before the Saxons, is said to have reached America. There are persons who hold that the descendants of his followers built the mounds in the Mississippi Valley, and that some of them became the white Mandans of the upper Missouri, and that others founded this old Mexican civilization. Of course it is all guess-work. There's nothing about it in the Regulations."

"I consider it highly probable," asserted Aunt Maria, forgetting her Scandinavian hypothesis. "I don't see how you can doubt that that flaxen-haired girl is a descendant of Medoc, Prince of Wales."

"Madoc," corrected Thurstane.

"Well, Madoc then," replied Aunt Maria rather pettishly, for she was dreadfully tired, and moreover she didn't like Thurstane.

A few minutes' walk brought them to the rampart which surrounded the pueblo. Its foundation was a solid blind wall, fifteen feet or so in height, and built of hewn stone laid in clay cement. Above was a second wall, rising from the first as one terrace rises from another, and surmounted by a third, which was also in terrace fashion. The ground tier of this stair-like structure contained the storerooms of the Moquis, while the upper tiers were composed of their two-story houses, the entire mass of masonry being upward of thirty feet high, and forming a continuous line of fortification. This rampart of dwellings was in the shape of a rectangle, and enclosed a large square or plaza containing a noble reservoir. Compact and populous, at once a castle and a city, the place could defy all the horse Indians of North America.

"Bless me! this is sublime but dreadful," said Aunt Maria when she learned that she must ascend to the landing of the lower wall by a ladder. "No gate? Isn't there a window somewhere that I could crawl through? Well, well! Dear me! But it's delightful to see how safe these excellent people have made themselves."

So with many tremblings, and with the aid of a lariat fastened around her waist and vigorously pulled from above by two Moquis, Aunt Maria clutched and scraped her way to the top of the foundation terrace.

"I shall never go down in the world," she remarked with a shuddering glance backward. "I shall pass the rest of my days here."

From the first platform the travellers were led to the second and third by stone stairways. They were now upon the inside of the rectangle, and could see two stories of doors facing the plaza and the reservoir in its centre, the whole scene cheerful with the gay garments and smiling faces of the Moquis.

"Beautiful!" said Aunt Maria. "That court is absolutely swept and dusted. One might give a ball there. I should like to hear Lucretia Mott speak in it."

Her reflections were interrupted by the courteous gestures of a middle-aged, dignified Moqui, who was apparently inviting the party to enter one of the dwellings.

Pepita and the other two Indian women, with the wounded muleteers, were taken to another house. Aunt Maria, Clara, Thurstane, and Phineas Glover entered the residence of the chief, and found themselves in a room six or seven feet high, fifteen feet in length and ten in breadth. The floor was solid, polished clay; the walls were built of the large, sunbaked bricks called adobes; the ceilings were of beams, covered by short sticks, with adobes over all. Skins, bows and arrows, quivers, antlers, blankets, articles of clothing, and various simple ornaments hung on pegs driven into the walls or lay packed upon shelves.

"They are a musical race, I see," observed Aunt Maria, pointing to a pair of painted drumsticks tipped with gay feathers, and a reed wind-instrument with a bell-shaped mouth like a clarionet. "Of course they are. The Welsh were always famous for their bards and their harpers. Does anybody in our party speak Welsh? What a pity we are such ignoramuses! We might have an interesting conversation with these people. I should so like to hear their traditions about the voyage across the Atlantic and the old mill at Newport."

Her remarks were interrupted by a short speech from the chief, whom she at first understood as relating the adventures of his ancestors, but who finally made it clear that he was asking them to take seats. After they were arranged on a row of skins spread along the wall, a shy, meek, and pretty Moqui woman passed around a vase of water for drinking and a tray which contained something not unlike a bundle of blue wrapping paper.

"Is this to wipe our hands on?" inquired Aunt Maria, bringing her spectacles to bear on the contents of the tray.

"It smells like corn bread," said Clara.

So it was. The corn of the Moquis is blue, and grinding does not destroy the color. The meal is stirred into a thin gruel and cooked by pouring over smooth, flat, heated stones, the light shining tissues being rapidly taken off and folded, and subsequently made up in bundles.

The party made a fair meal off the blue wrapping paper. Then the meek-eyed woman reappeared, removed the dishes, returned once more, and looked fixedly at Thurstane's bloody sleeve.

"Certainly!" said Aunt Maria. "Let her dress your arm. I have no doubt that unpretending woman knows more about surgery than all the men doctors in New York city. Let her dress it."

Thurstane partially threw off his coat and rolled up his shirt sleeve. Clara gave one glance at the huge white arm with the small crimson hole in it, and turned away with a thrill which was new to her. The Moqui woman washed the wound, applied a dressing which looked like chewed leaves, and put on a light bandage.

"Does it feel any better?" asked Aunt Maria eagerly.

"It feels cooler," said Thurstane.

Aunt Maria looked as if she thought him very ungrateful for not saying that he was entirely well.

"An' my nose," suggested Glover, turning up his lacerated proboscis.

"Yes, certainly; your poor nose," assented Aunt Maria. "Let the lady cure it."

The female surgeon fastened a poultice upon the tattered cartilage by passing a bandage around the skipper's sandy and bristly head.

"Works like a charm 'n' smells like peach leaves," snuffled the patient. "It's where it's handy to sniff at—that's a comfort."

After much dumb show, arrangements were made for the night. One of the inner rooms was assigned to Mrs. Stanley and Clara, and another to Thurstane and Glover. Bedding, provisions, and some small articles as presents for the Moquis were sent up from the train by Coronado.

But would the wagons, the animals, and the human members of the party below be safe during the night? Young as he was, and wounded as he was, Thurstane was so badgered by his army habit of incessant responsibility that he could not lie down to rest until he had visited the camp and examined personally into probabilities of attack and means of defence. As he descended the stony path which scored the side of the butte, his anxiety was greatly increased by the appearance of a party of armed Moquis rushing like deer down the steep slope, as if to repel an attack.

CHAPTER XIV.

Thurstane found the caravan in excellent condition, the mules being tethered at the reservoir half-way up the acclivity, and the wagons parked and guarded as usual, with Weber for officer of the night.

"We are in no tanger, Leftenant," said the sergeant. "A large barty of these bueplo beeble has shust gone to the vront. They haf daken atfandage of our bresence to regover a bortion of the blain. I haf sent Kelly along to look after them a leetle und make them keep a goot watch. We are shust as safe as bossible. Und to-morrow we will basture the animals. It is a goot blace for a gamp, Leftenant, und we shall pe all right in a tay or two."

"Does Shubert's leg need attention?"

"No. It is shust nothing. Shupert is for tuty."

"And you feel perfectly able to take care of yourselves here?"

"Berfectly, Leftenant."

"Forty rounds apiece!"

"They are issued, Leftenant."

"If you are attacked, fire heavily; and if the attack is sharp, retreat to the bluff. Never mind the wagons; they can be recovered."

"I will opey your instructions, Leftenant."

Thurstane was feverish and exhausted; he knew that Weber was as good a soldier as himself; and still he went back to the village with an anxious heart; such is the tenderness of the military conscience as to *duty*.

By the time he reached the upper landing of the wall of the pueblo it was sunset, and he paused to gaze at a magnificent landscape, the *replica* of the one which he had seen at sunrise. There were buttes, valleys, and cañons, the vast and lofty plateaus of the north, the ranges of the Navajo country, the Sierra del Carrizo, and the ice peaks of Monte San Francisco. It was sublime, savage, beautiful, horrible. It seemed a revelation from some other world. It was a nightmare of nature.

Clara met him on the landing with the smile which she now often gave him. "I was anxious about you," she said. "You were too weak to go down there. You look very tired. Do come and eat, and then rest. You will make yourself sick. I was quite anxious about you."

It was a delightful repetition. How his heart and his eyes thanked her for being troubled for his sake! He was so cheered that in a moment he did not seem to be tired at all. He could have watched all that night, if it had been necessary for her safety, or even for her comfort. The soul certainly has a great deal to do with the body.

While our travellers sleep, let us glance at the singular people among whom they have found refuge.

It is said hesitatingly, by scholars who have not yet made comparative studies of languages, that the Moquis are not *red men*, like the Algonquins, the Iroquois, the Lenni Lenape, the Sioux, and in general those whom we know as *Indians*. It is said, moreover, that they are of the same generic stock with the Aztecs of Mexico, the ancient Peruvians, and all the other city-building peoples of both North and South America.

It was an evil day for the brown race of New Mexico when horses strayed from the Spanish settlements into the desert, and the savage red tribes became cavalry. This feeble civilization then received a more cruel shock than that which had been dealt it by the storming columns of the conquistadors. The horse transformed the Utes, Apaches, Comanches, and Navajos from snapping-turtles into condors. Thenceforward, instead of crawling in slow and feeble bands to tease the dense populations of the pueblos, they could come like a tornado, and come in a swarm. At no time were the Moquis and their fellow agriculturists and herdsmen safe from robbery and slaughter. Such villages as did not stand upon buttes inaccessible to horsemen, and such as did not possess fertile lands immediately under the shelter of their walls, were either abandoned or depopulated by slow starvation.

It is thus that we may account for many of the desolate cities which are now found in Arizona, New Mexico, and Utah. Not of course for all; some, we know, were destroyed by the early Spaniards; others may have been forsaken because their tillable lands became exhausted; others doubtless fell during wars between different tribes of the brown race. But the cavalry of the desert must necessarily have been a potent instrument of destruction.

It is a pathetic spectacle, this civilization which has perished, or is perishing, without the poor consolation of a history to record its sufferings. It comes near to being a repetition of the silent death of the flint and bronze races, the mound-raisers, and cave-diggers, and cromlech-builders of Europe.

Captain Phineas Glover, rising at an early hour in the morning, and having had his nosebag of medicament refilled and refitted, set off on an appetizer around the ramparts of the pueblo, and came back marvelling.

"Been out to shake hands with these clever critters," he said. "Best behavin' 'n' meekest lookin' Injuns I ever see. Put me in mind o' cows 'n' lambs. An' neat! 'Most equal to Amsterdam Dutch. Seen a woman sweepin' up her husband's tobacco ashes 'n' carryin' 'em out to throw over the wall. Jest what they do in Broek. Ever been in Broek? Tell ye 'bout it some time. But how d'ye s'pose this town was built? *I* didn't see no stun up here that was fit for quarryin'. So I put it to a lot of fellers where they got their buildin' m'ter'ls. Wal, after figurin' round a spell, 'n' makin' signs by the schuner load, found out the hull thing. Every stun in this place was whittled out 'f the ruff-scuff at the bottom of the mounting, 'n' fetched up here in blankets on men's shoulders. All the mud, too, to make their bricks, was backed up in the same way. Feller off with his blanket 'n' showed me how they did it. Beats all. Wust of it was, couldn't find out how long it took 'em, nor how the job was lotted out to each one."

"I suppose they made their women do it," said Aunt Maria grimly. "Men usually put all the hard work on women."

"Wal, women folks do a heap," admitted Glover, who never contradicted anybody. "But there's reason to entertain a hope that they didn't take the brunt of it here. I looked over into the gardens down b'low the town, 'n' see men plantin' corn, 'n' tendin' peach trees, but didn't see no women at it. The women was all in the houses, spinnin', weavin', sewin', 'n' fixin' up ginerally."

"Remarkable people!" exclaimed Aunt Maria. "They are at least as civilized as we. Very probably more so. Of course they are. I must learn whether the women vote, or in any way take part in the government. If so, these Indians are vastly our superiors, and we must sit humbly at their feet."

During this talk the worn and wounded Thurstane had been lying asleep.

He now appeared from his dormitory, nodded a hasty good-morning, and pushed for the door.

"Train's all right," said Glover. "Jest took a squint at it. Peaceful 's a ship becalmed. Not a darned Apache in sight."

"You are sure?" demanded the young officer.

"Better get some more peach-leaf pain-killer on your arm 'n' set straight down to breakfast."

"If the Apaches have vamosed, Coronado might join us," suggested Thurstane.

"Never!" answered Mrs. Stanley with solemnity. "His ancestor stormed Cibola and ravaged this whole country. If these people should hear his name pronounced, and suspect his relationship to their oppressor, they might massacre him."

"That was three hundred years ago," smiled the wretch of a lieutenant.

"It doesn't matter," decided Mrs. Stanley.

And so Coronado, thanks to one of his splendid inventions, was not invited up to the pueblo.

The travellers spent the day in resting, in receiving a succession of pleasant, tidy visitors, and in watching the ways of the little community. The weather was perfect, for while the season was the middle of May, and the latitude that of Algeria and Tunis, they were nearly six thousand feet above the level of the sea, and the isolated butte was wreathed with breezes. It was delightful to sit or stroll on the landings of the ramparts, and overlook the flourishing landscape near at hand, and the peaceful industry which caused it to bloom.

Along the hillside, amid the terraced gardens of corn, pumpkins, guavas, and peaches, many men and children were at work, with here and there a woman.

The scene had not only its charms, but its marvels. Besides the grand environment of plateaus and mountains in the distance, there were near at hand freaks of nature such as one might look for in the moon. Nowhere perhaps has the great water erosion of bygone æons wrought more grotesquely and fantastically than in the Moqui basin. To the west rose a series of detached buttes, presenting forms of castles, towers, and minarets, which looked more like the handiwork of man than the pueblo itself. There were piles of variegated sandstone, some of them four hundred feet in height, crowned by a hundred feet of sombre trap. Internal fire had found vent here; its outflowings had crystallized into columnar trap; the trap had protected the underlying sandstone from cycles of water-flow; thus had been fashioned these sublime donjons and pinnacles.

They were not only sublime but beautiful. The sandstone, reduced by ages to a crumbling marl, was of all colors. There were layers of green, reddish-brown, drab, purple, red, yellow, pinkish, slate, light-brown, orange, white, and banded. Nature, not contented with building enchanted palaces, had frescoed them. At this distance, indeed, the separate tints of the strata could not be discerned, but their general effect of variegation was distinctly visible, and the result was a landscape of the Thousand and One Nights.

To the south were groups of crested mounds, some of them resembling the spreading stumps of trees, and others broad-mouthed bells, all of vast magnitude. These were of sandstone marl, the caps consisting of hard red and green shales, while the swelling boles, colored by gypsum, were as white as loaf-sugar. It was another specimen of the handiwork of deluges which no man can number.

Far away to the southwest, and yet faintly seen through the crystalline atmosphere, were the many-colored knolls and rolls and cliffs of the Painted Desert.

Marls, shales, and sandstones, of all tints, were strewn and piled into a variegated vista of sterile splendor. Here surely enchantment and glamour had made undisputed abode.

All day the wounded and the women reposed, gazing a good deal, but sleeping more. During the afternoon, however, our wonder-loving Mrs. Stanley roused herself from her lethargy and rushed into an adventure such as only she knew how to find. In the morning she had noticed, at the other end of the pueblo from her quarters, a large room which was frequented by men alone. It might be a temple; it might be a hall for the transaction of public business; such were the diverse guesses of the travellers. Into the mysteries of this apartment Aunt Maria resolved to poke.

She reached it; nobody was in it; suspicious circumstance! Aunt Maria put an end to this state of questionable solitude by entering. A dark room; no light except from a trap door; a very proper place for improper doings. At one end rose a large, square block of red sandstone, on which was carved a round face environed by rays, probably representing the sun. Aunt Maria remembered the sacrificial altars of the Aztecs, and judged that the old sanguinary religion of Tenochtitlan was not yet extinct. She became more convinced of this terrific fact when she discovered that the red tint of the stone was deepened in various places by stains which resembled blood.

Three or four horrible suggestions arose in succession to jerk at her heartstrings. Were these Moquis still in the habit of offering human sacrifices? Would a woman answer their purpose, and particularly a white woman? If they should catch her there, in the presence of their deity, would they consider it a leading of Providence? Aunt Maria, notwithstanding her curiosity and courage, began to feel a desire to retreat.

Her reflections were interrupted and her emotions accelerated by darkness. Evidently the door had been shut; then she heard a rustling of approaching feet and an awful whispering; then projected hands impeded her gropings toward safety. While she stood still, too completely blinded to fly and too frightened to scream, a light gleamed from behind the altar and presently rose into a flame. The sacred fire!—she knew it as soon as she saw it; she remembered Prescott, and recognized it at a glance.

By its flickering rays she perceived that the apartment was full of men, all robed in blankets of ebony blackness, and all gazing at her in solemn silence. Two of them, venerable elders with long white hair, stood in front of the others, making genuflexions and signs of adoration toward the carved face on the altar. Presently they advanced to her, one of them suddenly seizing her by the shoulders and pinioning her arms behind her, while the other drew from beneath his robe a long sharp knife of the glassy flint known as obsidian.

At this point the horrified Aunt Maria found her voice, and uttered a piercing scream.

At the close of her scream she by a supreme effort turned on her side, raised her hands to her face, rubbed her eyes open, stared at Clara, who was lying near her, and mumbled, "I've had an awful nightmare."

That was it. There was no altar, nor holy fire, nor high priest, nor flint lancet. She hadn't been anywhere, and she hadn't even screamed, except in imagination. She was on her blanket, alongside of her niece, in the house of the Moqui chief, and as safe as need be.

CHAPTER XV.

BUT the visionary terror had scarcely gone when a real one came. Coronado appeared—Coronado, the descendant of the great Vasquez—Coronado, whom the Moquis would destroy if they heard his name—of whom they would not leave two limbs or two fingers together. From her dormitory she saw him walk into the main room of the house in his airiest and cheeriest manner, bowing and smiling to right, bowing and smiling to left, winning Moqui hearts in a moment, a charmer of a Coronado. He shook hands with the chief; he shook hands with all the head men ; next a hand to Thurstane and another to Glover. Mrs. Stanley heard him addressed as Coronado ; she looked to see him scattered in rags on the floor ; she tried to muster courage to rush to his rescue.

There was no outcry of rage at the sound of the fatal name, and she could not perceive that a Moqui countenance smiled the less for it.

Coronado produced a pipe, filled it, lighted it, and handed it to the chief. That dignitary took it, bowed gravely to each of the four points of the compass, exhaled a few whiffs, and passed it to his next blanketed neighbor, who likewise saluted the four cardinal points, smoked a little, and sent it on. Mrs. Stanley drew a sigh of relief; the pipe of peace had been used, and there would be no bloodshed ; she saw the whole bearing of her favorite's audacious manœuvre at a glance.

Coronado now glided into the obscure room where she and Clara were sitting on their blankets and skins. He kissed his hand to the one and the other, and rolled out some melodious congratulations.

"You reckless creature!" whispered Aunt Maria. "How dared you come up here?"

"Why so?" asked the Mexican, for once puzzled.

"Your name! Your ancestor!"

"Ah!!" and Coronado smiled mysteriously. "There is no danger. We are under the protection of the American eagle. Moreover, hospitalities have been interchanged."

Next the experiences of the last twenty-four hours, first Mrs. Stanley's version and then Coronado's, were related. He had little to tell: there had been a quiet night and much slumber; the Moquis had stood guard and been every way friendly ; the Apaches had left the valley and gone to parts unknown.

The truth is that he had slept more than half of the time. Journeying, fighting, watching, and anxiety had exhausted him as well as every one else, and enabled him to plunge into slumber with a delicious consciousness of it as a restorative and a luxury.

Now that he was himself again, he wondered at what he had been. For two days he had faced death, fighting like a legionary or a knight-errant, and in short playing the hero. What was there in his nature, or what had there been in his selfish and lazy life, that was akin to such fine frenzies? As he remembered it all, he hardly knew himself for the same old Coronado.

Well, being safe again, he was a devoted lover again, and he must get on with his courtship. Considering that Clara and Thurstane, if left much together here in the pueblo, might lead each other into the temptation of a betrothal, he decided that he must be at hand to prevent such a catastrophe, and so here he was. Presently he began to talk to the girl in Spanish; then he begged the aunt's pardon for speaking what was to her an unknown tongue; but he had, he said, some family matters for his cousin's ear; would Mrs. Stanley be so good as to excuse him?

"Certainly," returned that far-sighted woman, guessing what the family matters might be, and approving them. "By the way, I have something to do," she added. "I must attend to it immediately."

By this time she remembered all about her nightmare, and she was in a state of inflammation as to the Moqui religion. If the dream were true, if the Moquis were in the habit of sacrificing strong-minded women or any kind of women, she must know it and put a stop to it. Stepping into the central room, where Thurstane and Glover were smoking with a number of Indians, she said in her prompt, positive way, "I must look into these people's religion. Does anybody know whether they have any?"

The Lieutenant had a spark or two of information on the subject. Through the medium of a Navajo who had strolled into the pueblo, and who spoke a little Spanish and a good deal of Moqui, he had been catechising the chief as to manners, customs, etc.

"I understand," he said, "that they have a sacred fire which they never suffer to go out. They are believed to worship the sun, like the ancient Aztecs. The sacred fire seems to confirm the suspicion."

"Sacred fire! vestal virgins, too, I suppose! can they be Romans?" reasoned Aunt Maria, beginning to doubt Prince Madoc.

"The vestal virgins here are old men," replied Ralph, wickedly pleased to get a joke on the lady.

"Oh! The Moquis are not Romans," decided Mrs Stanley. "Well, what do these old men do?"

"Keep the fire burning."

"What if it should go out? What would happen?"

"I don't know," responded the sub-acid Thurstane.

"I didn't suppose you did," said Aunt Maria pettishly. "Captain Glover, I want you to come with me."

Followed by the subservient skipper, she marched to the other end of the pueblo. There was the mysterious apartment; it was not really a temple, but a sort of public hall and general lounging place; such rooms exist in the Spanish-speaking pueblos of Zuni and Laguna, and are there called *estufas*. The explorers soon discovered that the only entrance into the estufa was by a trapdoor and a ladder. Now Aunt Maria hated ladders: they were awkward for skirts, and moreover they made her giddy; so she simply got on her knees and peeped through the trap-door. But there was a fire directly below, and there was also a pretty strong smell of pipes of tobacco, so that she saw nothing and was stifled and disgusted. She sent Glover down, as people lower a dog into a mine where gases are suspected. After a brief absence the skipper returned and reported.

"Pooty sizable room. Dark 's a pocket 'n' hot 's a footstove. Three or four Injuns talkin' 'n' smokin'. Scrap 'f a fire smoulderin' in a kind 'f standee fireplace without any top."

"That's the sacred fire," said Aunt Maria. "How many old men were watching it?"

"Didn't see *any*."

"They must have been there. Did you put the fire out?"

"No water handy," explained the prudent Glover.

"You might have—expectorated on it."

"Reckon I didn't miss it," said the skipper, who was a chewer of tobacco and a dead shot with his juice.

"Of course nothing happened."

"Nary."

"I knew there wouldn't," declared the lady triumphantly. "Well, now let us go back. We know something about the religion of these people. It is certainly a very interesting study."

"Didn't appear to me much l'k a temple," ventured Glover. "Sh'd say t'was a kind 'f gineral smokin' room 'n' jawin' place. Git together there 'n' talk crops 'n' 'lections 'n' the like."

"You must be mistaken," decided Aunt Maria. "There was the sacred fire."

She now led the willing captain (for he was as inquisitive as a monkey) on a round of visits to the houses of the Moquis. She poked smiling through their kitchens and bedrooms, and gained more information than might have been expected concerning their spinning and weaving, cheerfully spending ten minutes in signs to obtain a single idea.

"Never shear their sheep till they are dead!" she exclaimed when that fact had been gestured into her understanding. "Absurd! There's another specimen of masculine stupidity. I'll warrant you, if the women had the management of things, the good-for-nothing brutes would be sheared every day."

"Jest as they be to hum," slily suggested Glover, who knew better.

"Certainly," said Aunt Maria, aware that cows were milked daily.

The Moquis were very hospitable; they absolutely petted the strangers. At nearly every house presents were offered, such as gourds full of corn, strings of dried peaches, guavas as big as pomegranates, or bundles of the edible wrapping paper, all of which Aunt Maria declined with magnanimous waves of the hand and copious smiles. Curious and amiable faces peeped at the visitors from the landings and doorways.

"How mild and good they all look!" said Aunt Maria. "They put me in mind somehow of Shenstone's pastorals. How humanizing a pastoral life is, to be sure! On the whole, I admire their way of not shearing their sheep alive. It isn't stupidity, but goodness of heart. A most amiable people!"

"Jest so," assented Glover. "How it must go ag'in the grain with 'em to take a skelp when it comes in the way of dooty! A man oughter feel willin' to be skelped by sech tender-hearted critters."

"Pshaw!" said Aunt Maria. "I don't believe they ever scalp anybody—unless it is in self-defence."

"Dessay. Them fellers that went down to fight the Apaches was painted up 's savage 's meat-axes. Probably though 'twas to use up some 'f their paint that was a wastin'. Equinomical, I sh'd say."

Mrs. Stanley did not see her way clear to comment either upon the fact or the inference. There were times when she did not understand Glover, and this was one of the times. He had queer twistical ways of reasoning which often proved the contrary of what he seemed to want to prove; and she had concluded that he was a dark-minded man who did not always know what he was driving at; at all events, a man not invariably comprehensible by clear intellects.

Her attention was presently engaged by a stir in the pueblo. Great things were evidently at hand; some spectacle was on the point of presentation; what was it? Aunt Maria guessed marriage, and Captain Glover guessed a war-dance; but they had no argument, for the skipper gave in. Meantime the Moquis, men, women, and children, all dressed in their gayest raiment, were gathering in groups on the landings and in the square. Presently there was a crowd, a thousand or fifteen hundred strong; at last appeared the victims, the performers, or whatever they were.

"Dear me!" murmured Aunt Maria. "Twenty weddings at once! I hope divorce is frequent."

Twenty men and twenty women advanced to the centre of the plaza in double file and faced each other.

The dance began; the performers furnished their own music; each rolled out a deep *aw aw aw* under his visor.

"Sounds like a swarm of the biggest kind of blue-bottle flies inside 'f the biggest kind 'f a sugar hogset," was Glover's description.

The movement was as monotonous as the melody. The men and women faced each other without changing positions; there was an alternate lifting of the feet, in time with the *aw aw* and the rattling of the gourds; now and then there was a simultaneous about face.

After a while, open ranks; then rugs and blankets were brought; the maidens sat down and the men danced at them; trot trot, aw aw, and rattle rattle.

Every third girl now received a large empty gourd, a grooved board, and the dry shoulder-bone of a sheep. Laying the board on the gourd, she drew the bone sharply across the edges of the wood, thus producing a sound like a watchman's rattle.

They danced once on each side of the square; then retired to a house and rested fifteen minutes; then recommenced their trot. Meanwhile maidens with large baskets ran about among the spectators, distributing meat, roasted ears of corn, sheets of bread, and guavas.

So the gayety went on until the sun and the visitors alike withdrew.

"After all, I think it is more interesting than our marriages," declared Aunt Maria. "I wonder if we ought to make presents to the wedded couples. There are a good many of them."

She was quite amazed when she learned that this was not a wedding, but a rain-dance, and that the maidens whom she had admired were boys dressed up in female raiment, the customs of the Moquis not allowing women to take part in public spectacles.

"What exquisite delicacy!" was her consolatory comment. "Well, well, this is the golden age, truly."

When further informed that in marriage among the Moquis it is woman who takes the initiative, the girl pointing out the young man of her heart and the girl's father making the offer, which is never refused, Mrs. Stanley almost shed tears of gratification. Here was something like woman's rights; here was a flash of the glorious dawn of equality between the sexes; for when she talked of equality she meant female preëminence.

"And divorces?" she eagerly asked.

"They are at the pleasure of the parties," explained Thurstane, who had been catechising the chief at great length through his Navajo.

"And who, in case of a divorce, cares for the children?"

"The grandparents."

Aunt Maria came near clapping her hands. This was better than Connecticut or Indiana. A woman here might successively marry all the men whom she might successively fancy, and thus enjoy a perpetual gush of the affections and an unruffled current of happiness.

To such extreme views had this excellent creature been led by brooding over what she called the wrongs of her sex and the legal tyranny of the other.

But we must return to Coronado and Clara. The man had come up to the pueblo on purpose to have a plain talk with the girl and learn exactly what she meant to do with him. It was now more than a week since he had offered himself, and in that time she had made no sign which indicated her purpose. He had looked at her and sighed at her without getting a response of any sort. This could not go on; he must know how she felt towards him; he must know how much she cared for Thurstane. How else could he decide what to do with her and with *him?*

Thus, while the other members of the party were watching the Moqui dances, Coronado and Clara were talking matters of the heart, and were deciding, unawares to her, questions of life and death.

CHAPTER XVI.

IT must be remembered that when Mrs. Stanley carried off skipper Glover to help her investigate the religion of the Moquis, she left Coronado alone with Clara in one of the interior rooms of the chief's house.

Thurstane, to be sure, was in the next room and in sight; but he had with him the chief, two other leading Moquis, and his chance Navajo interpreter; they were making a map of the San Juan country by scratching with an arrow-point on the clay floor; everybody was interested in the matter, and there was a pretty smart jabbering. Thus Coronado could say his say without being overheard or interrupted.

For a little while he babbled commonplaces. The truth is that the sight of the girl had unsettled his resolutions a little. While he was away from her, he could figure to himself how he would push her into taking him at once, or how, if she refused him, he would let loose upon her the dogs of fate. But once face to face with her, he found that his resolutions had dispersed like a globule of mercury under a hammer, and that he needed a few moments to scrape them together again. So he prattled nothings while he meditated; and you would have thought that he cared for the nothings. He had that faculty; he could mentally ride two horses at once; he would have made a good diplomatist.

His mind glanced at the past while it peered into the future. What a sinuous underground plot the superficial incidents of this journey covered! To his fellow-travellers it was a straight line; to him it was a complicated and endless labyrinth. How much more he had to think of than they! Only he knew that Pedro Muñoz was dead, that Clara Van Dieman was an heiress, that she was in danger of being abandoned to the desert, that Thurstane was in danger of assassination. Nothing that he had set out to do was yet done, and some of it he must absolutely accomplish, and that shortly. How much? That depended upon this girl. If she accepted him, his course would be simple, and he would be spared the perils of crime.

Meantime, he looked at Clara even more frankly and calmly than she looked at him. He showed no guilt or remorse in his face, because he felt none in his heart. It must be understood distinctly that the man was almost as destitute of a conscience as it is possible for a member of civilized society to be. He knew what the world called right and wrong; but the mere opinion of the world had no weight with him; that is, none as against his own opinion. His rule of life was to do what he wanted to do, providing he could accomplish it without receiving a damage. You can hardly imagine a being whose interior existence was more devoid of complexity and of mixed motives than was Coronado's. Thus he was quite able to contemplate the possible death of Clara, and still look her calmly in the face and tell her that he loved her.

The girl returned his gaze tranquilly, because she had no suspicions of his profound wickedness. By nature confiding and reverential, she trusted those who professed friendship, and respected those who were her elders, especially if they belonged in any manner to her own family. Considering herself under obligations to Coronado, and not guessing that he was capable of doing her a harm, she was truly grateful to him and wished him well with all her heart. If her eye now and then dropped under his, it was because she feared a repetition of his offer of marriage, and hated to pain him with a refusal.

The commonplaces lasted longer than the man had meant, for he could not bring himself promptly to take the leap of fate. But at last came the dance; the chief and his comrades led Thurstane away to look at it; now was the time to talk of this fateful betrothal.

"Something is passing outside," observed Clara. "Shall we go to see?"

"I am entirely at your command," replied Coronado, with his charming air of gentle respect. "But if you can give me a few minutes of your time, I shall be very grateful."

Clara's heart beat violently, and her cheeks and neck flushed with spots of red, as she sank back upon her seat. She guessed what was coming; she had been a good deal afraid of it all the time; it was her only cause of dreading Coronado.

"I venture to hope that you have been good enough to think of what I said to you a week ago," he went on. "Yes, it was a week ago. It seems to me a year."

"It seems a long time," stammered Clara. So it did, for the days since had been crammed with emotions and events, and they gave her young mind an impression of a long period passed.

"I have been so full of anxiety!" continued Coronado. "Not about our dangers," he asserted with a little bravado. "Or, rather, not about mine. For you I have been fearful. The possibility that you might fall into the hands of the Apaches was a horror to me. But, after all, my chief anxiety was to know what would be your final answer to me. Yes, my beautiful and very dear cousin, strange as it may seem under our circumstances, this thought has always outweighed with me all our dangers."

Coronado, as we have already declared, was really in love with Clara. It seems incredible, at first glance, that a man who had no conscience could have a heart. But the assertion is not a fairy story; it is founded in solid philosophy. It is true that Coronado's moral education had been neglected or misdirected; that he was either born indifferent to the idea of duty, or had become indifferent to it; and that he was an egotist of the first water, bent solely upon favoring and gratifying himself. But while his nature was somewhat chilled by these things, he had the hottest of blood in his veins, he possessed a keen perception of the beautiful, and so he could desire with fury. His love could not be otherwise than selfish; but it was none the less capable of ruling him tyrannically.

Just at this moment his intensity of feeling made him physically imposing and almost fascinating. It seemed to remove a veil from his usually filmy black eyes, and give him power for once to throw out all of truth that there was in his soul. It communicated to his voice a tremor which made it eloquent. He exhaled, as it were, an aroma of puissant emotion which was intoxicating, and which could hardly fail to act upon the sensitive nature of woman. Clara was so agitated by this influence, that for the moment she seemed to herself to know no man in the world but Coronado. Even while she tried to remember Thurstane, he vanished as if expelled by some enchantment, and left her alone in life with her tempter. Still she could not or would not answer; though she trembled, she remained speechless.

"I have asked you to be my wife," resumed Coronado, seeing that he must urge her. "I venture now to ask you again. I implore you not to refuse me. I cannot be refused. It would make me utterly wretched. It might perhaps bring wretchedness upon you. I hope not. I could not wish you a pain, though you should give me many. My very dear Clara, I offer you the only love of my life, and the only love that I shall ever offer to any one. Will you take it?"

Clara was greatly moved. She could not doubt his sincerity; no one who heard him could have doubted it; he *was* sincere. To her, young, tender-hearted, capable of loving earnestly, beginning already to know what love is, it seemed a horrible thing to spurn affection. If it had not been for Thurstane, she would have taken Coronado for pity.

"Oh, my cousin!" she sighed, and stopped there.

Coronado drew courage from the kindly title of relationship, and, leaning gently towards her, attempted to take her hand. It was a mistake; she was strangely shocked by his touch; she perceived that she did not like him, and she drew away from him.

"Thank you for that word," he whispered. "Is it the kindest that you can give me? Is there——?"

"Coronado!" she interrupted. "This is all an error. See here. I am not an independent creature. I am a young girl. I owe some duty somewhere. My father and mother are gone, but I have a grandfather. Coronado, he is the head of my family, and I ought not to marry without his permission. Why can you not wait until we are with Muñoz?"

There she suddenly dropped her head between the palms of her hands. It struck her that she was hypocritical; that even with the consent of Muñoz she would not marry Coronado; that it was her duty to tell him so.

"My cousin, I have not told the whole truth," she added, after a terrible struggle. "I would not marry any one without first laying the case before my grandfather. But that is not all. Coronado, I cannot—no, I cannot marry you."

The man without a conscience, the man who was capable of planning and ordering murder, turned pale under this announcement.

Notwithstanding its commonness, notwithstanding that it has been described until the subject is hackneyed, notwithstanding that it has become a laughing-stock for many, even including poets and novelists, there is probably no heart-pain keener than disappointment in love. The shock of it is like a deep stab; it not merely tortures, but it instantly sickens; the anguish is much, but the sense of helplessness is more; the lover who is refused feels not unlike the soldier who is wounded to death.

This sorrow compares in dignity and terror with the most sublime sorrows of which humanity is capable. The death of a parent or child, though rendered more imposing to the spectator by the ceremonies of the sepulchre, does not chill the heart more deeply than the death of love. It lasts also; many a human being has carried the marks of it for life; and surely duration of effect is proof of power. We are serious in making these declarations, strange as they may seem to a satirical age. What we have said is strictly true, notwithstanding the mockery of those who have never loved, or the incredulity of those who, having loved, have never lost. But probably only the wretchedly initiated will believe.

Coronado, though selfish, infamous, and atrocious, was so far susceptible of affection that he was susceptible of suffering. The simple fact of pallor in that hardened face was sufficient proof of torture.

However, it stood him in hand to recover his self-possession and plead his suit. There was too much at stake in this cause for him to let it go without a struggle and a vehement one. Although he had seen at once that the girl was in earnest, he tried to believe that she was not so, and that he could move her.

"My dear cousin!" he implored in a voice that was mellow with agitation, "don't decide against me at once and forever. I must have some hope. Pity me."

"Ah, Coronado! Why will you?" urged Clara, in great trouble.

"I must! You must not stop me!" he persisted eagerly. "My life is in it. I love you so that I don't know how I shall end if you will not hearken to me. I shall be driven to desperation. Why do you turn away from me? Is it my fault that I care for you? It is your own. You are *so* beautiful!"

"Coronado, I wish I were very ugly," murmured Clara, for the moment sincere in so wishing.

"Is there anything you dislike in me? I have been as kind as I knew how to be."

"It is true, Coronado. You have overwhelmed me with your goodness. I could go on my knees to thank you."

"Then—why?"

"Ah! why will you force me to say hard things? Don't you see that it tortures me to refuse you?"

"Then why refuse me? Why torture us both?"

"Better a little pain now than much through life."

"Do you mean to say that you never can——?" He could not finish the question.

"It is so, Coronado. I never could have said it myself. But you have said it. I never shall love you."

Once more the man felt a cutting and sickening wound, as of a bullet penetrating a vital part. Unable for the moment to say another word, he rose and walked the room in silence.

"Coronado, you don't know how sorry I am to grieve you so," cried the girl, almost sobbing. "It seems, too, as if I were ungrateful. I can only beg your pardon for it, and pray that Heaven will reward you."

"Heaven!" he returned impatiently. "You are my heaven. You are the only heaven that I know."

"Oh, Coronado! Don't say that. I am a poor, sinful, unworthy creature. Perhaps I could not make any one happy long. Believe me, Coronado, I am not worthy to be loved as you love me."

"You are!" he said, turning on her passionately and advancing close to her. "You are worthy of my life-long love, and you shall have it. You shall have it, whether you wish it or not. You shall not escape it. I will pursue you with it wherever you go and as long as you live."

"Oh! You frighten me. Coronado, I beg of you not to talk to me in that way. I am afraid of you."

"What is the cause of this?" he demanded, hoping to daunt her into submission. "There is something in my way. What is it? Who is it?"

Clara's paleness turned in an instant to scarlet.

"Who is it?" he went on, his voice suddenly becoming hoarse with excitement. "It is some one. Is it this American? This boy of a lieutenant?"

Clara, trembling with an agitation which was only in part dismay, remained speechless.

"Is it?" he persisted, attempting to seize her hands and looking her fiercely in the eyes. "Is it?"

"Coronado, stand back!" said Clara. "Don't you try to take my hands!"

She was erect, her eyes flashing, her cheeks spotted with crimson, her expression strangely imposing.

The man's courage drooped the moment he saw that she had turned at bay. He walked to the other side of the room, pressed his temples between his palms to quiet their throbbing, and made an effort to recover his self-possession. When he returned to her, after nearly a minute of silence, he spoke quite in his natural manner.

"This must pass for the present," he said. "I see that it is useless to talk to you of it now."

"I hope you are not angry with me, Coronado."

"Let it go," he replied, waving his hand. "I can't speak more of it now."

She wanted to say, "Try never to speak of it again;" but she did not dare to anger him further, and she remained silent.

"Shall we go to see the dance?" he asked.

"I will, if you wish it."

"But you would rather stay alone?"

"If you please, Coronado."

Bowing with an air of profound respect, he went his way alone, glanced at the games of the Moquis, and hurried back to camp, meditating as he went.

What now should be done? He was in a state of fury, full of plottings of desperation, swearing to himself that he would show no mercy. Thurstane must die at the first opportunity, no matter if his death should kill Clara. And she? There he hesitated; he could not yet decide what to do with her; could not resolve to abandon her to the wilderness.

But to bring about any part of his projects he must plunge still deeper into the untraversed. To him, by the way, as to many others who have had murder at heart, it seemed as if the proper time and place for it would never be found. Not now, but by and by; not here, but further on. Yes, it must be further on; they must set out as soon as possible for the San Juan country; they must get into wilds never traversed by civilized man.

To go thither in wagons he had already learned was impossible. The region was a mass of mountains and rocky plateaux, almost entirely destitute of water and forage, and probably forever impassable by wheels. The vehicles must be left here; the whole party must take saddle for the northern desert; and then must come death—or deaths.

But while Coronado was thus planning destruction for others, a noiseless, patient, and ferocious enmity was setting its ambush for him.

CHAPTER XVII.

SHORTLY after the safe arrival of the train at the base of the Moqui bluff, and while the repulsed and retreating warriors of Delgadito were still in sight two strange Indians cantered up to the park of wagons.

They were fine-looking fellows, with high aquiline features, the prominent cheek-bones and copper complexion of the red race, and a bold, martial, trooper-like expression, which was not without its wild good-humor and gayety. One was dressed in a white woollen hunting-shirt belted around the waist, white woollen trousers or drawers reaching to the knee, and deerskin leggins and moccasins. The other had the same costume, except that his drawers were brown and his hunting-shirt blue, while a blanket of red and black stripes drooped from his shoulders to his heels. Their coarse black hair was done up behind in thick braids, and kept out of their faces by a broad band around the temples. Each had a lance eight or ten feet long in his hand, and a bow and quiver slung at his waist-belt. These men were Navajos (Na-va-hos).

Two jolly and impudent braves were these visitors. They ate, smoked, lounged about, cracked jokes, and asked for liquor as independently as if the camp were a tavern. Rebuffs only made them grin, and favors only led to further demands. It was hard to say whether they were most wonderful for good-nature or impertinence.

Coronado was civil to them. The Navajos abide or migrate on the south, the north, and the west of the Moqui pueblas. He was in a manner within their country, and it was still necessary for him to traverse a broad stretch of it, especially if he should attempt to reach the San Juan. Besides, he wanted them to warn the Apaches out of the neighborhood and thus avert from his head the vengeance of Manga Colorada. Accordingly he gave this pair of roystering troopers a plentiful dinner and a taste of aguardiente. Toward sunset they departed in high good-humor, promising to turn back the hoofs of the Apache horses; and when in the morning Coronado saw no Indians on the plain, he joyously trusted that his visitors had fulfilled their agreement.

Somewhere or other, within the next day or two, there was a grand council of the two tribes. We know little of it; we can guess that Manga Colorada must have made great concessions or splendid promises to the Navajos; but it is only certain that he obtained leave to traverse their country. Having secured this privilege, he posted himself fifteen or twenty miles to the southwest of Tegua, behind a butte which was extensive enough to conceal his wild cavalry, even in its grazings. He undoubtedly supposed that, when the train should quit its shelter, it would go to the west or to the south. In either case he was in a position to fall upon it.

Did the savage know anything about Coronado? Had he attacked his wagons without being aware that they belonged to the man who had paid him five hundred dollars and sent him to harry Bernalillo? Or had he attacked in full knowledge of this fact, because he had been beaten off the southern trail. and believed that he had been lured thither to be beaten? Had he learned. either from Apaches or Navajos, whose hand it was that slew his boy? We can only ask these questions.

One thing alone is positive: there was a debt of blood to be paid. An Indian war is often the result of a private vendetta. The brave is bound, not only by natural affection and family pride, but still more powerfully by sense of honor and by public opinion, to avenge the slaughter of a relative. Whether he wishes it or not, and frequently no doubt when he does not wish it, he must black his face, sing his death-song, set out alone if need be, encounter labors, hardships, and dangers, and never rest until his sanguinary account is settled. The tyranny of Mrs. Grundy in civilized cities and villages is nothing to the despotism which she exercises among those slaves of custom, the red men of the American wildernesses. Manga Colorada, bereaved and with blackened face, lay in wait for the first step of the emigrants outside of their city of refuge.

We must return to Coronado. Although Clara's rejection of his suit left him vindictively and desperately eager for a catastrophe of some sort, a week elapsed before he dared take his mad plunge into the northern desert. It was a hundred miles to the San Juan; the intervening country was a waste of rocks, almost entirely destitute of grass and water; the mules and horses must recruit their full strength before they could undertake such a journey. They must not only be strong enough to go, but they must have vital force left to return.

It is astonishing what labors and dangers the man was willing to face in his vain search for a spot where he might commit a crime in safety. Such a spot is as difficult to discover as the Fountain of Youth or the Terrestrial Paradise. More than once Coronado sickened of his seemingly hopeless and ever lengthening pilgrimage of sin. Not because it was sinful—he had little or no conscience, remember—only because it was perplexing and perilous.

It was in vain that Thurstane protested against the crazy trip northward. Coronado sometimes argued for his plan; said the route improved as it approached the river; hoped the party would not be broken up in this manner; declared that he could not spare his dear friend the lieutenant. Another time he calmly smoked his cigarito, looked at Thurstane with filmy, expressionless eyes, and said, "Of course you are not obliged to accompany us."

"I have not the least intention of quitting you," was the rather indignant reply of the young fellow.

At this declaration Coronado's long black eyebrows twitched, and his lips curled with the smile of a puma, showing his teeth disagreeably.

"My dear lieutenant, that is so like you!" he said. "I own that I expected it. Many thanks."

Thurstane's blue-black eyes studied this enigmatic being steadily and almost angrily. He could not at all comprehend the fellow's bland obstinacy and recklessness.

"Very well," he said sullenly. "Let us start on our wild-goose chase. What I object to is taking the women with us. As for myself, I am anxious to reach the San Juan and get something to report about it."

"The ladies will have a day or two of discomfort," returned Coronado; "but you and I will see that they run no danger."

Nine days after the arrival of the emigrants at Tegua they set out for the San Juan. The wagons were left parked at the base of the butte under the care of the Moquis. The expedition was reorganized as follows: On horseback, Clara, Coronado, Thurstane, Texas Smith, and four Mexicans; on mules, Mrs. Stanley, Glover, the three Indian women, the four soldiers, and the ten drivers and muleteers. There were besides eighteen burden mules loaded with provisions and other baggage. In all, five women, twenty-two men, and forty-five animals.

The Moquis, to whom some stores and small presents were distributed, overflowed with hospitable offices. The chief had a couple of sheep slaughtered for the travellers, and scores of women brought little baskets of meal, corn, guavas, etc. As the strangers left the pueblo both sexes and all ages gathered on the landings, grouped about the stairways and ladders which led down the rampart, and followed for some distance along the declivity of the butte, holding out their simple offerings and urging acceptance. Aunt Maria was more than ever in raptures with Moquis and women.

The chief and several others accompanied the cavalcade for eight or ten miles in order to set it on the right trail for the river. But not one would volunteer as a guide; all shook their heads at the suggestion. "Navajos! Apaches! Comanches!"

They had from the first advised against the expedition, and they now renewed their expostulations. Scarcely any grass; no water except at long distances; a barren, difficult, dangerous country: such was the meaning of their dumb show. On the summit of a lofty bluff which commanded a vast view toward the north, they took their leave of the party, struck off in a rapid trot toward the pueblo, and never relaxed their speed until they were out of sight.

The adventurers now had under their eyes a large part of the region which they were about to traverse. For several miles the landscape was rolling; then came elevated plateaux rising in successive steps, the most remote being apparently sixty miles away; and the colossal scene was bounded by isolated peaks, at a distance which could not be estimated with anything like accuracy. Ranges, buttes, pinnacles, monumental crags, gullies, shadowy chasms, the beds of perished rivers, the stony wrecks left by unrecorded deluges, diversified this monstrous, sublime, and savage picture. Only here and there, separated by vast intervals of barrenness, could be seen minute streaks of verdure. In general the landscape was one of inhospitable sterility. It could not be imagined by men accustomed only to fertile regions. It seemed to have been taken from some planet not yet prepared for human, nor even for beastly habitation. The emotion which it aroused was not that which usually springs from the contemplation of the larger aspects of nature. It was not enthusiasm; it was aversion and despair.

Clara gave one look, and then drew her hat over her eyes with a shudder, not wishing to see more. Aunt Maria, heroic and constant as she was or tried to be, almost lost faith in Coronado and glanced at him suspiciously. Thurstane, sitting bolt upright in his saddle, stared straight before him with a grim frown, meanwhile thinking of Clara. Coronado's eyes were filmy and incomprehensible; he was planning, querying, fearing, almost trembling; when he gave the word to advance, it was without looking up. There was a general feeling that here before them lay a fate which could only be met blindfold.

Now came a long descent, avoiding precipices and impracticable slopes, winding from one stony foot-hill to another, until the party reached what had seemed a plain. It was a plain because it was amid mountains; a plain consisting of rolls, ridges, ravines, and gullies; a plain with hardly an acre of level land. All day they journeyed through its savage interstices and struggled with its monstrosities of trap and sandstone. Twice they halted in narrow valleys, where a little loam had collected and a little moisture had been retained, affording meagre sustenance to some thin grass and scattered bushes. The animals browsed, but there was nothing for them to drink, and all began to suffer with thirst.

It was seven in the evening, and the sun had already gone down behind the sullen barrier of a gigantic plateau, when they reached the mouth of the cañon which had once contained a river, and discovered by the merest accident that it still treasured a shallow pool of stagnant water. The fevered mules plunged in headlong and drank greedily; the riders were perforce obliged to slake their thirst after them. There was a hastily eaten supper, and then came the only luxury or even comfort of the day, the sound and delicious sleep of great weariness.

Repose, however, was not for all, inasmuch as Thurstane had reorganized his system of guard duty, and seven of the party had to stand sentry. It was Coronado's *tour;* he had chosen to take his watch at the start; there would be three nights on this stretch, and the first would be the easiest. He was tired, for he had been fourteen hours in the saddle, although the distance covered was only forty miles. But much as he craved rest, he kept awake until midnight, now walking up and down, and now smoking his eternal cigarito.

There was a vast deal to remember, to plan, to hope for, to dread, and to hate. Once he sat down beside the unconscious Thurstane, and meditated shooting him through the head as he lay, and so making an end of that obstacle. But he immediately put this idea aside as a frenzy, generated by the fever of fatigue and sleeplessness. A dozen times he was assaulted by a lazy or cowardly temptation to give up the chances of the desert, push back to the Bernalillo route, leave everything to fortune, and take disappointment meekly if it should come. When the noon of night arrived, he had decided upon nothing but to blunder ahead by sheer force of momentum, as if he had been a rolling bowlder instead of a clever, resolute Garcia Coronado.

The truth is, that his circumstances were too mighty for him. He had launched them, but he could not steer them as he would, and they were carrying him he knew not whither. At one o'clock he awoke Texas Smith, who was now his sergeant of the guard; but instead of enjoining some instant atrocity upon him, as he had more than once that night purposed, he merely passed the ordinary instructions of the watch; then, rolling himself in his blankets, he fell asleep as quickly and calmly as an infant.

At daybreak commenced another struggle with the desert. It was still sixty miles to the San Juan, over a series of savage sandstone plateaux, said to be entirely destitute of water. If the animals could not accomplish the distance in two days, it seemed as if the party must perish. Coronado went at his work, so to speak, head foremost and with his hat over his eyes. Nevertheless, when it came to the details of his mad enterprise, he managed them admirably. He was energetic, indefatigable, courageous, cheerful. All day he was hurrying the cavalcade, and yet watching its ability to endure. His "Forward, forward," alternated with his "Carefully, carefully." Now "*Adelante,*" and now "*Con juicio.*"

About two in the afternoon they reached a little nook of sparse grass, which the beasts gnawed perfectly bare in half an hour. No water; the horses were uselessly jaded in searching for it; beds of trap and gullies of ancient rivers were explored in vain; the horrible rocky wilderness was as dry as a bone. Meanwhile, the fatigue of scrambling and stumbling thus far had been enormous.

It had been necessary to ascend plateau after plateau by sinuous and crumbling ledges, which at a distance looked impracticable to goats. More than once, in face of some beetling precipice, or on the brink of some gaping chasm, it seemed as if the journey had come to an end. Long detours had to be made in order to connect points which were only separated by slight intervals. The whole region was seamed by the jagged zigzags of cañons worn by rivers which had flowed for thousands of years, and then for thousands of years more had been non-existent. If, at the commencement of one of these mighty grooves, you took the wrong side, you could not regain the trail without returning to the point of error, for crossing was impossible.

A trail there was. It is by this route that the Utes and Payoches of the Colorado come to trade with the Moquis or to plunder them. But, as may be supposed, it is a journey which is not often made even by savages; and the cavalcade, throughout the whole of its desperate push, did not meet a human being. Amid the monstrous expanse of uninhabited rock it seemed lost beyond assistance, forsaken and cast out by mankind, doomed to a death which was to have no spectator. Could you have seen it, you would have thought of a train of ants endeavoring to cross a quarry; and you would have judged that the struggle could only end in starvation, or in some swifter destruction.

The most desperate venture of the travellers was amid the wrecks of an extinct volcano. It seemed here as if the genius of fire had striven to outdo the grotesque extravagances of the genii of the waters. Crags, towers, and pinnacles of porphyry were mingled with huge convoluted masses of light brown trachyte, of tufa either pure white or white veined with crimson, of black and gray columnar basalts, of red, orange, green, and black scoria, with adornments of obsidian, amygdaloids, rosettes of quartz crystal and opalescent chalcedony. A thousand stony needles lifted their ragged points as if to defy the lightning. The only vegetation was a spiny cactus, clinging closely to the rocks, wearing their grayish and yellowish colors, lending no verdure to the scene, and harmonizing with its thorny inhospitality.

As the travellers gazed on this wilderness of scorched summits, glittering in the blazing sunlight, and yet drawing from it no life—as stark, still, unsympathizing, and cruel as death—they seemed to themselves to be out of the sweet world of God, and to be in the power of malignant genii and demons. The imagination cannot realize the feeling of depression which comes upon one who finds himself imprisoned in such a landscape. Like uttermost pain, or like the extremity of despair, it must be felt in order to be known.

"It seems as if Satan had chosen this land for himself," was the perfectly serious and natural remark of Thurstane.

Clara shuddered; the same impression was upon her mind; only she felt it more deeply than he. Gentle, somewhat timorous, and very impressionable, she was almost overwhelmed by the terrific revelations of a nature which seemed to have no pity, or rather seemed full of malignity. Many times that day she had prayed in her heart that God would help them. Apparently detached from earth, she was seeking nearness to heaven. Her look at this moment was so awe-struck and piteous, that the soul of the man who loved her yearned to give her courage.

"Miss Van Diemen, it shall all turn out well," he said, striking his fist on the pommel of his saddle.

"Oh! why did we come here?" she groaned.

"I ought to have prevented it," he replied, angry with himself. "But never mind. Don't be troubled. It shall all be right. I pledge my life to bring it all to a good end."

She gave him a look of gratitude which would have repaid him for immediate death. This is not extravagant; in his love for her he did not value himself; he had the sublime devotion of immense adoration.

That night another loamy nook was found, clothed with a little thin grass, but waterless. Some of the animals suffered so with thirst that they could not graze, and uttered doleful whinneys of distress. As it was the Lieutenant's tour on guard, he had plenty of time to study the chances of the morrow.

"Kelly, what do you think of the beasts?" he said to the old soldier who acted as his sergeant.

"One more day will finish them, Leftenant."

"We have been fifteen hours in the saddle. We have made about thirty-five miles. There are twenty-five miles more to the river. Do you think we can crawl through?"

"I should say, Leftenant, we could just do it."

At daybreak the wretched animals resumed their hideous struggle. There was a plateau for them to climb at the start, and by the time this labor was accomplished they were staggering with weakness, so that a halt had to be ordered on the windy brink of the acclivity. Thurstane, according to his custom, scanned the landscape with his field-glass, and jotted down topographical notes in his journal. Suddenly he beckoned to Coronado, quietly put the glass in his hands, nodded toward the desert which lay to the rear, and whispered, "Look."

Coronado looked, turned slightly more yellow than his wont, and murmured "Apaches!"

"How far off are they?"

"About ten miles," judged Coronado, still gazing intently.

"So I should say. How do you know they are Apaches?"

"Who else would follow us?" asked the Mexican, remembering the son of Manga Colorada.

"It is another race for life," calmly pronounced Thurstane, facing about toward the caravan and making a signal to mount.

CHAPTER XVIII.

Yes, it was a life and death race between the emigrants and the Apaches for the San Juan. Positions of defence were all along the road, but not one of them could be held for a day, all being destitute of grass and water.

"There is no need of telling the ladies at once," said Thurstane to Coronado, as they rode side by side in rear of the caravan. "Let them be quiet as long as they can be. Their trouble will come soon enough."

"How many were there, do you think?" was the reply of a man who was much occupied with his own chances. "Were there a hundred?"

"It's hard to estimate a mere black line like that. Yes, there must be a hundred, besides stragglers. Their beasts have suffered, of course, as well as ours. They have come fast, and there must be a lot in the rear. Probably both bands are along."

"The devils!" muttered Coronado. "I hope to God they will all perish of thirst and hunger. The stubborn, stupid devils! Why should they follow us *here?*" he demanded, looking furiously around upon the accursed landscape.

"Indian revenge. We killed too many of them."

"Yes," said Coronado, remembering anew the son of the chief. "Damn them! I wish we could have killed them all."

"That is just what we must try to do," returned Thurstane deliberately.

"The question is," he resumed after a moment of business-like calculation of chances—"the question is mainly this, whether we can go twenty-five miles quicker than they can go thirty-five. We must be the first to reach the river."

"We can spare a few beasts," said Coronado. "We must leave the weakest behind."

"We must not give up provisions."

"We can eat mules."

"Not till the last moment. We shall need them to take us back."

Coronado inwardly cursed himself for venturing into this inferno, the haunting place of devils in human shape. Then his mind wandered to Saratoga, New York, Newport, and the other earthly heavens that were known to him. He hummed an air; it was the *brindisi* of Lucrezia Borgia; it reminded him of pleasures which now seemed lost forever; he stopped in the middle of it. Between the associations which it excited—the images of gayety and splendor, real or feigned—a commingling of kid gloves, bouquets, velvet cloaks, and noble names—between these glories which so attracted his hungry soul and the present environment of hideous deserts and savage pursuers, what a contrast there was! There, far away, was the success for which he longed; here, close at hand, was the peril which must purchase it. At that moment he was willing to deny his bargain with Garcia and the devil. His boldest desire was, "Oh that I were in Santa Fé!"

By Coronado's side rode a man who had not a thought for himself. A person who has not passed years in the army can hardly imagine the sense of *responsibility* which is ground into the character of an officer. He is a despot, but a despot who is constantly accountable for the welfare of his subjects, and who never passes a day without many grave thoughts of the despots above him. Superior officers are in a manner his deities, and the Army Regulations have for him the weight of Scripture. He never forgets by what solemn rules of duty and honor he will be judged if he falls short of his obligations. This professional conscience becomes a destiny to him, and guides his life to an extent inconceivable by most civilians. He acquires a habit of watching and caring for others; he cannot help assuming a charge which falls in his way. When he is not governed by the rule of obedience, he is governed by the rule of responsibility. The two make up his duty, and to do his duty is his existence.

At this moment our young West Pointer, only twenty-three or four years old, was gravely and grimly anxious for his four soldiers, for all these people whom circumstance had placed under his protection, and even for his army mules, provisions, and ammunition. His only other sentiment was a passionate desire to prevent harm or even fear from approaching Clara Van Diemen. These two sentiments might be said to make up for the present his entire character. As we have already observed, he had not a thought for himself.

Presently it occurred to the youngster that he ought to cheer on his fellow-travellers.

Trotting up with a smile to Mrs. Stanley and Clara, he asked, "How do you bear it?"

"Oh, I am almost dead," groaned Aunt Maria. "I shall have to be tied on before long."

The poor woman, no longer youthful, it must be remembered, was indeed badly jaded. Her face was haggard; her general get-up was in something like scarecrow disorder; she didn't even care how she looked. So fagged was she that she had once or twice dozed in the saddle and come near falling.

"It was outrageous to bring us here," she went on pettishly. "Ladies shouldn't be dragged into such hardships."

Thurstane wanted to say that he was not responsible for the journey; but he would not, because it did not seem manly to shift all the blame upon Coronado.

"I am very, very sorry," was his reply. "It is a frightful journey."

"Oh, frightful, frightful!" sighed Aunt Maria, twisting her aching back.

"But it will soon be over," added the officer. "Only twenty miles more to the river."

"The river! It seems to me that I could live if I could see a river. Oh, this desert! These perpetual rocks! Not a green thing to cool one's eyes. Not a drop of water. I seem to be drying up, like a worm in the sunshine."

"Is there no water in the flasks?" asked Thurstane.

"Yes," said Clara. "But my aunt is feverish with fatigue."

"What I want is the sight of it—and rest," almost whimpered the elder lady.

"Will our horses last?" asked Clara. "Mine seems to suffer a great deal."

"They *must* last," replied Thurstane, grinding his teeth quite privately. "Oh, yes, they will last," he immediately added. "Even if they don't, we have mules enough."

"But how they moan! It makes me cringe to hear them."

"Twenty miles more," said Thurstane. "Only six hours at the longest. Only half a day."

"It takes less than half a day for a woman to die," muttered the nearly desperate Aunt Maria.

"Yes, when she sets about it," returned the officer. "But we haven't set about it, Mrs. Stanley. And we are not going to."

The weary lady had no response ready for words of cheer; she leaned heavily over the pommel of her saddle and rode on in silence.

"Ain't the same man she was," slyly observed Phineas Glover with a twist of his queer physiognomy.

Thurstane, though not fond of Mrs. Stanley, would not now laugh at her expense, and took no notice of the sarcasm. Glover, fearful lest he had offended, doubled the gravity of his expression and tacked over to a fresh subject.

"Shouldn't know whether to feel proud 'f myself or not, 'f I'd made this country, Capm. Depends on what 'twas meant for. If 'twas meant to live in, it's the poorest outfit I ever did see. If 'twas meant to scare folks, it's jest up to the mark. 'Nuff to frighten a crow into fits. Capm, it fairly seems more than airthly; puts me in mind 'f things in the Pilgrim's Progress—only worse. Sh'd say it was like five thousin' Valleys 'f the Shadow 'f Death tangled together. Tell ye, believe Christian 'd 'a' backed out 'f he'd had to travel through here. Think Mr. Coronado 's all right in his top hamper, Capm? Do, hey? Wal, then I'm all wrong; guess I'm 's crazy 's a bedbug. Wouldn't 'a'ketched me steerin' this course of my own free will 'n' foreknowledge. Jest look at the land now. Don't it look like the bottomless pit blowed up 'n' gone to smash? Tell ye, 'f the Old Boy himself sh'd ride up alongside, shouldn't be a mite s'prised to see him. Sh'd reckon he had a much bigger right to be s'prised to ketch me here."

After some further riding, shaking his sandy head, staring about him and whistling, he broke out again.

"Tell ye, Capm, this beats my imagination. Used to think I c'd yarn it pooty consid'able. But never can tell this. Never can do no manner 'f jestice to it. Look a there now. There's a nateral bridge, or 'n unnateral one. There's a hole blowed through a forty foot rock 's clean 's though 'twas done with Satan's own field-piece, sech 's Milton tells about. An' there's a steeple higher 'n our big one in Fair Haven. An' there's a church, 'n' a haystack. If the devil hain't done his biggest celebratin' 'n' carpenterin' 'n' farmin' round here, d'no 's I know where he has done it. Beats *me*, Capm; cleans me out. Can't do no jestice to it. Can't talk about it. Seems to me 's though I was a fool."

Yes, even Phineas Glover's small and sinewy soul (a psyche of the size, muscular force, and agility of a flea) had been seized, oppressed, and in a manner smashed by the hideous sublimity of this wilderness of sandstone, basalt, and granite.

Two hours passed, during which, from the nature of the ground, the travellers could neither see nor be seen by their pursuers. Then came a breathless ascent up another of the monstrous sandstone terraces. Thurstane ordered every man to dismount, so as to spare the beasts as much as possible. He walked by the side of Clara, patting, coaxing, and cheering her suffering horse, and occasionally giving a heave of his solid shoulder against the trembling haunches.

"Let me walk," the girl presently said. "I can't bear to see the poor beast so worried."

"It would be better, if you can do it," he replied, remembering that she might soon have to call upon the animal for speed.

She dismounted, clasped her hands over his arm, and clambered thus. From time to time, when some rocky step was to be surmounted, he lifted her bodily up it.

"How can you be so strong?" she said, looking at him wonderingly and gratefully.

"Miss Van Diemen, you give me strength," he could not help responding.

At last they were at the summit of the rugged slope. The animals were trembling and covered with sweat; some of them uttered piteous whinnyings, or rather bleatings, like distressed sheep; five or six lay down with hollow moans and rumblings. It was absolutely necessary to take a short rest.

Looking ahead, Thurstane saw that they had reached the top of the table-land which lies south of the San Juan, and that nothing was before them for the rest of the day but a rolling plateau seamed with meandering fissures of undiscoverable depth. Traversable as the country was, however, there was one reason for extreme anxiety. If they should lose the trail, if they should get on the wrong side of one of those profound and endless chasms, they might reach the river at a point where descent to it would be impossible, and might die of thirst within sight of water. For undoubtedly the San Juan flowed at the bottom of one of those amazing cañons which gully this Mer de Glace in stone.

An error of direction once committed, the enemy would not give them time to retrieve it, and they would be slaughtered like mad dogs with the foam on their mouths.

Thurstane remembered that it would be his terrible duty in the last extremity to send a bullet through the heart of the woman he worshipped, rather than let her fall into the hands of brutes who would only grant her a death of torture and dishonor. Even his steady soul failed for a moment, and tears of desperation gathered in his eyes. For the first time in years he looked up to heaven and prayed fervently.

From the unknown destiny ahead he turned to look for the fate which pursued. Walking with Coronado to the brink of the colossal terrace, and sheltering himself from the view of the rest of the party, he scanned the trail with his glass. The dark line had now become a series of dark specks, more than a hundred and fifty in number, creeping along the arid floor of the lower plateau, and reminding him of venomous insects.

"They are not five miles from us," shuddered the Mexican. "Cursed beasts! Devils of hell!"

"They have this hill to climb," said Thurstane, "and, if I am not mistaken, they will have to halt here, as we have done. Their ponies must be pretty well fagged by this time."

"They will get a last canter out of them," murmured Coronado. His soul was giving way under his hardships, and it would have been a solace to him to weep aloud. As it was, he relieved himself with a storm of blasphemies. Oaths often serve to a man as tears do to a woman.

"We must trot now," he said presently.

"Not yet. Not till they are within half a mile of us. We must spare our wind up to the last minute."

They were interrupted by a cry of surprise and alarm. Several of the muleteers had strayed to the edge of the declivity, and had discovered with their unaided eyesight the little cloud of death in the distance. Texas Smith approached, looked from under his shading hand, muttered a single curse, walked back to his horse, inspected his girths, and recapped his rifle. In a minute it was known throughout the train that Apaches were in the rear. Without a word of direction, and in a gloomy silence which showed the general despair, the march was resumed. There was a disposition to force a trot, which was promptly and sternly checked by Thurstane. His voice was loud and firm; he had instinctively assumed responsibility and command; no one disputed him or thought of it.

Three mules which could not rise were left where they lay, feebly struggling to regain their feet and follow their comrades, but falling back with hollow groanings and a kind of human despair in their faces. Mile after mile the retreat continued, always at a walk, but without halting. It was long before the Apaches were seen again, for the ascent of the plateau lost them a considerable space, and after that they were hidden for a time by its undulations. But about four in the afternoon, while the emigrants were still at least five miles from the river, a group of savage horsemen rose on a knoll not more than three miles behind, and uttered a yell of triumph. There was a brief panic, and another attempt to push the animals, which Thurstane checked with levelled pistol.

The train had already entered a gully. As this gully advanced it rapidly broadened and deepened into a cañon. It was the track of an extinct river which had once flowed into the San Juan on its way to the distant Pacific. Its windings hid the desired goal; the fugitives must plunge into it blindfold; whatever fate it brought them, they must accept it. They were like men who should enter the cavern of unknown goblins to escape from demons who were following visibly on their footsteps.

From time to time they heard ferocious yells in their rear, and beheld their fiendish pursuers, now also in the cañon. It was like Christian tracking the Valley of the Shadow of Death, and listening to the screams and curses of devils. At every reappearance of the Apaches they had diminished the distance between themselves and their expected prey, and at last they were evidently not more than a mile behind. But there in sight was the river; there, enclosed in one of its bends, was an alluvial plain; rising from the extreme verge of the plain, and overhanging the stream, was a bluff; and on this bluff was what seemed to be a fortress.

Thurstane sent all the horsemen to the rear of the train, took post himself as the rearmost man, measured once more with his eye the space between his charge and the enemy, cast an anxious glance at the reeling beast which bore Clara, and in a firm ringing voice commanded a trot.

The order and the movement which followed it were answered by the Indians with a yell. The monstrous and precipitous walls of the cañon clamored back a fiendish mockery of echoes which seemed to call for the prowlers of the air to arrive quickly and devour their carrion.

CHAPTER XIX.

THE scene was like one of Doré's most extravagant designs of abysses and shadows. The gorge through which swept this silent flight and screaming chase was not more than two hundred feet wide, while it was at least fifteen hundred feet deep, with walls that were mainly sheer precipices.

As the fugitives broke into a trot, the pursuers quickened their pace to a slow canter. No faster; they were too wise to rush within range of riflemen who could neither be headed off nor flanked; and their hardy mustangs were nearly at the last gasp with thirst and with the fatigue of this tremendous journey. Four hundred yards apart the two parties emerged from the sublime portal of the cañon and entered upon the little alluvial plain.

To the left glittered the river; but the trail did not turn in that direction; it led straight at the bluff in the elbow of the current. The mules and horses followed it in a pack, guided by their acute scent toward the nearest water, a still invisible brooklet which ran at the base of the butte. Presently, while yet a mile from the stream, they were seized by a mania. With a loud beastly cry they broke simultaneously into a run, nostrils distended and quivering, eyes bloodshot and protruding, heads thrust forward with fierce eagerness, ungovernably mad after water. There was no checking the frantic stampede which from this moment thundered with constantly increasing speed across the plain. No order; the stronger jostled the weaker; loads were flung to the ground and scattered; the riders could scarcely keep their seats. Spun out over a line of twenty rods, the cavalcade was the image of senseless rout.

Of course Thurstane was furious at this seemingly fatal dispersion; and he trumpeted forth angry shouts of "Steady there in front! Close up in the rear!"

But before long he guessed the truth—water! "They will rally at the drinking place," he thought. "Forward the mules!" he yelled. "Steady, you men here! Hold in your horses. Keep in rear of the women. I'll shoot the man who takes the lead."

But even Spanish bits could do no more than detain the horses a rod or two behind the beasts of burden, and the whole panting, snorting mob continued to rush over the loamy level with astonishing swiftness.

Meanwhile the leading Apaches, not now more than fifty in number, were swept along by tne same whirlwind of brute instinct. They diverged a little from the trail; their object apparently was to overlap the train and either head it off or divide it; but their beasts were too frantic to be governed fully. Before long there were two lines of straggling flight, running parallel with each other at a distance of perhaps one hundred yards, and both storming toward the still unseen rivulet. A few arrows were thrown; four or five unavailing shots were fired in return; the hiss of shaft and *ping* of ball crossed each other in air; but no serious and effective fight commenced or could commence. Both parties, guided and mastered by their lolling beasts, almost without conflict and almost without looking at each other, converged helplessly toward a verdant, shallow depression, through the centre of which loitered a clear streamlet scarcely less calm than the heaven above. Next they were all together, panting, plunging, splashing, drinking, mules and horses, white men and red men, all with no other thought than to quench their thirst.

The Apaches, who had probably made their cruel journey without flasks, seemed for the moment insatiable and utterly reckless. Many of them rolled off their tottering ponies into the rivulet, and plunging down their heads drank like beasts. There were a few minutes of the strangest peace that ever was seen. It was in vain that two or three of the hardier or fiercer chiefs and braves shouted and gestured to their comrades, as if urging them to commence the attack. Manga Colorada, absorbed by a thirst which was more burning than revenge, did not at first see the slayer of his boy, and when he did could not move toward him because of fevered mustangs, who would not budge from their drinking, or who were staggering blind with hunger. Thurstane, keeping his horse beside Clara's, watched the lean figure and restless, irritable face of Delgadito, not ten yards distant. Mrs. Stanley had halted helplessly so near an Apache boy that he might have thrust her through with his lance had he not been solely intent upon water.

It was fortunate for the emigrants that they had reached the stream a few seconds the sooner. Their thirst was first satiated; and then men and animals began to draw away from their enemies; for even the mules of white men instinctively dread and detest the red warriors. This movement was accelerated by Thurstane, Coronado, Texas Smith, and Sergeant Meyer calling to one and another in English and Spanish, "This way! this way!" There seemed to be a chance of massing the party and getting it to some distance before the Indians could turn their thoughts to blood.

But the manœuvre was only in part accomplished when battle commenced. Little Sweeny, finding that his mule was being crowded by an Apache's horse, uttered some indignant yelps. "Och, ye bloody naygur! Get away wid yerself. Get over there where ye b'long."

This request not being heeded, he made a clumsy punch with his bayonet and brought the blood. The warrior uttered a grunt of pain, cast a surprised angry stare at the shaveling of a Paddy, and thrust with his lance. But he was probably weak and faint; the weapon merely tore the uniform. Sweeny instantly fired, and brought down another Apache, quite accidentally. Then, banging his mule with his heels, he splashed up to Thurstane with the explanation, "Liftinant, they're the same bloody naygurs. Wan av um made a poke at me, Liftinant."

"Load your beece!" ordered Sergeant Meyer sternly, "und face the enemy."

By this time there was a fierce confusion of plungings and outcries. Then came a hiss of arrows, followed instantaneously by the scream of a wounded man, the report of several muskets, a pinging of balls, more yells of wounded, and the splash of an Apache in the water. The little streamlet, lately all crystal and sunshine, was now turbid and bloody. The giant portals of the cañon, although more than a mile distant, sent back echoes of the musketry. Another battle rendered more horrible the stark, eternal horror of the desert.

"This way!" Thurstane continued to shout. "Forward, you women; up the hill with you. Steady, men. Face the ene[illegible] away a shot. Steady with the firing. Steady!"

The hostile parties were alrea[illegible]rty or forty yards apart; and the emigrants, drawing loosely up the slope, were increasing the distance[illegible] Colorada spurred to the front of his people, sh[illegible] yelling for a charge. Only half a dozen followed him; his horse fell almost immediately under a rifle ball; one of the braves picked up the chief and bore him away; the rest dispersed, prancing and curveting. The opportunity for mingling with the emigrants and destroying them in a series of single combats was lost.

Evidently the Apaches, and their mustangs still more, were unfit for fight. The forty-eight hours of hunger and thirst, and the prodigious burst of one hundred and twenty miles up and down rugged terraces, had nearly exhausted their spirits as well as their strength, and left them incapable of the furious activity necessary in a cavalry battle. The most remarkable proof of their physical and moral debilitation was that in all this mêlée not more than a dozen of them had discharged an arrow.

If they would not attack they must retreat, and that speedily. At fifty yards' range, armed only with bows and spears, they were at the mercy of riflemen and could stand only to be slaughtered. There was a hasty flight, scurrying zigzag, right and left, rearing and plunging, spurring the last caper out of their mustangs, the whole troop spreading widely, a hundred marks and no good one. Nevertheless Texas Smith's miraculous aim brought down first a warrior and then a horse

By the time the Apaches were out of range the emigrants were well up the slope of the hill which occupied the extreme elbow of the bend in the river. It was a bluff or butte of limestone which innumerable years had converted into marl, and for the most part into earth. A thin turf covered it; here and there were thickets; more rarely trees. Presently some one remarked that the sides were terraced. It was true; there were the narrow flats of soil which had once been gardens; there too were the supporting walls, more or less ruinous. Curious eyes now turned toward the seeming mound on the summit, querying whether it might not be the remains of an antique pueblo.

At this instant Clara uttered a cry of anxiety, "Where is Pepita?'

The girl was gone; a hasty looking about showed that; but whither? Alas! the only solution to this enigma must be the horrible word, "Apaches." It seemed the strangest thing conceivable; one moment with the party, and the next vanished; one moment safe, and the next dead or doomed. Of course the kidnapping must have been accomplished during the frenzied riot in the stream, when the two bands were disentangling amid an uproar of plungings, yells, and musket shots. The girl had probably been stunned by a blow, and then either left to float down the brook or dragged off by some muscular warrior.

There was a halt, an eager and prolonged lookout over the plain, a scanning of the now distant Indians through field glasses. Then slowly and sadly the train resumed its march and mounted to the summit of the butte.

Here, in this land of marvels, there was a new marvel. Incredible as the thing seemed, so incredible that they had not at first believed their eyes, they were at the base of the walls of a fortress. A confused, general murmur broke forth of "Ruins! Pueblos! Casas Grandes! Casas de Montezuma!"

The architecture, unlike that of Tegua, but similar to that of the ruins of the Gila, was of adobes. Large cakes of mud, four or five feet long and two feet thick, had been moulded in cases, dried in the sun, and laid in regular courses to the height of twenty feet. Centuries (perhaps) of exposure to weather had so cracked, guttered, and gnawed this destructible material, that at a distance the pile looked not unlike the natural monuments which fire and water have builded in this enchanted land, and had therefore not been recognized by the travellers as human handiwork.

What they now saw was a rampart which ran along the brow of the bluff for several hundred yards. Originally twenty feet high, it had been so fissured by the rains and crumbled by the winds, that it resembled a series of peaks united here and there in a plane surface. Some of the gaps reached nearly to the ground, and through these it could be seen that the wall was five feet across, a single adobe forming the entire thickness. All along the base the dampness of the earth had eaten away the clay, so that in many places the structure was tottering to its fall.

Filing to the left a few yards, the emigrants found a deep fissure through which the animals stumbled one by one over mounds of crumbled adobes. Thurstane, entering last, looked around him in wonder. He was inside a quadrilateral enclosure, apparently four hundred yards in length by two hundred and fifty in breadth, the walls throughout being the same mass of adobe work, fissured, jagged, gray, solemn, and in their utter solitariness sublime.

But this was not the whole ruin; the fortress had a citadel. In one corner of the enclosure stood a tower-like structure, forty-five or fifty feet square and thirty in altitude, surmounted on its outer angle by a smaller tower, also four-sided, which rose some twelve or fourteen feet higher. It was not isolated, but built into an angle of the outer rampart, so as to form with it one solid mass of fortification. The material was adobe; but, unlike the other ruins, it was in good condition; some species of roofing had preserved the walls from guttering; not a crevice deformed their gray, blank, dreary faces.

Instinctively and without need of command the emigrants had pushed on toward this edifice. It was to be their fortress; in it and around it they must fight for life against the Apaches; here, where a nameless people had perished, they must conquer or perish also. Thurstane posted Kelly and one of the Mexicans on the exterior wall to watch the movements of the savage horde in the plain below. Then he followed the others to the deserted citadel.

Two doorways, one on each of the faces which looked into the enclosure, offered ingress. They were similar in size and shape, seven feet and a half in height by four in breadth, and tapering toward the summit like the portals of the temple-builders of Central America. Inside were solid mud floors, strewn with gray dust and showing here and there a gleam of broken pottery, the whole brooded over by obscurity. It was discoverable, however, that the room within was of considerable height and size.

There was a hesitation about entering. It seemed as if the ghosts of the nameless people forbade it. This had been the abode of men who perhaps inhabited America before the coming of Columbus. Here possibly the ancestors of Montezuma had stayed their migrations from the mounds of the Ohio to the pyramids of Cholula and Tenochtitlan. Or here had lived the Moquis, or the Zunians, or the Lagunas, before they sought refuge from the red tribes of the north upon the buttes south of the Sierra del Carrizo. Here at all events had once palpitated a civilization which was now a ghost.

"This is to be our home for a little while," said Thurstane to Clara. "Will you dismount? I will run in and turn out the snakes, if there are any. Sergeant, keep your men and a few others ready to repel an attack. Now, fellows, off with the packs."

Producing a couple of wax tapers, he lighted them, handed one to Coronado, and led the way into the silent Casa de Montezuma. They were in a hall about ten feet high, fifteen feet broad, and forty feet long, which evidently ran across the whole front of the building. The walls were hard-finished and adorned with etchings in vermilion of animals, geometrical figures, and nondescript grotesques, all of the rudest design and disposed without regard to order. A doorway led into a small central room, and from that doorways opened into three more rooms, one on each side.

The ceilings of all the rooms were supported by unhewn beams, five or six inches thick, deeply inserted into the adobe walls. In the ceiling of the rearmost hall (the one which had no direct outlet upon the enclosure) was a trapdoor which offered the only access to the stories above. A rude but solid ladder, consisting of two beams with steps chopped into them, was still standing here. With a vague sense of intrusion, half expecting that the old inhabitants would appear and order them away, Thurstane and Coronado ascended. The second story resembled the first, and above was another of the same pattern. Then came a nearly flat roof; and here they found something remarkable. It was a solid sheathing or tiling, made of slates of baked and glazed pottery, laid with great exactness, admirably cemented and projecting well over the eaves. This it was which had enabled the adobes beneath to endure for years, and perhaps for centuries, in spite of the lapping of rains and the gnawing of winds.

On the outermost corner of the structure, overlooking the eddying, foaming bend of the San Juan, rose the isolated tower. It contained a single room, walled with hard-finish and profusely etched with figures in vermilion. No furniture anywhere, nor utensils, nor relics, excepting bits of pottery, precisely such as is made now by the Moquis, various in color, red, white, grayish, and black, much of it painted inside as well as out, and all adorned with diamond patterns and other geometrical outlines.

"I have seen Casas Grandes in other places," said Coronado, "but nothing like this. This is the only one that I ever found entire. The others are in ruins, the roofs fallen in, the beams charred, etc."

"This was not taken," decided the Lieutenant, after a tactical meditation. "This must have been abandoned by its inhabitants. Pestilence, or starvation, or migration."

"We can beat off all the Apaches in New Mexico," observed Coronado, with something like cheerfulness.

"We can whip everything but our own stomachs," replied Thurstane.

"We have as much food as those devils."

"But water?" suggested the forethoughted West Pointer.

It was a horrible doubt, for if there was no water in the enclosure, they were doomed to speedy and cruel death, unless they could beat the Indians in the field and drive them away from the rivulet.

CHAPTER XX.

WHEN Thurstane came out of the Casa Grande he would have given some years of his life to know that there was water in the enclosure.

Yet so well disciplined was the soul of this veteran of twenty-three, and so thoroughly had he acquired the wise soldierly habit of wearing a mask of cheer over trouble, that he met Clara and Mrs. Stanley with a smile and a bit of small talk.

"Ladies, can you keep house?" he said. "There are sixteen rooms ready for you. The people who moved out haven't left any trumpery. Nothing wanted but a little sweeping and dusting and a stair carpet."

"We will keep house," replied Clara with a laugh, the girlish gayety of which delighted him.

Assuming a woman's rightful empire over household matters, she began to direct concerning storage, lodgment, cooking, etc. Sharp as the climbing was, she went through all the stories and inspected every room, selecting the chamber in the tower for herself and Mrs. Stanley.

"I never can get up in this world," declared Aunt Maria, staring in dismay at the rude ladder. "So this is what Mr. Thurstane meant by talking about a stair carpet! It was just like him to joke on such a matter. I tell you I never can go up."

"Av coorse ye can get up," broke in little Sweeny impatiently. "All ye've got to do is to put wan fut above another an' howld on wid yer ten fingers."

"I should like to see *you* do it," returned Aunt Maria, looking indignantly at the interfering Paddy.

Sweeny immediately shinned up the stepped beam, uttered a neigh of triumphant laughter from the top, and then skylarked down again.

"Well, *you* are a man," observed the strong-minded lady, somewhat discomfited.

"Av coorse I'm a man," yelped Sweeny. "Who said I wasn't? He's a lying informer. Ha ha, hoo hoo, ho ho!"

Thus incited, pulled at moreover from above and boosted from below, Aunt Maria mounted ladder after ladder until she stood on the roof of the Casa Grande.

"If I ever go down again, I shall have to drop," she gasped. "I never expected when I came on this journey to be a sailor and climb maintops."

"Lieutenant Thurstane is waving his hand to us," said Clara, with a smile like sunlight.

"Let him wave," returned Mrs. Stanley, weary, disconsolate, and out of patience with everything. "I must say it's a poor place to be waving hands."

Meantime Thurstane had beckoned a couple of muleteers tc follow him, and set off to beat the enclosure for a spring, or for a spot where it would be possible to sink a well with good result. Although the search seemed absurd on such an isolated hill, he had some hopes; for in the first place, the old inhabitants must have had a large supply of water, and they could not have brought it up a steep slope of two hundred feet without great difficulty; in the second place, the butte was of limestone, and in a limestone region water makes for itself strange reservoirs and outlets.

His trust was well-grounded. In a sharply indented hollow, twenty feet below the general surface of the enclosure, and not more than thirty yards from the Casa Grande, he found a copious spring. About it were traces of stone work, forming a sort of ruinous semicircle, as though a well had been dug, the neighboring earth scooped out, and the sides of the opening fenced up with masonry. By the way, he was not the first to discover the treasure, for the acute senses of the mules had been beforehand with him, and a number of them were already there drinking.

Calling Meyer, he said, "Sergeant, get a fatigue party to work here. I want a transverse trench cut below the spring for the animals, and a guard at the spring itself to keep it clear for the people."

Next he hurried away to the spot where he had posted Kelly to watch the Apaches.

Climbing the wall, he looked about for the Apaches, and discovered them about half a mile distant, bivouacked on the bank of the rivulet.

"They have been reinforced, sir," said Kelly. "Stragglers are coming up every few minutes."

"So I perceive. Have you seen anything of the girl Pepita?"

"There's a figure there, sir, against that sapling, that hasn't moved for half an hour. I've an idea it's the girl, sir, tied to the sapling."

Thurstane adjusted his glass, took a long steady look, and said sombrely, "It's the girl. Keep an eye on her. If they start to do anything with her, let me know. Signal with your cap."

As he hurried back to the Casa Grande he tried to devise some method of saving this unfortunate. A rescue was impossible, for the savages were numerous, watchful, and merciless, and in case they were likely to lose her they would brain her. But she might be ransomed: blankets, clothing, and perhaps a beast or two could be spared for that purpose; the gold pieces that he had in his waist-belt should all go of course. The great fear was lest the brutes should find all bribes poor compared with the joys of a torture dance. Querying how he could hide this horrible affair from Clara, and shuddering at the thought that but for favoring chances she might have shared the fate of Pepita, he ran on toward the Casa, waving his hand cheerfully to the two women on the roof

Meantime Clara had been attending to her housekeeping and Mrs. Stanley had been attending to her feelings. The elder lady (we dare not yet call her an old lady) was in the lowest spirits. She tried to brace herself; she crossed her hands behind her back, man-fashion; she marched up and down the roof man-fashion. All useless; the transformation didn't work; or, if she was a man, she was a scared one.

She could not help feeling like one of the spirits in prison as she glanced at the awful solitude around her. Notwithstanding the river, there still was the desert. The little plain was but an oasis. Two miles to the east the San Juan burst out of a defile of sandstone, and a mile to the west it disappeared in a similar chasm. The walls of these gorges rose abruptly two thousand feet above the hurrying waters. All around were the monstrous, arid, herbless, savage, cruel ramparts of the plateau. No outlook anywhere; the longest reach of the eye was not five miles; then came towering precipices. The travellers were like ants gathered on an inch of earth at the bottom of a fissure in a quarry. The horizon was elevated and limited, resting everywhere on harsh lines ot rock which were at once near the spectator and far above him. The overhanging plateaux strove to shut him out from the sight of heaven.

What variety there was in the grim monotony appeared in shapes that were horrible to the weary and sorrowful. On the other side of the San Juan towered an assemblage of pinnacles which looked like statues.; but these statues were a thousand feet above the stream, and the smallest of them was at least four hundred feet high. To a lost wanderer, and especially to a dispirited woman, such magnitude was not sublime, but terrifying. It seemed as if these shapes were gods who had no mercy, or demons who were full of malevolence. Still higher, on a jutting crag which overhung the black river, was a castle a hundred fold huger than man ever built, with ramparts that were dizzy precipices and towers such as no daring could scale. It faced the horrible group of stony deities as if it were their pandemonium.

The whole landscape was a hideous Walhalla, a fit abode for the savage giant gods of the old Scandinavians. Thor and Woden would have been at home in it. The Cyclops and Titans would have been too little for it. The Olympian deities could not be conceived of as able or willing to exist in such a hideous chaos. No creature of the Greek imagination would have been a suitable inhabitant for it except Prometheus alone. Here his eternal agony and boundless despair might not have been out of place.

There was no comfort in the river. It came out of unknown and inhospitable mystery, and went into a mystery equally unknown and inhospitable. To what fate it might lead was as uncertain as whence it arrived. A sombre flood, reddish brown in certain lights, studded with rocks which raised ghosts of unmoving foam, flowing with a speed which perpetually boiled and eddied, promising nothing to the voyager but thousand-fold shipwreck, a breathless messenger from the mountains to the ocean, it wheeled incessantly from stony portal to stony portal, a brief gleam of power and cruelty. The impression which it produced was in unison with the sublime malignity and horror of the landscape.

Depressed by fatigue, the desperate situation of the party, and the menace of the frightful scene around her, Mrs. Stanley could not and would not speak to Thurstane when he mounted the roof, and turned away to hide the tears in her eyes.

"You see I am housekeeping," said Clara with a smile. "Look how clean the room in the tower has been swept. I had some brooms made of tufted grass.

There are our beds in the corners. These hard-finished walls are really handsome."

She stopped, hesitated a moment, looked at him anxiously, and then added, "Have you seen Pepita?"

"Yes," he replied, deciding to be frank. "I think I have discovered her tied to a tree."

"Oh! to be tortured!" exclaimed Clara, wringing her hands and beginning to cry.

"We will ransom her," he hurried on. "I am going down to hold a par ley with the Apaches."

"*You!*" exclaimed the girl, catching his arm. "Oh no! Oh, why did we come here!"

Fearing lest he should be persuaded to evade what he considered his duty, he pressed her hand fervently and hurried away. Yes, he repeated, it was *his* duty; to parley with the Apaches was a most dangerous enterprise; he did not feel at liberty to order any other to undertake it.

Finding Coronado, he said to him, "I am going down to ransom Pepita. You know the Indians better than I do. How many people shall I take?"

A gleam of satisfaction shot across the dark face of the Mexican as he replied, "Go alone."

"Certainly," he insisted, in response to the officer's stare of surprise. "If you take a party, they'll doubt you. If you go alone, they'll parley. But, my dear Lieutenant, you are magnificent. This is the finest moment of your life. Ah! only you Americans are capable of such impulses. We Spaniards haven't the nerve."

"I don't know their scoundrelly language."

"Manga Colorada speaks Spanish. I dare say you'll easily come to an understanding with him. As for ransom, anything that we have, of course, excepting food, arms, and ammunition. I can furnish a hundred dollars or so. Go, my dear Lieutenant; go on your noble mission. God be with you."

"You will see that I am covered, if I have to run for it."

"I'll see to everything. I'll line the wall with sharpshooters."

"Post your men. Good-by."

"Good-by, my dear Lieutenant."

Coronado did post his men, and among them was Texas Smith. Into the ear of this brute, whom he placed quite apart from the other watchers, he whispered a few significant words.

"I told ye, to begin with, I didn't want to shute at brass buttons," growled Texas. "The army's a big thing. I never wanted to draw a bead on that man, and I don't want to now more 'n ever. Them army fellers hunt together. You hit one, an' you've got the rest after ye; an' four to one 's a mighty slim chance."

"Five hundred dollars down," was Coronado's only reply.

After a moment of sullen reflection the desperado said, "Five hundred dollars! Wal, stranger, I'll take yer bet."

Coronado turned away trembling and walked to another part of the wall. His emotions were disordered and disagreeable; his heart throbbed, his head was a little light, and he felt that he was pale; he could not well bear any more excitement, and he did not want to see the deed done. Rifle in hand, he was pretending to keep watch through a fissure, when he observed Clara following the line of the wall with the obvious purpose of finding a spot whence she could see the plain. It seemed to him that he ought to stop her, and then it seemed to him that he had better not. With such a horrible drumming in his ears how could he think clearly and decide wisely?

Clara disappeared; he did not notice where she went; did not think of looking. Once he thrust his head through his crevice to watch the course of Thurstane, but drew it back again on discovering that the brave lad had not yet reached the Apaches, and after that looked no more. His whole strength seemed to be absorbed in merely listening and waiting. We must remember that, although Coronado had almost no conscience, he had nerves.

Let us see what happened on the plain through the anxious eyes of Clara.

CHAPTER XXI.

In the time-eaten wall Clara had found a fissure through which she could watch the parley between Thurstane and the Apaches. She climbed into it from a mound of disintegrated adobes, and stood there, pale, tremulous, and breathless, her whole soul in her eyes.

Thurstane, walking his horse and making signs of amity with his cap, had by this time reached the low bank of the rivulet, and halted within four hundred yards of the savages. There had been a stir immediately on his appearance: first one warrior and then another had mounted his pony; a score of them were now prancing hither and thither. They had left their lances stuck in the earth, but they still carried their bows and quivers.

When Clara first caught sight of Thurstane he was beckoning for one of the Indians to approach. They responded by pointing to the summit of the hill, as if signifying that they feared to expose themselves to rifle shot from the ruins. He resumed his march, forded the shallow stream, and pushed on two hundred yards.

"O Madre de Dios!" groaned Clara, falling into the language of her childhood. "He is going clear up to them."

She was on the point of shrieking to him, but she saw that he was too far off to hear her, and she remained silent, just staring and trembling.

Thurstane was now about two hundred yards from the Apaches. Except the twenty who had first mounted, they were sitting on the ground or standing by their ponies, every face set towards the solitary white man and every figure as motionless as a statue. Those on horseback, moving slowly in circles, were spreading out gradually on either side of the main body, but not advancing. Presently a warrior in full Mexican costume, easily recognizable as Manga Colorada himself, rode straight towards Thurstane for a hundred yards, threw his bow and quiver ten feet from him, dismounted and lifted both hands. The officer likewise lifted his hands, to show that he too was without arms, moved forward to within thirty feet of the Indian, and thence advanced on foot, leading his horse by the bridle.

Clara perceived that the two men were conversing, and she began to hope that all might go well, although her heart still beat suffocatingly. The next moment she was almost paralyzed with horror. She saw Manga Colorada spring at Thurstane; she saw his dark arms around him, the two interlaced and reeling; she heard the triumphant yell of the Indian, and the response of his fellows; she saw the officer's startled horse break loose and prance away. In the same instant the mounted Apaches, sending forth their war-whoop and unslinging their bows, charged at full speed toward the combatants.

Thurstane had but five seconds in which to save his life. Had he been a man of slight or even moderate physical and moral force, there would not nave been the slightest chance for him. But he was six feet high, broad in the shoulders, limbed like a gladiator, solidified by hardships and marches, accustomed to danger, never losing his head in it, and blessed with lots of pugnacity. He was pinioned; but with one gigantic effort he loosened the Indian's lean sinewy arms, and in the next breath he laid him out with a blow worthy ot Heenan.

Thurstane was free; now for his horse. The animal was frightened and capering wildly; but he caught him and flung himself into the saddle without minding stirrups; then he was riding for life. Before he had got fairly under headway the foremost Apaches were within fifty paces of him, yelling like demons and letting fly their arrows. But every weapon is uncertain on horseback, and especially every missile weapon, the bow as well as the rifle. Thus, although a score of shafts hissed by the fugitive, he still kept his seat; and as his powerful beast soon began to draw ahead of the Indian ponies, escape seemea probable.

He had, however, to run the gauntlet of another and even a greater peril. In a crevice of the ruined wall which crested the hill crouched a pitiless assassin and an almost unerring shot, waiting the right moment to send a bullet through his head. Texas Smith did not like the job; but he had said "You bet," and had thus pledged his honor to do the murder; and moreover, he sadly wanted the five hundred dollars. If he could have managed it, he would have preferred to get the officer and some "Injun" in a line, so as to bring them down together. But that was hopeless; the fugitive was increasing his lead; now was the time to fire—now or never.

When Clara beheld Manga Colorada seize Thurstane, she had turned instinctively and leaped into the enclosure, with a feeling that, if she did not see the tragedy, it would not be. In the next breath she was wild to know what was passing, and to be as near to the officer and his perils as possible. A little further along the wall was a fissure which was lower and broader than the one she had just quitted. She had noticed it a minute before, but had not gone to it because a man was there. Towards this man she now rushed, calling out, "Oh, do save him!"

Her voice and the sound of her footsteps were alike drowned by a rattle of musketry from other parts of the ruin. She reached the man and stood behind him; it was Texas Smith, a being from whom she had hitherto shrunk with instinctive aversion; but now he seemed to her a friend in extremity. He was aiming; she glanced over his shoulder along the levelled rifle; in one breath she saw Thurstane and saw that the weapon was pointed at *him*. With a shriek she sprang forward against the kneeling assassin, and flung him clean through the crevice upon the earth outside the wall, the rifle exploding as he fell and sending its ball at random.

Texas Smith was stupefied and even profoundly disturbed. After rolling over twice, he picked himself up, picked up his gun also, and while hastily reloading it clambered back into his lair, more than ever confounded at seeing no one. Clara, her exploit accomplished, had instantly turned and fled along the course of the wall, not at all with the idea of escaping from the bushwhacker, but merely to meet Thurstane. She passed a dozen men, but not one of them saw her, they were all so busy in popping away at the Apaches. Just as she reached the large gap in the rampart, her hero cantered through it, erect, unhurt, rosy, handsome, magnificent. The impassioned gesture of joy with which she welcomed him was a something, a revelation perhaps, which the youngster saw and understood afterwards better than he did then. For the present he merely waved her towards the Casa, and then turned to take a hand in the fighting.

But the fighting was over. Indeed the Apaches had stopped their pursuit as soon as they found that the fugitive was beyond arrow shot, and were now prancing slowly back to their bivouac. After one angry look at them from the wall, Thurstane leaped down and ran after Clara.

"Oh!" she gasped, out of breath and almost faint. "Oh, how it has frightened me!"

"And it was all of no use," he answered, passing her arm into his and supporting her.

"No. Poor Pepita! Poor little Pepita! But oh, what an escape you had!"

"We can only hope that they will adopt her into the tribe," he said in answer to the first phrase, while he timidly pressed her arm to thank her for the second.

Coronado now came up, ignorant of Texas Smith's misadventure, and puzzled at the escape of Thurstane, but as fluent and complimentary as usual.

"My dear Lieutenant! Language is below my feelings. I want to kneel down and worship you. You ought to have a statue—yes, and an altar. If your humanity has not been successful, it has been all the same glorious."

"Nonsense," answered Thurstane. "Every one of us has done well in his turn! It was my tour of duty to-day. Don't praise me. I haven't accomplished anything."

"Ah, the scoundrels!" declaimed Coronado. "How could they violate a truce! It is unknown, unheard of. The miserable traitors! I wish you could have killed Manga Colorada."

From this dialogue he hurried away to find and catechise Texas Smith. The desperado told his story: "Jest got a bead on him—had him sure pop—never see a squarer mark—when somebody mounted me—pitched me clean out of my hole."

"Who?" demanded Coronado, a rim of white showing clear around his black pupils.

"Dunno. Didn't see nobody. 'Fore I could reload and git in it was gone."

"What the devil did you stop to reload for?"

"Stranger, I *allays* reload."

Coronado flinched under the word *stranger* and the stare which accompanied it.

"It was a woman's yell," continued Texas.

Coronado felt suddenly so weak that he sat down on a mouldering heap of adobes. He thought of Clara; was it Clara? Jealous and terrified, he for an instant, only for an instant, wished she were dead.

"See here," he said, when he had restrung his nerves a little. "We must separate. If there is any trouble, call on me. I'll stand by you."

"I reckon you'd better," muttered Smith, looking at Coronado as if he were already drawing a bead on him.

Without further talk they parted. The Texan went off to rub down his horse, mend his accoutrements, squat around the cooking fires, and gamble with the drivers. Perhaps he was just a bit more fastidious than usual about having his weapons in perfect order and constantly handy; and perhaps too he looked over his shoulder a little oftener than common while at his work or his games; but on the whole he was a masterpiece of strong, serene, ferocious self-possession. Coronado also, as unquiet at heart as the devil, was outwardly as calm as Greek art. They were certainly a couple of almost sublime scoundrels.

It was now nightfall; the day closed with extraordinary abruptness; the sun went down as though he had been struck dead; it was like the fall of an ox under the axe of the butcher. One minute he was shining with an intolerable, feverish fervor, and the next he had vanished behind the lofty ramparts of the plateau.

It was Sergeant Meyer's tour as officer of the day, and he had prepared for the night with the thoroughness of an old soldier. The animals were picketed in the innermost rooms of the Casa Grande, while the spare baggage was neatly piled along the walls of the central apartment. Thurstane's squad was quartered in one of the two outer rooms, and Coronado's squad in the other, each man having his musket loaded and lying beside him, with the butt at his feet and the muzzle pointing toward the wall. One sentry was posted on the roof of the building, and one on the ground twenty yards or so from its salient angle, while further away were two fires which partially lighted up the great enclosure. The sergeant and such of his men as were not on post slept or watched in the open air at the corner of the Casa.

The night passed without attack or alarm. Apache scouts undoubtedly prowled around the enclosure, and through its more distant shadows, noting avenues and chances for forlorn hopes. But they were not ready as yet to do any nocturnal spearing, and if ever Indians wanted a night's rest they wanted it. The garrison was equally quiet. Texas Smith, too familiar with ugly situations to lie awake when no good was to be got by it, chose his corner, curled up in his blanket and slept the sleep of the just. Overwhelming fatigue soon sent Coronado off in like manner. Clara, too; she was querying how much she should tell Thurstane; all of a sudden she was dreaming.

When broad daylight opened her eyes she was still lethargic and did not know where she was. A stretch; a long wondering stare about her; then she sprang up, ran to the edge of the roof, and looked over. There was Thurstane, alive, taking off his hat to her and waving her back from the brink. It was a second and more splendid sun-rising; and for a moment she was full of happiness.

At dawn Meyer had turned out his squad, patrolled the enclosure, made sure that no Indians were in or around it, and posted a single sentry on the southeastern angle of the ruins, which commanded the whole of the little plain. He discovered that the Apaches, fearful like all cavalry of a night attack, had withdrawn to a spot more than a mile distant, and had taken the precaution of securing their retreat by garrisoning the mouth of the cañon. Having made his dispositions and his reconnoissance, the sergeant reported to Thurstane.

"Turn out the animals and let them pasture," said the officer, waking up promptly to the situation, as a soldier learns to do. "How long will the grass in the enclosure last them?"

"Not three days, Leftenant."

"To-morrow we will begin to pasture them on the slope. How about fishing?"

"I cannot zay, Leftenant."

"Take a look at the Buchanan boat and see if it can be put together. We may find a chance to use it."

"Yes, Leftenant."

The Buchanan boat, invented by a United States officer whose name it bears, is a sack of canvas with a frame of light sticks; when put together it is about twelve feet long by five broad and three deep, and is capable of sustaining a weight of two tons. Thurstane, thinking that he might have rivers to cross in his explorations, had brought one of these coracles. At present it was a bundle, weighing one hundred and fifty pounds, and forming the load of a single mule. Meyer got it out, bent it on to its frame, and found it in good condition.

"Very good," said Thurstane. "Roll it up again and store it safely. We may want it to-morrow."

Meantime Clara had thought out her problem. In her indignation at Texas Smith she had contemplated denouncing him before the whole party, and had found that she had not the courage. She had wanted to make a confidant of her relative, and had decided that nothing could be more unwise. Aunt Maria was good, but she lacked practical sense; even Clara, girl as she was, could see the one fact as well as the other. Her final and sagacious resolve was to tell the tale to Thurstane alone.

Mrs. Stanley, still jaded through with her forced march, fell asleep immediately after breakfast. Clara went to the brink of the roof, caught the officer's eye, and beckoned him to come to her.

"We must not be seen," she whispered when he was by her side. "Come inside the tower. There has been something dreadful. I must tell you."

Then she narrated how she had surprised and interrupted Texas Smith in his attempt at murder; for the time she was all Spanish in feeling, and told the story with fervor, with passion; and the moment she had ended it she began to cry. Thurstane was so overwhelmed by her emotion that he no more thought of the danger which he had escaped than if it had been the buzzing of a mosquito. He longed to comfort her; he dared to put his hand upon her waist; rather, we should say, he could not help it. If she noticed it she had no objection to it, for she did not move; but the strong and innocent probability is that she really did not notice it.

"Oh, what can it mean?" she sobbed. "Why did he do it? What will you do?"

"Never mind," he said, his voice tender, his blue-black eyes full of love, his whole face angelic with affection. "Don't be troubled. Don't be anxious. I will do what is right. I will put him under arrest and try him, if it seems best. But I don't want you to be troubled. It shall all come out right. I mean to live till you are safe."

After a time he succeeded in soothing her, and then there came a moment in which she seemed to perceive that his arm was around her waist, for she drew a little away from him, coloring splendidly. But he had held her too long to be able to let her go thus; he took her hands and looked in her face with the solemnity of a love which pleads for life.

"Will you forgive me?" he murmured. "I must say it. I cannot help it. I love you with all my soul. I dare not ask you to be my wife. I am not fit for you. But have pity on me. I couldn't help telling you."

He just saw that she was not angry; yes, he was so shy and humble that he could not see more; but that little glimpse of kindliness was enough to lure him forward. On he went, hastily and stammeringly, like a man who has but a moment in which to speak, only a moment before some everlasting farewell.

"Oh, Miss Van Diemen! Is there—can there ever be—any hope for me?"

It was one of the questions which arise out of great abysses from men who in their hopelessness still long for heaven. No prisoner at the bar, faintly trusting that in the eyes of his judge he might find mercy, could be more anxious than was Thurstane at that moment. The lover who does not yet know that he will be loved is a figure of tragedy.

CHAPTER XXII.

Although Thurstane did not perceive it, his question was answered the instant it was asked. The answer started like lightning from Clara's heart, trembled through all her veins, flamed in her cheeks, and sparkled in her eyes.

Such a moment of agitation and happiness she had never before known, and had never supposed that she could know. It was altogether beyond her control. She could have stopped her breathing ten times easier than she could have quelled her terror and her joy. She was no more master of the power and direction of her feelings, than the river below was master of its speed and course. One of the mightiest of the instincts which rule the human race had made her entirely its own. She was not herself; she was Thurstane; she was love. The love incarnate is itself, and not the person in whom it is embodied.

There was but one answer possible to Clara. Somehow, either by look or word, she must say to Thurstane, "Yes." Prudential considerations might come afterward—might come too late to be of use; no matter. The only thing now to be done, the only thing which first or last must be done, the only thing which fate insisted should be done, was to say "Yes."

It was said. Never mind how. Thurstane heard it and understood it. Clara also heard it, as if it were not she who uttered it, but some overruling power, or some inward possession, which spoke for her. She heard it and she acquiesced in it. The matter was settled. Her destiny had been pronounced. The man to whom her heart belonged had his due.

Clara passed through a minute which was in some respects like a lifetime, and in some respects like a single second. It was crowded and encumbered with emotions sufficient for years; it was the scholastic needle-point on which stood a multitude of angels. It lasted, she could not say how long; and then of a sudden she could hardly remember it. Hours afterwards she had not fully disentangled from this minute and yet monstrous labyrinth a clear recollection of what he had said and what she had answered. Only the splendid exit of it was clear to her, and that was that she was his affianced wife.

"But oh, my friend—one thing!" she whispered, when she had a little regained her self-possession. "I must ask Muñoz."

"Your grandfather? Yes."

"But what if he refuses?" she added, looking anxiously in his eyes. She was beginning to lay her troubles on his shoulders, as if he were already her husband.

"I will try to please him," replied the young fellow, gazing with almost equal anxiety at her. It was the beautiful union of the man-soul and woman-soul, asking courage and consolation the one of the other, and not only asking but receiving.

"Oh! I think you must please him," said Clara, forgetting how Muñoz had driven out his daughter for marrying an American. "He can't help but like you."

"God bless you, my darling!" whispered Thurstane, worshipping her for worshipping him.

After a while Clara thought of Texas Smith, and shuddered out, "But oh, how many dangers! Oh, my friend, how will you be safe?"

"Leave that to me," he replied, comprehending her at once. "I will take care of that man."

"Do be prudent."

"I will. For *your* sake, my dear child, I promise it. Well, now we must part. I must rouse no suspicions."

"Yes. We must be prudent."

He was about to leave her when a new and terrible thought struck him, and made him look at her as though they were about to part forever.

"If Muñoz leaves you his fortune," he said firmly, "you shall be free."

She stared; after a moment she burst into a little laugh; then she shook her finger in his face and said, blushing, "Yes, free to be—your wife."

He caught the finger, bent his head over it and kissed it, ready to cry upon it. It was the only kiss that he had given her; and what a world-wide event it was to both! Ah, these lovers! They find a universe where others see only trifles; they are gifted with the second-sight and live amid miracles.

"Do be careful, oh my dear friend!" was the last whisper of Clara as Thurstane quitted the tower. Then she passed the day in ascending and descending between heights of happiness and abysses of anxiety. Her existence henceforward was a Jacob's ladder, which had its foot on a world of crime and sorrow, and its top in heavens passing description.

As for Thurstane, he had to think and act, for something must be done with Texas Smith. He queried whether the fellow might not have seen Clara when she pushed him out of the crevice, and would not seize the first opportunity to kill her. Angered by this supposition, he at first resolved to seize him, charge him with his crime, and turn him loose in the desert to take his chance among the Apaches. Then it occurred to him that it might be possible to change this enemy into a partisan. While he was pondering these matters his eye fell upon the man. His army habit of authority and of butting straight at the face of danger immediately got the better of his wish to manage the matter delicately, and made him forget his promises to be prudent. Beckoning Texas to follow him, he marched out of the plaza through the nearest gap, faced about upon his foe with an imperious stare, and said abruptly, "My man, do you want to be shot?"

Texas Smith had his revolver and long hunting-knife in his waist-belt. He thought of drawing both at once and going at Thurstane, who was certainly in no better state for battle, having only revolver and sabre. But the chance of combat was even; the certainty of being slaughtered after it by the soldiers was depressing; and, what was more immediately to the point, he was cowed by that stare of habitual authority.

"Capm——I don't," he said, watching the officer with the eye of a lynx, for, however unwilling to fight as things were, he meant to defend himself.

"Because I could have you set up by my sergeant and executed by my privates," continued Thurstane.

"Capm, I reckon you're sound there," admitted Texas, with a slight flinch in his manner.

"Now, then, do you want to fight a duel?" broke out the angry youngster, his pugnacity thoroughly getting the better of his wisdom. "We both have pistols."

"Capm," said the bravo, and then came to a pause—"Capm, I ain't a gentleman," he resumed, with the sulky humility of a bulldog who is beaten by his master. "I own up to it, Capm. I ain't a gentleman"

He was a "poor white" by birth; he remembered still the "high-toned gentlemen" who used to overawe his childhood; he recognized in Thurstane that unforgotten air of domination, and he was thoroughly daunted by it. Moreover, there was his acquired and very rational fear of the army—a fear which had considerably increased upon him since he had joined this expedition, for he had noted carefully the disciplined obedience of the little squad of regulars, and had been much struck with its obvious potency for offence and defence.

"You won't fight?" said the officer. "Well, then, will you stop hunting me?"

"Capm, I'll go that much."

"Will you pledge yourself not to harm any one in this party, man or woman?"

"I'll go that much, too."

"I don't want to get any tales out of you. You can keep your secrets. Damn your secrets!"

"Capm, you're jest the whitest man I ever see."

"Will you pledge yourself to keep dark about this talk that we've had?"

"You bet!" replied Texas Smith, with an indescribable air of humiliation. "I'm outbragged. I shan't tell of it."

"I shall give orders to my men. If anything queer happens, you won't live the day out."

"The keerds is stocked agin me, Capm. I pass. You kin play it alone."

"Now, then, walk back to the Casa, and keep quiet during the rest of this journey."

The most humbled bushwhacker and cutthroat between the two oceans, Texas Smith stepped out in front of Thurstane and returned to the cooking-fire, not quite certain as he marched that he would not get a pistol-ball in the back of his head, but showing no emotion in his swarthy, sallow, haggard countenance.

Although Thurstane trusted that danger from that quarter was over, he nevertheless called Meyer aside and muttered to him, "Sergeant, I have some confidential orders for you. If murder happens to me, or to any other person in this party, have that Texan shot immediately."

"I will addend to it, Leftenant," replied Meyer with perfect calmness and with his mechanical salute.

"You may give Kelly the same instructions, confidentially."

"Yes, Leftenant."

Texas Smith, fifteen or twenty yards away, watched this dialogue with an interest which even his Indian-like stoicism could hardly conceal. When the sergeant returned to the cooking-fire, he gave him a glance which was at once watchful and deprecatory, made place for him to sit down on a junk of adobe, and offered him a corn-shuck cigarito. Meyer took it, saying, "Thank you, Schmidt," and the two smoked in apparently amicable silence.

Nevertheless, Texas knew that his doom was sealed if murder should occur in the expedition; for, as to the protection of Coronado, he did not believe that that could avail against the uniform; and as to finding safety in flight, the cards there were evidently "stocked agin him." Indeed, what had quelled him more than anything else was the fear lest he should be driven out to take his luck among the Apaches. Suppose that Thurstane had taken a fancy to swap him for that girl Pepita? What a bright and cheerful fire there would have been for him before sundown! How thoroughly the skin would have been peeled off his muscles! What neat carving at his finger joints and toe joints! Coarse, unimaginative, hardened, and beastly as Texas Smith was, his flesh crawled a little at the thought of it. Presently it struck him that he had better do some thing to propitiate a man who could send him to encounter such a fate.

"Sergeant," he said in his harsh, hollow croak of a voice.

"Well, Schmidt?"

"Them creeturs oughter browse outside."

"So. You are right, Schmidt."

"If the Capm 'll let me have three good men, I'll take 'em out."

Meyer's light-blue eyes, twinkling from under his sandy eyelashes, studied the face of the outlaw.

"I should zay it was a goot blan, Schmidt," he decided. "I'll mention it to the leftenant."

Thurstane, on being consulted, gave his consent. Meyer detailed Shubert and two of the Mexican cattle-drivers to report to Smith for duty. The Texan mounted his men on horses, separated one-third of the mules from the others, drove them out of the enclosure, and left them on the green hillside, while he pushed on a quarter of a mile into the plain and formed his line of four skirmishers. When a few of the Apaches approached to see what was going on, he levelled his rifle, knocked over one of the horses, and sent the rest off capering. After four or five hours he drove in his mules and took out another set. The Indians could only interrupt his pastoral labors by making a general charge; and that would expose them to a fire from the ruin, against which they could not retaliate. They thought it wise to make no trouble, and all day the foraging went on in peace.

Peace everywhere. Inside the fortress sleeping, cooking, mending of equipments, and cleaning of arms. Over the plain mustangs filling themselves with grass and warriors searching for roots. Not a movement worth heeding was made by the Apaches until the herders drove in their first relay of mules, when a dozen hungry braves lassoed the horse which Smith had shot, dragged him away to a safe distance, and proceeded to cut him up into steaks. On seeing this, the Texan cursed himself to all the hells that were known to him.

"It's the last time they'll catch me butcherin' for 'em," he growled. "If I can't hit a man, I won't shute."

One more night in the Casa de Montezuma, with Thurstane for officer of the guard. His arrangements were like Meyer's: the animals in the rear rooms of the Casa; Coronado's squad in one of the outer rooms, and Meyer's in the other; a sentry on the roof, and another in the plaza. The only change was that, owing to scarcity of fuel, no watch-fires were built. As Thurstane expected an attack, and as Indian assaults usually take place just before daybreak, he chose the first half of the night for his tour of sleep. At one he was awakened by Sweeny, who was sergeant of his squad, Kelly being with Meyer and Shubert with Coronado.

"Well, Sweeny, anything stirring?" he asked.

"Divil a stir, Liftinant."

"Did nothing happen during your guard?"

"Liftinant," replied Sweeny, searching his memory for an incident which should prove his watchfulness—"the moon went down."

"I hope you didn't interfere."

"Liftinant, I thought it was none o' my bizniss."

"Send a man to relieve the sentry on the roof, and let him come down here."

"I done it, Liftinant, before I throubled ye. Where shall we slape? Jist by the corner here?"

"No. I'll change that. Two just inside of one doorway and two inside the other. I'll stay at the angle myself."

Three hours passed as quietly as the wool-clad footsteps of the Grecian Fate. Then, stealing through the profound darkness, came the faintest rustle imaginable. It was not the noise of feet, but rather that of bodies slowly dragging through herbage, as if men were crawling or rolling toward the Casa. Thurstane, not quite sure of his hearing, and unwilling to disturb the garrison without cause, cocked his revolver and listened intently.

Suddenly the sentry in the plaza fired, and, rushing in upon him, fell motionless at his feet, while the air was filled in an instant with the whistling of arrows, the trampling of running men, and the horrible quavering of the war-whoop.

CHAPTER XXIII.

At the noise of the Apache charge Thurstane sprang in two bounds to Coronado's entrance, and threw himself inside of it with a shout of "Indians!"

It must be remembered that, while a doorway of the Casa was five feet in depth, it was only four feet wide at the base and less than thirty inches at the top, so that it was something in the way of a defile and easily defensible. The moment Thurstane was inside, he placed himself behind one of the solid jambs of the opening, and presented both sabre and revolver.

Immediately after him a dozen running Indians reached the portal, some of them plunging into it and the others pushing and howling close around it. Three successive shots and as many quick thrusts, all delivered in the darkness, but telling at close quarters on naked chests and faces, cleared the passage in half a minute. By this time Texas Smith, Coronado, and Shubert had leaped up, got their senses about them, and commenced a fire of rifle shot, pistol shot, and buck-and-ball. In another half minute nothing remained in the doorway but two or three corpses, while outside there were howls as of wounded. The attack here was repulsed, at least for the present.

But at the other door matters had gone differently, and, as it seemed, fatally ill. There had been no one fully awakened to keep the assailants at bay until the other defenders could rouse themselves and use their weapons. Half a dozen Apaches, holding their lances before them like pikes, rushed over the sleeping Sweeny and burst clean into the room before Meyer and his men were fairly on their feet. In the profound darkness not a figure could be distinguished; and there was a brief trampling and yelling, during which no one was hurt. Lances and bows were useless in a room fifteen feet by ten, without a ray of light. The Indians threw down their long weapons, drew their knives, groped hither and thither, struck out at random, and cut each other. Nevertheless, they were masters of the ground. Meyer and his people, crouching in corners, could not see and dared not fire. Sweeny, awakened by a kneading of Apache boots, was so scared that he lay perfectly still, and either was not noticed or was neglected as dead. His Mexican comrade had rushed along with the assailants, got ahead of them, gained the inner rooms, and hastened up to the roof. In short, it was a completely paralyzed defence.

Had the mass of the Apaches promptly followed their daring leaders, the garrison would have been destroyed. But, as so often happens in night attacks, there was a pause of caution and investigation. Fifty warriors halted around the doorway, some whooping or calling, and others listening, while the five or six within, probably fearful of being hit if they spoke, made no answer. The sentinel on the roof fired down without seeing any one, and had arrows sent back at him by men who were as blinded as himself. The darkness and mystery crippled the attack almost as completely as the defence.

Sweeny was the first to break the charm. A warrior who attempted to enter the doorway struck his boot against a pair of legs, and stooped down to feel if they were alive. By a lucky intuition of scared self-defence, the little Paddy made a furious kick into the air with both his solid army shoes, and sent the invader reeling into the outer darkness. Then he fired his gun just as it lay, and brought down one of the braves inside with a broken ankle. The blaze of the discharge faintly lighted up the room, and Meyer let fly instantly, killing another of the intruders. But the Indians also had been able to see. Those who survived uttered their yell and plunged into the corners, stabbing with their knives. There was a wild, blind, eager scuffling, mixed with another shot or two, oaths, whooping, screams, tramplings, and aimless blows with musket-butts.

Reinforcements arrived for both parties, four or five more Apaches stealing into the room, while Thurstane and Shubert came through from Coronado's side. Hitherto, it did not seem that the garrison had lost any killed except the sentry who had fallen outside; but presently the lieutenant heard Shubert cry out in that tone of surprise, pain, and anger, which announces a severe wound.

The scream was followed by a fall, a short scuffle, repeated stabbings, and violent breathing mixed with low groans. Thurstane groped to the scene of combat, put out his left hand, felt a naked back, and drove his sabre strongly and cleanly into it. There was a hideous yell, another fall, and then silence.

After that he stood still, not knowing whither to move. The trampling of feet, the hasty breathing of struggling men, the dull sound of blows upon living bodies, the yells and exclamations and calls, had all ceased at once. It seemed to him as if everybody in the room had been killed except himself. He could not hear a sound in the darkness besides the beating of his own heart, and an occasional feeble moan rising from the floor. In all his soldierly life he had never known a moment that was anything like so horrible.

At last, after what seemed minutes, remembering that it was his duty as an officer to be a rallying point, he staked his life on his very next breath and called out firmly, "Meyer!"

"Here!" answered the sergeant, as if he were at roll-call.

"Where are you?"

"I am near the toorway, Leftenant. Sweeny is with me."

"'Yis I be," interjected Sweeny.

Thurstane, feeling his way cautiously, advanced to the entrance and found the two men standing on one side of it.

"Where are the Indians?" he whispered.

"I think they are all out, except the tead ones, Leftenant."

Thurstane gave an order: "All forward to the door."

Steps of men stealing from the inner room responded to this command.

"Call the roll, Sergeant," said Thurstane.

In a low voice Meyer recited the names of the six men who belonged to his squad, and of Shubert. All responded except the last.

"I am avraid Shupert is gone, Leftenant," muttered the sergeant; and the officer replied, "I am afraid so."

All this time there had been perfect silence outside, as if the Indians also were in a state of suspense and anxiety. But immediately after the roll-call had ceased, a few arrows whistled through the entrance and struck with short sharp spats into the hard-finished partition within.

"Yes, they are all out," said Thurstane. "But we must keep quiet till daybreak."

There followed a half hour which seemed like a month. Once Thurstane stole softly through the Casa to Coronado's room, found all safe there, and returned, stumbling over bodies both going and coming. At last the slow dawn came and sent a faint, faint radiance through the door, enabling the benighted eyes within to discover one dolorous object after another. In the centre of the room lay the boy Shubert, perfectly motionless and no doubt dead. Here and there, slowly revealing themselves through the diminishing darkness, like horrible waifs left uncovered by a falling river, appeared the bodies of four Apaches, naked to the breechcloth and painted black, all quiet except one which twitched convulsively. The clay floor was marked by black pools and stains which were undoubtedly blood. Other fearful blotches were scattered along the entrance, as if grievously wounded men had tottered through it, or slain warriors had been dragged out by their comrades.

While the battle is still in suspense a soldier looks with but faint emotion, and almost without pity, upon the dead and wounded. They are natural; they belong to the scene; what else should he see? Moreover, the essential sentiments of the time and place are, first, a hard egoism which thinks mainly of self-preservation, and second, a stern sense of duty which regulates it. In the fiercer moments of the conflict even these feelings are drowned in a wild excitement which may be either exultation or terror. Thus it is that the ordinary sympathies of humanity for the suffering and for the dead are suspended.

Looking at Shubert, our lieutenant simply said to himself, "I have lost a man. My command is weakened by so much." Then his mind turned with promptness to the still living and urgent incidents of the situation. Could he peep out of the doorway without getting an arrow through the head? Was the roof of the Casa safe from escalade? Were any of his people wounded?

This last question he at once put in English and Spanish. Kelly replied, "Slightly, sir," and pointed to his left shoulder, pretty smartly laid open by the thrust of a knife. One of the Indian muleteers, who was sitting propped up in a corner, faintly raised his head and showed a horrible gash in his thigh. At a sign from Thurstane another muleteer bound up the wound with the sleeve of Shubert's shirt, which he slashed off for the purpose. Kelly said, "Never mind me, sir; it's no great affair, sir."

"Two killed and two wounded," thought the lieutenant. "We are losing more than our proportion."

As soon as it was light enough to distinguish objects clearly, a lively fire opened from the roof of the Casa. Judging that the attention of the assailants would be distracted by this, Thurstane cautiously edged his head forward and peeped through the doorway. The Apaches were still in the plaza; he discovered something like fifty of them; they were jumping about and firing arrows at the roof. He inferred that this could not last long; that they would soon be driven away by the musketry from above; that, in short, things were going well.

After a time, becoming anxious lest Clara should expose herself to the missiles, he went to Coronado's room, sent one of the Mexicans to reinforce Meyer, and then climbed rapidly to the tower, taking along sabre, rifle, and revolver.

He was ascending the last of the stepped sticks, and had the trap-door of the isolated room just above him, when he heard a shout, "Come up here, somebody!"

It was the snuffling utterance of Phineas Glover, who slept on the roof as permanent guard of the ladies. Tumbling into the room, Thurstane found the skipper and two muleteers defending the doorway against five Apaches, who had reached the roof, three of them already on their feet and plying their arrows, while the two others were clambering over the ledge. Clara and Mrs. Stanley were crouched on their beds behind the shelter of the wall.

The young man's first desperate impulse was to rush out and fight hand to hand. But remembering the dexterity of Indians in single combat, he halted just in time to escape a flight of missiles, placed himself behind the jamb of the doorway, and fired his rifle. At that short distance Sweeny would hardly have missed; and the nearest Apache, leaning forward with outspread arms, fell dead. Then the revolver came into play, and another warrior dropped his bow, his shoulder shattered. Glover and the muleteers, steadied by this opportune reinforcement, reloaded and resumed their file-firing. Guns were too much for archery; three Indians were soon stretched on the roof; the others slung themselves over the eaves and vanished.

"Darned if they didn't reeve a tackle to git up," exclaimed Glover in amazement.

It appeared that the savages had twisted lariats into long cords, fastened rude grapples to the end of them, flung them from the wall below the Casa, and so made their daring escalade.

"Look out!" called Thurstane to the investigating Yankee. But the warning came too late; Glover uttered a yell of surprise, pain, and rage; this time it was not his nose, but his left ear.

"Reckon they'll jest chip off all my feeturs 'fore they git done with me," he grinned, feeling of the wounded part. "Git my figgerhead smooth all round."

To favor the escalade, the Apaches in the plaza had renewed their war-whoop, sent flights of arrows at the Casa, and made a spirited but useless charge on the doorways. Its repulse was the signal for a general and hasty flight. Just as the rising sun spread his haze of ruddy gold over the east, there was a despairing yell which marked the termination of the conflict, and then a rush for the gaps in the wall of the enclosure. In one minute from the signal for retreat the top of the hill did not contain a single painted combatant. No vigorous pursuit; the garrison had had enough of fighting; besides, ammunition was becoming precious. Texas Smith alone, insatiably bloodthirsty and an independent fighter, skulked hastily across the plaza, ambushed himself in a crevice of the ruin, and took a couple of shots at the savages as they mounted their ponies at the foot of the hill and skedaddled loosely across the plain.

When he returned he croaked out, with an unusual air of excitement, "Big thing!"

"What is a pig ding?" inquired Sergeant Meyer.

"Never see Injuns make such a fight afore."

"Nor I," assented Meyer.

"Stranger, they fowt first-rate," affirmed Smith, half admiring the Apaches. "How many did we save?"

"Here are vour in our room, und the leftenant says there are three on the roof, und berhabs we killed vour or vive outside."

"A dozen!" chuckled Texas, "besides the wounded. Let's hev a look at the dead uns."

Going into Meyer's room, he found one of the Apaches still twitching, and immediately cut his throat. Then he climbed to the roof, gloated over the three bodies there, dragged them one by one to the ledge, and pitched them into the plaza.

"That'll settle 'em," he remarked with a sigh of intense satisfaction, like that of a baby when it has broken its rattle. Coming down again, he looked all the corpses over again, and said with an air of disappointment which was almost sentimental, "On'y a dozen!"

"I kin keer for the Injuns," he volunteered when the question came up of burying the dead. "I'd rather keer for 'em than not."

Before Thurstane knew what was going on, Texas had finished his labor of love. A crevice in the northern wall of the enclosure looked out upon a steep slope of marl, almost a precipice, which slanted sheer into the boiling flood of the San Juan. To this crevice Texas dragged one naked carcass after another, bundled it through, launched it with a vigorous shove, and then watched it with a pantherish grin, licking his chops as it were, as it rolled down the steep, splashed into the river, and set out on its swift voyage toward the Pacific.

"I s'pose you'll want to dig a hole for *him*," he said, coming into the Casa and looking wistfully at the body of poor young Shubert.

Sergeant Meyer motioned him to go away. Thurstane was entering in his journal an inventory of the deceased soldier's effects having already made a minute of the date and cause of his death. These with other facts, such as name, age, physical description, birthplace, time of service, amount of pay due, balance of clothing-account and stoppages, must be more or less repeated on various records, such as the descriptive book of the company, the daily return, the monthly return, the quarterly return, the muster-roll from which the name would be dropped, and the final statements which were to go to the Adjutant-General and the Paymaster-General. Even in the desert the monstrous accountability system of the army lived and burgeoned.

Nothing of importance happened until about noon, when the sentinel on the outer wall announced that the Apaches were approaching in force, and Thurstane gave orders to barricade one of the doors of the Casa with some large blocks of adobe, saying to himself, "I ought to have done it before."

This work well under way, he hastened to the brow of the hill and reconnoitred the enemy.

"They are not going to attack," said Coronado. "They are going to torture the girl Pepita."

Thurstane turned away sick at heart, observing, "I must keep the women in the Casa."

CHAPTER XXIV.

WHEN Thurstane, turning his back on the torture scene, had ascended to the roof of the Casa, he found the ladies excited and anxious.

"What is the matter?" asked Clara at once, taking hold of his sleeve with the tips of her fingers, in a caressing, appealing way, which was common with her when talking to those she liked.

Ordinarily our officer was a truth-teller; indeed, there was nothing which came more awkwardly to him than deception; he hated and despised it as if it were a personage, a criminal, an Indian. But here was a case where he must stoop to falsification, or at least to concealment.

"The Apaches are just below," he mumbled. "Not one of you women must venture out. I will see to everything. Be good now."

She gave his sleeve a little twitch, smiled confidingly in his face, and sat down to do some much-needed mending.

Having posted Sweeny at the foot of the ladders, with instructions to let none of the women descend, Thurstane hastened back to the exterior wall, drawn by a horrible fascination. With his field-glass he could distinguish every action of the tragedy which was being enacted on the plain. Pepita, entirely stripped of her clothing, was already bound to the sapling which stood by the side of the rivulet, and twenty or thirty of the Apaches were dancing around her in a circle, each one approaching her in turn, howling in her ears and spitting in her face. The young man had read and heard much of the horrors of that torture-dance, which stamps the American Indian as the most ferocious of savages; but he had not understood at all how large a part insult plays in this ceremony of deliberate cruelty; and, insulting a woman! he had not once dreamed it. Now, when he saw it done, his blood rushed into his head and he burst forth in choked incoherent curses.

"I can't stand this," he shouted, advancing upon Coronado with clenched fists. "We must charge."

The Mexican shook his head in a sickly, scared way, and pointed to the left. There was a covering party of fifty or sixty warriors; it was not more than a quarter of a mile from the eastern end of the enclosure; it was in position to charge either upon that, or upon the flank of any rescuing sally.

"We can do it," insisted the lieutenant, who felt as if he could fight twenty men.

"We can't," replied Coronado. "I won't go, and my men shan't go."

Thurstane thought of Clara, covered his face with his hands, and sobbed aloud. Texas Smith stared at him with a kind of contemptuous pity, and offered such consolation as it was in his nature to give.

"Capm, when they've got through this job they'll travel."

The hideous prelude continued for half an hour. The Apaches in the dance were relieved by their comrades in the covering party, who came one by one to take their turns in the round of prancing, hooting, and spitting. Then came a few minutes of rest; then insult was followed by outrage.

The girl was loosed from the sapling and lifted until her head was even with the lower branches, three warriors holding her while two others extended her arms and fixed them to two stout limbs. What the fastenings were Thurstane could guess from the fact that he saw blows given, and heard the long shrill scream of a woman in uttermost agony. Then there was more hammering around the sufferer's feet, and more shrill wailing. She was spiked through the palms and the ankles to the tree. It was a crucifixion.

"By ——!" groaned Thurstane, "I never will spare an Indian as long as I live."

"Capm, I'm with you," said Texas Smith. "I seen my mother fixed like that. I seen it from the bush whar I was a hidin'. I was a boy then. I've killed every Injun I could sence."

Now the dance was resumed. The Apaches pranced about their victim to the music of her screams. The movement quickened; at last they ran around the tree in a maddened crowd; at every shriek they stamped, gestured, and yelled demoniacally. Now and then one of them climbed the girl's body and appeared to stuff something into her mouth. Then the lamentable outcries sank to a gasping and sobbing which could only be imagined by the spectators on the hill.

"Can't you hit some of them?" Thurstane asked Texas Smith.

"Better let 'em finish," muttered the borderer. "The gal can't be helped. She's as good as dead, Capm."

After another rest came a fresh scene of horror. Several of the Apaches, no doubt chiefs or leading braves, caught up their bows and renewed the dance. Running in a circle at full speed about the tree, each one in turn let fly an arrow at the victim, the object being to send the missile clear through her.

"That's the wind-up," muttered Texas Smith. "It's my turn now."

He leaped from the wall to the ground, ran sixty or eighty yards down the hill, halted, aimed, and fired. One of the warriors, a fellow in a red shirt who had been conspicuous in the torture scene, rolled over and lay quiet. The Apaches, who had been completely absorbed by their frantic ceremony, and who had not looked for an attack at the moment, nor expected death at such a distance, uttered a cry of surprise and dismay. There was a scramble of ten or fifteen screaming horsemen after the audacious borderer. But immediately on firing he had commenced a rapid retreat, at the same time reloading. He turned and presented his rifle; just then, too, a protecting volley burst from the rampart; another Apache fell, and the rest retreated.

"Capm, it's all right," said Texas, as he reascended the ruin. "We're squar with 'em."

"We might have broken it up," returned Thurstane sullenly.

"No, Capm. You don't know 'em. They'd got thar noses p'inted to torture that gal. If they didn't do it thar, they'd a done it a little furder off. They was bound to do it. Now it's done, they'll travel."

Warned by their last misadventure, the Indians presently retired to their usual camping ground, leaving their victim attached to the sapling.

"I'll fotch her up," volunteered Texas, who had a hyena's hankering after dead bodies. "Reckon you'd like to bury her."

He mounted, rode slowly, and with prudent glances to right and left, down the hill, halted under the tree, stood up in his saddle and worked there for some minutes. The Apaches looked on from a distance, uttering yells of exultation and making opprobrious gestures. Presently Texas resumed his seat and cantered gently back to the ruins, bearing across his saddle-bow a fearful burden, the naked body of a girl of eighteen, pierced with more than fifty arrows, stained and streaked all over with blood, the limbs shockingly mangled, and the mouth stuffed with rags.

While nearly every other spectator turned away in horror, he glared steadily and calmly at the corpse, repeating, "That's Injin fun, that is. That's what they brag on, that is."

"Bury her outside the wall," ordered Thurstane, with averted face. "And listen, all you people, not a word of this to the women."

"We shall be catechised," said Coronado.

"You must do the lying," replied the officer. He was so shaken by what he had witnessed that he did not dare to face Clara for an hour afterward, lest his discomposure should arouse her suspicions. When he did at last visit the tower, she was quiet and smiling, for Coronado had done his lying, and done it well.

"So there was no attack," she said. "I am so glad!"

"Only a little skirmish. You heard the firing, of course."

"Yes. Coronado told us about it. What a horrible howling the Indians made! There were some screams that were really frightful."

"It was their last demonstration. They will probably be gone in the morning."

"Poor Pepita! She will be carried off," said Clara, a tear or two stealing down her cheek.

"Yes, poor Pepita!" sighed Thurstane.

The muleteer who had been killed in the assault was already buried. At sundown came the funeral of the soldier Shubert. The body, wrapped in a blanket, was borne by four Mexicans to the grave which had been prepared for it, followed by his three comrades with loaded muskets, and then by all the other members of the party, except Mrs. Stanley, who looked down from her roof upon the spectacle. Thurstane acted as chaplain, and read the funeral service from Clara's prayer-book, amidst the weeping of women and the silence of men. The dead young hero was lowered into his last resting-place. Sergeant Meyer gave the order: "Shoulder arms—ready—present—aim—fire!" The ceremony was ended; the muleteers filled the grave; a stone was placed to mark it; so slept a good soldier.

Now came another night of anxiety, but also of quiet. In the morning, when eager eyes looked through the yellow haze of dawn over the plain, not an Apache was to be seen.

"They are gone," said Coronado to Thurstane, after the two had made the tour of the ruins and scrutinized every feature of the landscape. "What next?"

Thurstane swept his field-glass around once more, searching for some outlet besides the horrible cañon, and searching in vain.

"We must wait a day or so for our wounded," he said. "Then we must start back on our old trail. I don't see anything else before us."

"It is a gloomy prospect," muttered Coronado, thinking of the hundred miles of rocky desert, and of the possibility that Apaches might be ambushed at the end of it.

He had been so anxious about himself for a few days that he had cared for little else. He had been humble, submissive to Thurstane, and almost entirely indifferent about Clara.

"We ought at least to try something in the way of explorations," continued the lieutenant. "To begin with, I shall sound the river. I shall be thought a devil of a failure if I don't carry back some information about the topography of this region."

"Can you paddle your boat against the current?" asked Coronado.

"I doubt it. But we can make a towing cord of lariats and let it out from the shore; perhaps swing it clear across the river in that way—with some paddling, you know."

"It is an excellent plan," said Coronado.

The day passed without movement, excepting that Texas Smith and two Mexicans explored the cañon for several miles, returning with a couple of lame ponies and a report that the Apaches had undoubtedly gone southward. At night, however, the animals were housed and sentries posted as usual, for Thurstane feared lest the enemy might yet return and attempt a surprise.

The next morning, all being quiet, the Buchanan boat was launched. A couple of fairish paddles were chipped out of bits of driftwood, and a towline a hundred feet long was made of lariats. Thurstane further provisioned the cockleshell with fishing tackle, a sounding line, his own rifle, Shubert's musket and accoutrements, a bag of hard bread, and a few pounds of jerked beef.

"You are not going to make a voyage!" stared Coronado.

"I am preparing for accidents. We may get carried down the river."

"I thought you proposed to keep fast to the shore."

"I do. But the lariats may break."

Coronado said no more. He lighted a cigarito and looked on with an air of dreamy indifference. He had hit upon a plan for getting rid of Thurstane.

The next question was, who could handle a boat? The lieutenant wanted two men to keep it out in the current while he used the sounding line and recorded results.

"Guess I'll do 's well 's the nex' hand," volunteered Captain Glover. "Got a sore ear, 'n' a hole in my nose, but reckon I'm 'n able-bodied seaman for all that. *Hev* rowed some in my time. Rowed forty mile after a whale onct, 'n' caught the critter—fairly rowed him down. Current's putty lively. Sh'd say 't was tearin' off 'bout five knots an hour. But guess I'll try it. Sh'd kinder like to feel water under me agin."

"Captain, you shall handle the ship," smiled Thurstane. "I'll mention you by name in my report. Who next?"

"Me," yelped Sweeny.

"Can you row, Sweeny?"

"I can, Liftinant."

"You may try it."

"Can I take me gun, Liftinant?" demanded Sweeny, who was extravagantly fond and proud of his piece, all the more perhaps because he held it in awe.

"Yes, you can take it, and Glover can have Shubert's. Though, 'pon my honor, I don't know why we should carry firearms. It's old habit, I suppose. It's a way we have in the army."

The lieutenant had no sort of anxiety on the score of his enterprise. His plan was to swing out into the current, and, if the boat proved perfectly manageable, to cut loose from the towline and paddle across, sounding the whole breadth of the channel. It seemed easy enough and safe enough. When he left the Casa Grande after breakfast he contrived to kiss Clara's hand, but it did not once occur to him that it would be proper to bid her farewell. He was very far indeed from guessing that in the knot of the lariat which was fast to the bow of his coracle there was a fatal gash. It was not suspicion of evil, but merely a habit of precaution, a prudential tone of mind which he had acquired in service, that led him at the last moment to say (making Coronado tremble in his boots), "Mr. Glover, have you thoroughly overhauled the cord?"

"Give her a look jest before we went up to breakfast," replied the skipper. "She'll hold."

Coronado, who stood three feet distant, blew a quiet little whiff of smoke through his thin purple lips, meanwhile dreamily contemplating the speaker.

"Git in, you paddywhack," said Glover to Sweeny. "Grab yer paddle. T'other end; that's the talk. Now then. All aboard that's goin'. Shove off."

In a few seconds, impelled from the shore by the paddles, the boat was at the full length of the towline and in the middle of the boiling current.

"Will it never break?" thought Coronado, smoking a little faster than usual, but not moving a muscle.

Yes. It had already broken. At the first pause in the paddling the mangled lariat had given way.

In spite of the renewed efforts of the oarsmen, the boat was flying down the San Juan.

CHAPTER XXV.

WHEN Thurstane perceived that the towline had parted and that the boat was gliding down the San Juan, he called sharply, "Paddle!"

He was in no alarm as yet. The line, although of rawhide, was switching on the surface of the rapid current; it seemed easy enough to recover it and make a new fastening. Passing from the stern to the bow, he knelt down and dipped one hand in the water, ready to clutch the end of the lariat.

But a boat five feet long and twelve feet broad, especially when made of canvas on a frame of light sticks, is not handily paddled against swift water; and the Buchanan (as the voyagers afterward named it) not only sagged awkwardly, but showed a strong tendency to whirl around like an egg-shell as it was. Moreover, the loose line almost instantly took the direction of the stream, and swept so rapidly shoreward that by the time Thurstane was in position to seize it, it was rods away.

"Row for the bank," he ordered. But just as he spoke there came a little noise which was to these three men the crack of doom. The paddle of that most unskilful navigator, Sweeny, snapped in two, and the broad blade of it was instantly out of reach. Next the cockle-shell of a boat was spinning on its keelless bottom, and whirling broadside on, bow foremost, stern foremost, any way, down the San Juan.

'Paddle away!" shouted Thurstane to Glover. "Drive her in shore! Pitch her in!"

The old coaster sent a quick, anxious look down the river, and saw at once that there was no chance of reaching the bank. Below them, not three hundred yards distant, was an archipelago of rocks, the *débris* of fallen precipices and pinnacles, through which, for half a mile or more, the water flew in whirlpools and foam. They were drifting at great speed toward this frightful rapid, and, if they entered it, destruction was sure and instant. Only the middle of the stream showed a smooth current; and there was less than half a minute in which to reach it. Without a word Glover commenced paddling as well as he could away from the bank.

"What are you about?" yelled Thurstane, who saw Clara on the roof of the Casa Grande, and was crazed at the thought of leaving her there. She would suspect that he had abandoned her; she would be massacred by the Apaches; she would starve in the desert, etc.

Glover made no reply. His whole being was engaged in the struggle of evading immediate death.

One more glance, one moment of manly, soldierly reflection, enabled Thurstane to comprehend the fate which was upon him, and to bow to it with resignation. Turning his back upon the foaming reefs which might the next instant be his executioners, he stood up in the boat, took off his cap, and waved a farewell to Clara. He was so unconscious of anything but her and his parting from her that for some time he did not notice that the slight craft had narrowly shaved the rocks, that it had barely crawled into the middle current, and that he was temporarily safe. He kept his eyes fixed upon the Casa and upon the girl's motionless figure until a monstrous, sullen precipice slid in between. He was like one who breathes his last with straining gaze settled on some loved face, parting from which is worse than death. When he could see her no longer, nor the ruin which sheltered her, and which suddenly seemed to him a paradise, he dropped his head between his hands, utterly unmanned.

"'Twon't dew to give it up while we float, Major," said Glover, breveting the lieutenant by way of cheering him.

"I don't give it up," replied Thurstane; "but I had a duty to do there, and now I can't do it."

"There's dooties to be 'tended to here, I reckon," suggested Glover.

"They will be done," said the officer, raising his head and settling his face. "How can we help you?"

"Don't seem to need much help. The river doos the paddlin'; wish it didn't. No 'casion to send anybody aloft. I'll take a seat in the stern 'n' mind the hellum. Guess that's all they is to be done."

"You dum paddywhack," he presently reopened, "what d'ye break yer paddle for?"

"I didn't break it," yapped Sweeny indignantly. "It broke itself."

"Well, what d'ye say y' could paddle for, when y' couldn't?"

"I can paddle. I paddled as long as I had anythin' but a sthick."

"Oh, you dum landlubber!" smirked Glover. "What if I should order ye to the masthead?"

"I wouldn't go," asseverated Sweeny. "I'll moind no man who isn't me suparior officer. I've moindin' enough to do in the arrmy. I wouldn't go onless the liftinint towld me. Thin I'd go."

"Guess y' wouldn't now."

"Yis I wud."

"But they an't no mast."

"I mane if there was one."

This kind of babble Glover kept up for some minutes, with the sole object of amusing and cheering Thurstane, whose extreme depression surprised and alarmed him. He knew that the situation was bad, and that it would take lots of pluck to bring them through it.

"Capm, where d'ye think we're bound?" he presently inquired. "Whereabouts doos this river come out?"

"It runs into the Colorado of the West, and that runs into the head of the Gulf of California."

"Californy! Reckon I'll git to the diggins quicker 'n I expected. Goin' at this rate, we'll make about a hundred 'n' twenty knots a day. What's the distance to Californy?"

"By the bends of the river it can't be less than twelve hundred miles to the gulf."

"Whew!" went Glover. "Ten days' sailin'. Wal, smooth water all the way?"

"The San Juan has never been navigated. So far as I know, we are the first persons who ever launched a boat on it."

"Whew! Why, it's like discoverin' Ameriky. Wal, what d'ye guess about the water? Any chance 'f its bein' smooth clear through?"

"The descent to the gulf must be two or three thousand feet, perhaps more. We can hardly fail to find rapids. I shouldn't be astonished by a cataract."

Glover gave a long whistle and fell into grave meditation. His conclusion was: "Can t navigate nights, that's a fact. Have to come to anchor. That makes twenty days on't. Wal, Capm, fust thing is to fish up a bit 'f driftwood 'n' whittle out 'nother paddle. Want a boat-pole, too, like thunder. We're awful short 'f spars for a long voyage."

His lively mind had hardly dismissed this subject before he remarked: "Dum cur'ous that towline breaking. I overhauled every foot on't. I'd a bet my bottom fo'pence on its drawin' ten ton. Haul in the slack end 'n' let's hev a peek at it."

The tip of the lariat, which was still attached to the boat, being handed to him, he examined it minutely, closed his eyes, whistled, and ejaculated, "Sawed!"

"What?" asked Thurstane.

"Sawed," repeated Glover. "That leather was haggled in tew with a jagged knife or a sharp flint or suthin 'f that sort. Done a purpose, 's sure 's I'm a sinner."

Thurstane took the lariat, inspected the breakage carefully, and scowled with helpless rage.

"That infernal Texan!" he muttered.

"Sho!" said Glover. "That feller? Anythin' agin ye? Wal, Capm, then all I've got to say is, you come off easy. That feller 'd cut a sleepin' man's throat. I sh'd say thank God for the riddance. Tell ye I've watched that cuss. Been blastedly afeard 'f him. Hev so, by George! The further I git from him the safer I feel."

"Not a nice man to leave *there*," muttered Thurstane, whose anxiety was precisely not for himself, but for Clara. The young fellow could not be got to talk much; he was a good deal upset by his calamity. The parting from Clara was an awful blow; the thought of her dangers made him feel as if he could jump overboard; and, lurking deep in his soul, there was an ugly fear that Coronado might now win her. He was furious moreover at having been tricked, and meditated bedlamite plans of vengeance. For a time he stared more at the mangled lariat than at the amazing scenery through which he was gliding.

And yet that scenery, although only a prelude, only an overture to the transcendent oratorios of landscape which were to follow, was in itself a horribly sublime creation. Not twenty minutes after the snapping of the towline the boat had entered one of those stupendous cañons which form the distinguishing characteristic of the great American table-land, and make it a region unlike any other in the world.

Remember that the cañon is a groove chiselled out of rock by a river. Although a groove, it is never straight for long distances. The river at its birth was necessarily guided by the hollows of the primal plateau; moreover, it was tempted to labor along the softest surfaces. Thus the cañon is a sinuous gully, cut down from the hollows of rocky valleys, and following their courses of descent from mountain-chain toward ocean.

In these channels the waters have chafed, ground, abraded, eroded for centuries which man cannot number. Like the Afreets of the Arabian Nights, they have been mighty slaves, subject to a far mightier master. That potent magician whose lair is in the centre of the earth, and whom men have vaguely styled the attraction of gravitation, has summoned them incessantly toward himself. In their struggle to render him obedience, they have accomplished results which make all the works of man insignificant by comparison.

To begin with, vast lakes, which once swept westward from the bases of the Rocky Mountains, were emptied into the Pacific. Next the draining currents transformed into rivers, cut their way through the soil which formerly covered the table-lands and commenced their attrition upon the underlying continent of sandstone. It was a grinding which never ceased; every pebble and every bowlder which lay in the way was pressed into the endless labor; mountains were used up in channelling mountains.

The central magician was insatiable and pitiless; he demanded not only the waters, but whatever they could bring; he hungered after the earth and all that covered it. His obedient Afreets toiled on, denuding the plateaux of their soil, washing it away from every slope and peak, pouring it year by year into the cañons, and whirling it on to the ocean. The rivers, the brooklets, the springs, and the rains all joined in this eternal robbery. Little by little an eighth of a continent was stripped of its loam, its forests, its grasses, its flowers, its vegetation of every species. What had been a land of fertility became an arid and rocky desert.

Then the minor Afreets perished of the results of their own obedience. There being no soil, the fountains disappeared; there being no evaporation, the rains diminished. Deprived of sustenance, nearly all the shorter streams dried up, and the channels which they had hewn became arid gullies. Only those rivers continued to exist which drew their waters from the snowy slopes of the Rocky Mountains or from the spurs and ranges which intersect the plateaux. The ages may come when these also will cease to flow, and throughout all this portion of the continent the central magician will call for his Afreets in vain.

For some time we must attend much to the scenery of the desert thus created. It has become one of the individuals of our story, and interferes with the fate of the merely human personages. Thurstane could not long ignore its magnificent, oppressive, and potent presence. Forgetting somewhat his anxieties about the loved one whom he had left behind, he looked about him with some such amazement as if he had been translated from earth into regions of supernature.

The cañon through which he was flying was a groove cut in solid sandstone, less than two hundred feet wide, with precipitous walls of fifteen hundred feet, from the summit of which the rock sloped away into buttes and peaks a thousand feet higher. On every side the horizon was half a mile above his head. He was in a chasm, twenty-five hundred feet below the average surface of the earth, the floor of which was a swift river.

He seemed to himself to be traversing the abodes of the Genii. Although he had only heard of "Vathek," he thought of the Hall of Eblis. It was such an abyss as no artist has ever hinted, excepting Doré in his picturings of Dante's "Inferno." Could Dante himself have looked into it, he would have peopled it with the most hopeless of his lost spirits. The shadow, the aridity, the barrenness, the solemnity, the pitilessness, the horrid cruelty of the scene, were more than might be received into the soul. It was something which could not be imagined, and which when seen could not be fully remembered. To gaze on it was like beholding the mysterious, wicked countenance of the father of all evil. It was a landscape which was a fiend.

The precipices were not bare and plain faces of rock, destitute of minor finish and of color. They had their horrible decorations; they showed the ingenuity and the artistic force of the Afreets who had fashioned them; they were wrought and tinted with a demoniac splendor suited to their magnitude. It seemed as if some goblin Michel Angelo had here done his carving and frescoing at the command of the lords of hell. Layers of brown, gray, and orange sandstone, alternated from base to summit; and these tints were laid on with a breadth of effect which was prodigious: a hundred feet in height and miles in length at a stroke of the brush.

The architectural and sculptural results were equally monstrous. There were lateral shelves twenty feet in width, and thousands of yards in length. There were towers, pilasters, and formless caryatides, a quarter of a mile in height. Great bulks projected, capped by gigantic mitres or diadems, and flanked by cavernous indentations. In consequence of the varying solidity of the stone, the river had wrought the precipices into a series of innumerable monuments, more or less enormous, commemorative of combats. There had been interminable strife here between the demons of earth and the demons of water, and each side had set up its trophies. It was the Vatican and the Catacombs of the Genii; it was the museum and the mausoleum of the forces of nature.

At various points tributary gorges, the graves of fluvial gods who had perished long ago, opened into the main cañon. In passing these the voyagers had momentary glimpses of sublimities and horrors which seemed like the handiwork of that "anarch old," who wrought before the shaping of the universe. One of these sarcophagi was a narrow cleft, not more than eighty feet broad, cut from surface to base of a bed of sandstone one-third of a mile in depth. It was inhabited by an eternal gloom which was like the shadow of the blackness of darkness. The stillness, the absence of all life whether animal or vegetable, the dungeon-like closeness of the monstrous walls, were beyond language.

Another gorge was a ruin. The rock here being of various degrees of density, the waters had essayed a thousand channels. All the softer veins had been scooped out and washed away, leaving the harder blocks and masses piled in a colossal grotesque confusion. Along the sloping sides of the gap stood bowlders, pillars, needles, and strange shapes of stone, peering over each other's heads into the gulf below. It was as if an army of misshapen monsters and giants had been petrified with horror, while staring at some inconceivable desolation and ruin. There was no hope for this concrete despair; no imaginable voice could utter for it a word of consolation; the gazer, like Dante amid the tormented, could only "look and pass on."

At one point two lateral cañons opened side by side upon the San Juan. The partition was a stupendous pile of rock fifteen hundred feet in altitude, but so narrow that it seemed to the voyagers below like the single standing wall of some ruined edifice. Although the space on its summit was broad enough for a cathedral, it did not appear to them that it would afford footing to a man, while the enclosing fissures looked narrow enough to be crossed at a bound. On either side of this isolated bar of sandstone a plumb-line might have been dropped straight to the level of the river. The two chasms were tombs of shadow, where nothing ever stirred but winds.

The solitude of this continuous panorama of precipices was remarkable. It was a region without man, or beast, or bird, or insect. The endless rocks, not only denuded, but eroded and scraped by the action of bygone waters, could furnish no support for animal life. A beast of prey, or even a mountain goat, would have starved here. Could a condor of the Andes have visited it, he would have spread his wings at once to leave it.

Yet horrible as the scene was, it was so sublime that it fascinated. For hours, gazing at lofty masses, vast outlines, prodigious assemblages of rocky imagery, endless strokes of natural frescoing, the three adventurers either exchanged-rare words of astonishment, or lay in reveries which transported them beyond earth. What Thurstane felt he could only express by recalling random lines of the "Paradise Lost." It seemed to him as if they might at any moment emerge upon the lake of burning marl, and float into the shadow of the walls ot Pandemonium. He would not have felt himself carried much beyond his present circumstances, had he suddenly beheld Satan,

High on a throne of royal state, which far
Outshone the wealth of Ormus and of Ind.

He was roused from his dreams by the quick, dry, grasshopper-like voice of Phineas Glover, asking, "What's that?"

A deep whisper came up the chasm. They could hardly distinguish it when they stretched their hearing to the utmost. It seemed to steal with difficulty against the rushing flood, and then to be swept down again. It sighed threateningly for a moment, and instantaneously became silence. One might liken it tc a ghost trying to advance through some castle hall, only to be borne backward by the fitful night-breeze, or by some mysterious ban. Was the desert inhabited, and by disembodied demons?

After a further flight of half a mile, this variable sigh changed to a continuous murmur. There was now before the voyagers a straight course of nearly two miles, at the end of which lay hid the unseen power which gave forth this solemn menace. The river, perfectly clear of rocks, was a sheet of liquid porphyry, an arrow of dark-red water slightly flecked with foam. The walls of the cañon, scarcely fifty yards apart and more stupendous than ever, rose in precipices without a landing-place or a foothold. So far as eye could pierce into the twilight of the sublime chasm, there was not a spot where the boat could be arrested in its flight, or where a swimmer could find a shelf of safety.

"It is a rapid," said Thurstane. "You did well, Captain Glover, to get another paddle."

"Lord bless ye!" returned the skipper impatiently, "it's lucky I was whittlin' while you was thinkin'. If we on'y had a boat-hook!"

From moment to moment the murmur came nearer and grew louder. It was smothered and then redoubled by the reverberations of the cañon, so that sometimes it seemed the tigerish snarl of a rapid, and sometimes the leonine roar of a cataract. A bend of the chasm at last brought the voyagers in sight of the monster, which was frothing and howling to devour them. It was a terrific spectacle. It was like Apollyon "straddling quite across the way," to intercept Christian in the Valley of the Shadow of Death. From one dizzy rampart to the other, and as far down the echoing cavern as eye could reach, the river was white with an arrowy rapid storming though a labyrinth of rocks.

Sweeny, evidently praying, moved his lips in silence. Glover's face had the keen, anxious, watchful look of the sailor affronting shipwreck; and Thurstane's the set, enduring rigidity of the soldier who is tried to his utmost by cannonade.

CHAPTER XXVI.

THE three adventurers were entering the gorge of an impassable rapid.

Here had once been the barrier of a cataract; the waters had ground through it, tumbled it down, and gnawed it to tatters; the scattered bowlders which showed through the foam were the remnants of the Cyclopean feast.

There appeared to be no escape from death. Any one of those stones would rend the canvas boat from end to end, or double it into a wet rag; and if a swimmer should perchance reach the bank, he would drown there, looking up at precipices; or, if he should find a footing, it would only be to starve.

"There is our chance," said Thurstane, pointing to a bowlder as large as a house which stood under the northern wall of the cañon, about a quarter of a mile above the first yeast of the rapid.

He and Glover each took a paddle. They had but one object: it was to get under the lee of the bowlder, and so stop their descent; after that they would see what more could be done. Danger and safety were alike swift here; it was a hurry as of battle or tempest. Almost before they began to hope for success, they were circling in the narrow eddy, very nearly a whirlpool, which wheeled just below the isolated rock. Even here the utmost caution was necessary, for while the Buchanan was as light as a bubble, it was also as fragile.

Sounding the muddy water with their paddles, they slowly glided into the angle between the bowlder and the precipice, and jammed the fragment of the towline in a crevice. For the first time in six hours, and in a run of thirty miles, they were at rest. Wiping the sweat of labor and anxiety from their brows, they looked about them, at first in silence, querying what next?

"I wish I was on an iceberg," said Glover in his despair.

"An' I wish I was in Oirland," added Sweeny. "But if the divil himself was to want to desart here, he couldn't."

Thurstane believed that he had seen Clara for the last time, even should she escape her own perils. Through his field-glass he surveyed the whole gloomy scene with microscopic attention, searching for an exit out of this monstrous man-trap, and searching in vain. It was as impossible to descend the rapid as it was to scale the walls of the cañon. He had just heard Sweeny say, "I wish I was bein' murthered by thim naygurs," and had smiled at the utterance of desperation with a grim sympathy, when a faint hope dawned upon him.

Not more than a yard above the water was a ledge or shelf in the face of the precipice. The layer of sandstone immediately over this shelf was evidently softer than the general mass; and in other days (centuries ago), when it had formed one level with the bed of the river, it had been deeply eroded. This erosion had been carried along the cañon on an even line of altitude as far as the softer layer extended. Thurstane could trace it with his glass for what seemed to him a mile, and there was of course a possibility that it reached below the foot of the rapid. The groove was everywhere about twenty feet high, while its breadth varied from a yard or so to nearly a rod.

Here, then, was a road by which they might perhaps turn the obstacle. The only difficulty was that while the bed of the river descended rapidly, the shelf kept on at the same elevation, so that eventually the travellers would come to a jumping-off place. How high would it be? Could they get down it so as to regain the stream and resume their navigation? Well, they must try it; there was no other road. With one eloquent wave of his hand Thurstane pointed out this slender chance of escape to his comrades.

"Hurray!" shouted Glover, after a long stare, in which the emotions succeeded each other like colors in a dolphin.

"Can we make the jump at the other end?" asked the lieutenant.

"Reckon so," chirruped Glover. "Look a here."

He exhibited a pile of unpleasant-looking matter which proved to be a mass of strips of fresh hide.

"Hoss skin," he explained. "Peeled off a mustang. Borrowed it from that Texan cuss. Thought likely we might want to splice our towline. 'Bout ten fathom, I reckon; 'n' there's the lariat, two fathom more. All we've got to do is to pack up, stick our backs under, 'n' travel.

It was three o'clock in the afternoon when they commenced their preparations for making this extraordinary portage. Sunk as they were twenty-five hundred feet in the bowels of the earth, the sun had already set for them; but they were still favored with a sort of twilight radiance, and they could count upon it for a couple of hours longer. Carefully the guns, paddles, and stores were landed on the marvellous causeway; and then, with still greater caution, the boat was lifted to the same support and taken to pieces. The whole mass of material, some two hundred pounds in weight, was divided into three portions. Each shouldered his pack, and the strange journey commenced.

"Sweeny, don't you fall off," said Glover. "We can't spare them sticks."

"If I fall off, ye may shute me where I stand," returned Sweeny. "I know better 'n to get drowned and starved to death in wan. I can take care av meself. I've sailed this a way many a time in th' ould counthry."

The road was a smooth and easy one, barring a few cumbering bowlders. To the left and below was the river, roaring, hissing, and foaming through its *chevaux de frise* of rocks. In front the cañon stretched on and on until its walls grew dim with shadow and distance. Above were overhanging precipices and a blue streak of sunlit sky.

It was quite dusk with the wanderers before they reached a point where the San Juan once more flowed with an undisturbed current.

"We can't launch by this light," said Thurstane. "We will sleep here."

"It'll be a longish night," commented Glover. "But don't see 's we can shorten it by growlin'. When fellahs travel in the bowels 'f th' earth, they've got to follow the customs 'f th' country. Puts me in mind of Jonah in the whale's belly. Putty short tacks, Capm. Nine hours a day won't git us along any too fast. But can't help it. Night travellin' ain't suited to our boat. Suthin' like a bladder football: one pin-prick 'd cowallapse it. Wal, so we'll settle. Lucky we wanted our blankets to set on. 'Pears to me this rock's a leetle harder'n a common deck plank. Unroll the boat, Capm? Wal, guess we'd better. Needs dryin' a speck. Too much soakin' an't good for canvas. Better dry it out, 'n' fold it up, 'n' sleep on't. This passageway that we're in, sh'd say it might git up a smart draught. What d'ye say to this spot for campin'? Twenty foot breadth of beam here. Kind of a stateroom, or bridal chamber. No need of fallin' out. Ever walk in yer sleep, Sweeny? Better cut it right square off to-night. Five fathom down to the river, sh'd say. Splash ye awfully, Sweeny."

Thus did Captain Glover prattle in his cheerful way while the party made its preparations for the night.

They were like ants lodged in some transverse crack of a lofty wall. They were in a deep cut of the shelf, with fifteen hundred or two thousand feet of sandstone above, and the porphyry-colored river thirty feet below. The narrow strip of sky far above their heads was darkening rapidly with the approach of night, and with an accumulation of clouds. All of a sudden there was a descent of muddy water, charged with particles of red earth and powdered sandstone, pouring by them down the overhanging precipice.

"Liftinant!" exclaimed Sweeny, "thim naygurs up there is washin' their dirty hides an' pourin' the suds down on us."

"It's the rain, Sweeny. There's a shower on the plateau above."

"The rain, is it? Thin all nate people in that counthry must stand in great nade of ombrellys."

The scene was more marvellous than ever. Not a drop of rain fell in the river; the immense façade opposite them was as dry as a skull; yet here was this muddy cataract. It fell for half an hour, scarcely so much as spattering them in their recess, but plunging over them into the torrent beneath. By the time it ceased they had eaten their supper of hard bread and harder beef, and lighted their pipes to allay their thirst. There was a laying of plans to regain the river to-morrow, a grave calculation as to how long their provisions would last, and in general much talk about their chances.

"Not a shine of a lookout for gittin' back to the Casa?" queried Captain Glover. "Knowed it," he added, when the lieutenant sadly shook his head. "Fool for talkin' 'bout it. How 'bout reachin' the trail to the Moqui country?"

"I have been thinking of it all day," said Thurstane. "We must give it up. Every one of the branch cañons on the other bank trends wrong. We couldn't cross them; we should have to follow them; it's an impassable hell of a country. We might by bare chance reach the Moqui pueblos; but the probability is that we should die in the desert of thirst. We shall have to run the river. Perhaps we shall have to run the Colorado too. If so, we had better keep on to Diamond creek, and from there push by land to Cactus Pass. Cactus Pass is on the trail, and we may meet emigrants there. I don't know what better to suggest."

"Dessay it's a tiptop idee," assented Glover cheeringly. "Anyhow, if we take on down the river, it seems like follyin' the guidings of Providence."

In spite of their strange situation and doubtful prospects, the three adventurers slept early and soundly. When they awoke it was daybreak, and after chewing the hardest, dryest, and rawest of breakfasts, they began their preparations to reach the river. To effect this, it was necessary to find a cleft in the ledge where they could fasten a cord securely, and below it a footing at the water's edge where they could put their boat together and launch it. It would not do to go far down the cañon, for the bed of the stream descended while the shelf retained its level, and the distance between them was already sufficiently alarming. After an anxious search they discovered a bowlder lying in the river beneath the shelf, with a flat surface perfectly suited to their purpose. There, too, was a cleft, but a miserably small one.

"We can't jam a cord in that," said Glover; "nor the handle of a paddle nuther."

"It 'll howld me bagonet," suggested Sweeny.

"It can be made to hold it," decided Thurstane. "We must drill away till it does hold it."

An hour's labor enabled them to insert the bayonet to the handle and wedge it with spikes split off from the precious wood of the paddles. When it seemed firm enough to support a strong lateral pressure, Glover knotted on to it, in his deft sailor fashion, a strip of the horse hide, and added others to that until he had a cord of some forty feet. After testing every inch and every knot, he said: "Who starts first?"

"I will try it," answered Thurstane.

"Lightest first, I reckon," observed Glover.

Sweeny looked at the precipice, skipped about the shelf uneasily, made a struggle with his fears, and asked, "Will ye let me down aisy?"

"Jest 's easy 's rollin' off a log."

"That's aisy enough. It's the lightin' that's har-rd. If it comes to rowlin' down, I'll let ye have the first rowl. I've no moind to git ahead of me betthers."

"Try it, my lad," said Thurstane. "The real danger comes with the last man. He will have to trust to the bayonet alone."

"An' what'll I do whin I get down there?"

"Take the traps off the cord as we send them down, and pile them on the rock."

"I'm off," said Sweeny, after one more look into the chasm. While the others held the cord to keep the strain from coming on the bayonet, he gripped it with both hands, edged stern foremost over the precipice, and slipped rapidly to the bowlder, whence he sent up a hoot of exultation. The cord was drawn back; the boat was made up in two bundles, which were lowered in succession; then the provisions, paddles, arms, etc. Now came the question whether Thurstane or Glover should remain last on the ledge.

"Lightest last," said the lean skipper. "Stands to reason."

"It's my duty to take the hot end of the poker," replied the officer.

"Loser goes first," said Glover, producing a copper. "Heads or tails?"

"Heads," guessed Thurstane.

"It's a tail. Catch hold, Capm. Slow 'n' easy till you get over."

The cord holding firm, Thurstane reached the bowlder, and was presently joined by Glover.

"Liftinant, I want me bagonet," cried Sweeny. "Will I go up afther it?"

"How the dickens 'd you git down again?" asked Glover. "Guess you'll have to leave your bayonet where it sticks. But, Capm, we want that line. Can't you shute it away, clost by th' edge?"

The third shot was a lucky one, and brought down the precious cord. Then came the work of putting the boat into shape, launching it, getting in the stores, and lastly the voyagers.

"Tight 's a drum yit," observed Glover, surveying the coracle admiringly. "Fust time I ever sailed *on* canvas. Great notion. Don't draw more'n three inches. Might sail acrost country with it. Capm, it's the only boat ever invented that could git down this blasted river."

Glover and Sweeny, two of the most talkative creatures on earth, chattered much to each other. Thurstane sometimes listened to them, sometimes lost himself in reveries about Clara, sometimes surveyed the scenery of the cañon.

The abyss was always the same, yet with colossal variety: here and there yawnings of veined precipices, followed by cavernous closings of the awful sides; breakings in of subsidiary cañons, some narrow clefts, and others gaping shattered mouths; the walls now presenting long lines of rampart, and now a succession of peaks. But still, although they had now traversed the chasm for seventy or eighty miles, they found no close and no declension to its solemn grandeur.

At last came another menace, a murmur deeper and hoarser than that of the rapid, steadily swelling as they advanced until it was a continuous thunder. This time there could be no doubt that they were entering upon a scene of yet undecided battle between the eternal assault of the river and the immemorial resistance of the mountains.

The quickening speed of the waters, and the ceaseless bellow of their charging trumpets as they tore into some yet unseen abyss, announced one of those struggles of nature in which man must be a spectator or a victim.

CHAPTER XXVII.

As Thurstane approached the cataract of the San Juan he thought of the rapids above Niagara, and of the men who had been whirled down them, foreseeing their fate and struggling against it, but unable to escape it.

"We must keep near one wall or the other," he said. "The middle of the river is sure death."

Paddling toward the northern bank, simply because it had saved them in their former peril, they floated like a leaf in the shadows of the precipices, watching for some footway by which to turn the lair of the monster ahead.

The scenery here did not consist exclusively of two lofty ramparts fronting each other. Before the river had established its present channel it had tried the strength of the plateau in various directions, slashing the upper strata into a succession of cañons, which were now lofty and arid gullies, divided from each other by every conceivable form of rocky ruin. Rotundas, amphitheatres, castellated walls, cathedrals of unparalleled immensity, façades of palaces huge enough to be the abodes of the principalities and powers of the air, far-stretching semblances of cities tottering to destruction, all fashions of domes, towers, minarets, spires, and obelisks, with a population of misshapen demons and monsters, looked down from sublime heights upon the voyagers. At every turn in the river the panorama changed, and they beheld new marvels of this Titanic architecture. There was no end to the gigantic and grotesque variety of the commingling outlines. The vastness, the loneliness, the stillness, the twilight sombreness, were awful. And through all reverberated incessantly the defiant clarion of the cataract.

The day was drawing to that early death which it has always had and must always have in these abysses. Knowing how suddenly darkness would fall, and not daring to attempt the unknown without light, the travellers looked for a mooring spot. There was a grim abutment at least eighteen hundred feet high; at its base two rocks, which had tumbled ages ago from the summit, formed a rude breakwater; and on this barrier had collected a bed of coarse pebbles, strewn with driftwood. Here they stopped their flight, unloaded the boat and beached it. The drift-wood furnished them a softer bed than usual, and materials for a fire.

Night supervened with the suddenness of a death which has been looked for, but which is at last a surprise. Shadow after shadow crept down the walls of the chasm, blurred its projections, darkened its faces, and crowded its recesses. The line of sky, seen through the jagged and sinuous opening above, changed slowly to gloom and then to blackness. There was no light in this rocky intestine of the earth except the red flicker of the camp-fire. It fought feebly with the powers of darkness; it sent tremulous despairing flashes athwart the swift ebony river; it reached out with momentary gleams to the nearer façades of precipice; it reeled, drooped, and shuddered as if in hopeless horror. Probably, since the world began, no other fire lighted by man had struggled against the gloom of this tremendous amphitheatre. The darknesses were astonished at it, but they were also uncomprehending and hostile. They refused to be dissipated, and they were victorious.

After two hours a change came upon the scene. The moon rose, filled the upper air with its radiance, and bathed in silver the slopes of the mountains. The narrow belt of visible sky resembled a milky way. The light continued to descend and work miracles. Isolated turrets, domes, and pinnacles came out in gleaming relief against the dark-blue background of the heavens. The opposite crest of the cañon shone with a broad illumination. All the uncouth demons and monsters of the rocks awoke, glaring and blinking, to menace the voyagers in the depths below. The contrast between this supereminent brilliancy and the sullen obscurity of the subterranean river made the latter seem more than ever like Styx or Acheron.

The travellers were awakened in the morning by the trumpetings of the cataract. They embarked and dropped down the stream, hugging the northern rampart and watching anxiously. Presently there was a clear sweep of a mile; the clamor now came straight up to them with redoubled vehemence; a ghost of spray arose and waved threateningly, as if forbidding further passage. It was the roar and smoke of an artillery which had thundered for ages, and would thunder for ages to come. It was a voice and signal which summoned reinforcements of waters, and in obedience to which the waters charged eternally.

The boat had shudders. Every spasm jerked it onward a little faster. It flew with a tremulous speed which was terrible. Thurstane, a good soldier, able to obey as well as to direct, knowing that if Glover could not steer wisely no one could, sat, paddle in hand, awaiting orders. Sweeny fidgeted, looked from one to another, looked at the mist ahead, cringed, wanted to speak, and said nothing. Glover, working hard with his paddle, and just barely keeping the coracle bows on, peered and grinned as if he were facing a hurricane. There was no time to have a care for sunken bowlders, reaching up to rend the thin bottom. The one giant danger of the cataract was enough to fill the mind and bar out every minor terror. Its deafening threats demanded the whole of the imagination. Compared with the probability of plunging down an unknown depth into a boiling hell of waters, all other peril seemed too trifling to attract notice. Such a fate is an enhancement of the horrors of death.

"Liftinant, let's go over with a whoop," called Sweeny. "It's much aisier."

"Keep quiet, my lad," replied the officer. "We must hear orders."

"All right, Liftinant," said Sweeny, relieved by having spoken.

At this moment Glover shouted cheerfully, "We ain't dead yit. There's a ledge."

"I see it," nodded Thurstane.

"Where there's a ledge there's an eddy," screamed Glover, raising his voice to pierce the hiss of the rapid and the roar of the cascade.

Below them, jutting out from the precipitous northern bank, was a low bar of rock over which the river did not sweep. It was the remnant of a once lofty barrier; the waters had, as it were, gnawed it to the bone, but they had not destroyed it. In two minutes the voyagers were beside it, paddling with all their strength against the eddy which whirled along its edge toward the cataract, and tossing over the short, spiteful ripples raised by the sudden turn of the current. With a "Hooroo!" Sweeny tumbled ashore, lariat in hand, and struck his army shoes into the crevices of the shattered sandstone. In five minutes more the boat was unloaded and lifted upon the ledge.

The travellers did not go to look at the cataract; their immediate and urgent need was to get by it. Making up their bundles as usual, they commenced a struggle with the intricacies and obstacles of the portage. The eroded, disintegrated plateau descended to the river in a huge confusion of ruin, and they had to pick their way for miles through a labyrinth of cliffs, needles, towers, and bowlders. Reaching the river once more, they found themselves upon a little plain of moderately fertile earth, the first plain and the first earth which they had seen since entering the cañon. The cataract was invisible; a rock cathedral several hundred feet high hid it; they could scarcely discern its lofty ghost of spray.

Two miles away, in the middle of the plain, appeared a ruin of adobe walls, guttered and fissured by the weather. It was undoubtedly a monument of that partially civilized race, Aztec, Toltec, or Moqui, which centuries ago dotted the American desert with cities, and passed away without leaving other record. With his field-glass Thurstane discovered what he judged to be another similar structure crowning a distant butte. They had no time to visit these remains, and they resumed their voyage.

After skirting the plain for several miles, they reëntered the cañon, drifted two hours or more between its solemn walls, and then came out upon a wide sweep of open country. The great cañon of the San Juan had been traversed nearly from end to end in safety. When the adventurers realized their triumph they rose to their feet and gave nine hurrahs.

"It's loike a rich man comin' through the oye av a needle," observed Sweeny.

"Only this haint much the air 'f the New Jerusalem," returned Glover, glancing at the arid waste of buttes and ranges in the distance.

"We oughter look up some huntin'," he continued. "Locker 'll begin to show bottom b'fore long. Sweeny, wouldn't you like to kill suthin?"

"I'd like to kill a pig," said Sweeny.

"Wal, guess we'll probably come acrost one. They's a kind of pigs in these deestricks putty nigh's long 's this boat."

"There ain't," returned Sweeny.

"Call 'em grizzlies when they call 'em at all," pursued the sly Glover.

"They may call 'em what they plaze if they won't call 'em as long as this boat."

Fortune so managed things, by way of carrying out Glover's joke, that a huge grizzly just then showed himself on the bank, some two hundred yards below the boat.

After easily slaughtering one bear, the travellers had a far more interesting season with another, who was allured to the scene by the smell of jerking meat, and who gave them a very lively half hour of it, it being hard to say which was the most hunted, the bruin or the humans.

"Look a' that now!" groaned Sweeny, when the victory had been secured. "The baste has chawed up me gun barrl loike it was a plug o' tobacky."

"Throw it away," ordered Thurstane, after inspecting the twisted and lacerated musket.

Tenderly and tearfully Sweeny laid aside the first gun that he had ever carried, went again and again to look at its mangled form as if it were a dead relative, and in the end raised a little mausoleum of cobble-stones over it.

"If there was any whiskey, I'd give um a wake," he sighed. "I'm a pratty soldier now, without a gun to me back."

"I'll let ye carry mine when we come to foot it," suggested Glover.

"Yis, an' ye may carry me part av the boat," retorted Sweeny.

The bear meat was tough and musky, but it could be eaten, must be eaten, and was eaten. During the time required for jerking a quantity of it, Glover made a boat out of the two hides, scraping them with a hunting knife, sewing them with a sailor's needle and strands of the sounding-line, and stretching them on a frame of green saplings, the result being a craft six feet long by nearly four broad, and about the shape of a half walnut-shell. The long hair was left on, as a protection against the rocks of the river, and the seams were filled and plastered with bear's grease.

"It's a mighty bad-smellin' thing," remarked Sweeny. "An who's goin' to back it over the portages?"

"Robinson Crusoe!" exclaimed Glover. "I never thought of that. Wal, let's see. Oh, we kin tow her astarn in plain sailin', 'n' when we come to a cataract we can put Sweeny in an' let her slide."

"No ye can't," said Sweeny. "It's big enough, an' yet it won't howld um, no more'n a tayspoon 'll howld a flay."

"Wal, we kin let her slide without a crew, 'n' pick her up arterwards," decided Glover.

We must hasten over the minor events of this remarkable journey. The travellers, towing the bearskin boat behind the Buchanan, passed the mouth of Cañon Bonito, and soon afterward beheld the San Juan swallowed up in the Grand River, a far larger stream which rises in the Rocky Mountains east of Utah. They swept by the horrible country of the Utes and Payoches, without holding intercourse with its squalid and savage inhabitants. Here and there, at the foot of some monstrous precipice, in a profound recess surrounded by a frenzy of rocks, they saw hamlets of a few miserable wigwams, with patches of starveling corn and beans. Sharp wild cries, like the calls of malicious brownies, or the shrieks of condemned spirits, were sent after them, without obtaining response.

"They bees only naygurs," observed Sweeny. "Niver moind their blaggard ways."

After the confluence with the Grand River came solitude. The land had been swept and garnished: swept by the waters and garnished with horrors; a land of cañons, plateaux, and ranges, all arid; a land of desolation and the shadow of death. There was nothing on which man or beast could support life; nature's power of renovation was for the time suspended, and seemed extinct. It was a desert which nothing could restore to fruitfulness except the slow mysterious forces of a geologic revolution.

Beyond the Sierra de Lanterna the Grand River was joined by the Green River, streaming down through gullied plateaux from the deserts of Utah and the mountains which tower between Oregon and Nebraska. Henceforward, still locked in Titanic defiles or flanked by Cyclopean *débris*, they were on the Colorado of the West.

Thurstane meditated as to what course he should follow. Should he strike southward by land for the Bernalillo trail, risking a march through a wide, rocky, lifeless, and perhaps waterless wilderness? Or should he attempt to descend a river even more terrible to navigate than the San Juan? It seemed to him that the hardships and dangers of either plan were about the same.

But the Colorado route would be the swiftest; the Colorado would take him quickest to Clara. For he trusted that she had long before this got back to the Moqui country and resumed her journey across the continent. He could not really fear that any deadly harm would befall her. He had the firmness of a soldier and the faith of a lover.

At last, silently and solemnly, through a portal thousands of feet in height, the voyagers glided into the perilous mystery of the Great Cañon of the Colorado, the most sublime and terrible waterway of this planet.

CHAPTER XXVIII.

THURSTANE had strange emotions as he swept into the "caverns measureless to man" of the Great Cañon of the Colorado.

It seemed like a push of destiny rather than a step of volition. An angel or a demon impelled him into the unknown; a supernatural portal had opened to give him passage; then it had closed behind him forever.

The cañon, with all its two hundred and forty miles of marvels and perils, presented itself to his imagination as a unity. The first step within it placed him under an enchantment from which there was no escape until the whole circuit of the spell should be completed. He was like Orlando in the magic garden, when the gate vanished immediately upon his entrance, leaving him no choice but to press on from trial to trial. He was no more free to pause or turn back than Grecian ghosts sailing down Acheron toward the throne of Radamanthus.

Direct statement, and even the higher speech of simile, fail to describe the Great Cañon and the emotion which it produces. Were its fronting precipices organs, with their mountainous columns and pilasters for organ-pipes, they might produce a *de profundis* worthy of the scene and of its sentiments, its inspiration. This is not bombast; so far from exaggerating it does not even attain to the subject; no words can so much as outline the effects of eighty leagues of mountain sculptured by a great river.

Let us venture one comparison. Imagine a groove a foot broad and twenty feet deep, with a runnel of water trickling at the bottom of it and a fleck of dust floating down the rivulet. Now increase the dimensions until the groove is two hundred and fifty feet in breadth by five thousand feet in depth, and the speck a boat with three voyagers. You have the Great Cañon of the Colorado and Thurstane and his comrades seeking its issue.

"Do you call this a counthry?" asked Sweeny, after an awe-stricken silence. "I'm thinkin' we're gittin' outside av the worrld like."

"An' I'm thinkin' we're gittin' too fur inside on't," muttered Glover. "Look's 's though we might slip clean under afore long. Most low-spirited hole I ever rolled into. 'Minds me 'f that last ditch people talk of dyin' in. Must say I'd rather be in the trough 'f the sea."

"An' what kind av a trough is that?" inquired Sweeny, inquisitive even in his dumps.

"It's the trough where they feed the niggers out to the sharks."

"Faix, an' I'd loike to see it at feedin' time," answered Sweeny with a feeble chuckle.

Nature as it is is one image; nature as it appears is a thousand; or rather it is infinite. Every soul is a mirror, reflecting what faces it; but the reflections differ as do the souls that give them. To the three men who now gazed on the Great Cañon it was far from being the same object.

Sweeny surveyed it as an old Greek or Roman might, with simple distaste and horror. Glover, ignorant and limited as he was, received far more of its inspiration. Even while "chirking up" his companions with trivial talk and jests he was in his secret soul thinking of Bunyan's Dark Valley and Milton's Hell, the two sublimest landscapes that had ever been presented to his imagination. Thurstane, gifted with much of the sympathy of the great Teutonic race for nature, was far more profoundly affected. The overshadowing altitudes and majesties of the chasm moved him as might oratorios or other solemn music. Frequently he forgot hardships, dangers, isolation, the hard luck of the past, the ugly prospects of the future in reveries which were a succession of such emotions as wonder, worship, and love.

No doubt the scenery had the more power over him because, by gazing at it day after day while his heart was full of Clara, he got into a way of animating it with her. Far away as she was, and divided from him perhaps forever, she haunted the cañon, transformed it and gave it grace. He could see her face everywhere; he could see it even without shutting his eyes; it made the arrogant and malignant cliffs seraphic. By the way, the vividness of his memory with regard to that fair, sweet, girlish countenance was wonderful, only that such a memory, the memory of the heart, is common. There was not one of her expressions which was not his property. Each and all, he could call them up at will, making them pass before him in heavenly procession, surrounding himself with angels. It was the power of the ring which is given to the slaves of lcve.

He had some vagaries (the vagaries of those who are subjugated by a strong and permanent emotion) which approached insanity. For instance, he selected a gigantic column of sandstone as bearing some resemblance to Clara, and sc identified it with her that presently he could see her face crowning it, though concealed by the similitude of a rocky veil. This image took such possession of him that he watched it with fascination, and when a monstrous cliff slid between it and him he felt as if here were a new parting; as if he were once more bidding her a speechless, hopeless farewell.

During the greater part of this voyage he was a very uninteresting companion. He sat quiet and sllent; sometimes he slightly moved his lips; he was whispering a name. Glover and Sweeny, who had only known him for a month, and supposed that he had always been what they saw him, considered him an eccentric.

"Naterally not quite himself," judged the skipper. "Some folks is born knocked on the head."

"May be officers is always that a way," was one of Sweeny's suggestions. "It must be mighty dull bein' an officer."

We must not forget the Great Cañon. The voyagers were amid magnitudes and sublimities of nature which oppressed as if they were powers and principalities of supernature. They were borne through an architecture of aqueous and plutonic agencies whose smallest fantasies would be belittled by comparisons with coliseums, labyrinths, cathedrals, pryamids, and stonehenges.

For example, they circled a bend of which the extreme delicate angle was a jutting pilaster five hundred feet broad and a mile high, its head towering in a sharp tiara far above the brow of the plateau, and its sides curved into extravagances of dizzy horror. It seemed as if it might be a pillar of confinement and punishment for some Afreet who had defied Heaven. On either side of this monster fissures a thousand feet deep wrinkled the forehead of the precipice. Armies might have been buried in their abysses; yet they scarcely deformed the line of the summits. They ran back for many miles; they had once been the channels of streams which helped to drain the plateau; yet they were merely superficial cracks in the huge mass of sandstone and limestone; they were scarcely noticeable features of the Titanic landscape.

From this bend forward the beauty of the cañon was sublime, horrible, satanic. Constantly varying, its transformations were like those of the chief among demons, in that they were always indescribably magnificent and always indescribably terrible. Now it was a straight, clean chasm between even hedges of cliff which left open only a narrow line of the beauty and mercy of the heavens. Again, where it was entered by minor cañons, it became a breach through crowded pandemoniums of ruined architectures and forsaken, frowning imageries. Then it led between enormous pilasters, columns, and caryatides, mitred with conical peaks which had once been ranges of mountains. Juttings and elevations, which would have been monstrous in other landscapes, were here but minor decorations.

Something like half of the strata with which earth is sheathed has been cut through by the Colorado, beginning at the top of the groove with hundreds of feet of limestone, and closing at the bottom with a thousand feet of granite. Here, too, as in many other wonder-spots of the American desert, nature's sculpture is rivalled by her painting. Bluish-gray limestone, containing corals; mottled limestone, charged with slates, flint, and chalcedony; red, brown, and blue limestone, mixed with red, green, and yellow shales; sandstone of all tints, white, brown, ochry, dark red, speckled and foliated; coarse silicious sandstone, and red quartzose sandstone beautifully veined with purple; layers of conglomerate, of many colored shales, argillaceous iron, and black oxide manganese; massive black and white granite, traversed by streaks of quartz and of red sienite; coarse red felspathic granite, mixed with large plates of silver mica; such is the masonry and such the frescoing.

Through this marvellous museum our three spectators wandered in hourly peril of death. The Afreets of the waters and the Afreets of the rocks, guarding the gateway which they had jointly builded, waged incessant warfare with the intruders. Although the current ran five miles an hour, it was a lucky day when the boat made forty miles. Every evening the travellers must find a beach or shelf where they could haul up for the night. Darkness covered destruction, and light exposed dangers. The bubble-like nature of the boat afforded at once a possibility of easy advance and of instantaneous foundering. Every hour that it floated was a miracle, and so they grimly and patiently understood it.

A few days in the cañon changed the countenances of these men. They looked like veterans of many battles. There was no bravado in their faces. The expression which lived there was a resigned, suffering, stubborn courage. It was the "silent berserker rage" which Carlyle praises. It was the speechless endurance which you see in portraits of the Great Frederick, Wellington, and Grant.

They relieved each other. The bow was guard duty; the steering was light duty; the midships off duty. It must be understood that, the great danger being sunken rocks, one man always crouched in the bow, with a paddle plunged below the surface, feeling for ambushes of the stony bushwhackers. Occasionally all three had to labor, jumping into shallows, lifting the boat over beds of pebbles, perhaps lightening it of arms and provisions, perhaps carrying all ashore to seek a portage.

"It's the best canew 'n' the wust canew I ever see for sech a voyage," observed Clover. "Navigatin' in it puts me in mind 'f angels settin' on a cloud. The cloud can go anywhere; but what if ye should slump through?"

"Och! ye're a heretic, 'n' don't belave angels can fly," put in Sweeny.

"Can't ye talk without takin' out yer paddle?" called Glover. "Mind yer soundings."

Glover was at the helm just then, while Sweeny was at the bow. Thurstane, sitting cross-legged on the light wooden flooring of the boat, was entering topographical observations in his journal. Hearing the skipper's warning, he looked up sharply; but both the call and the glance came too late to prevent a catastrophe. Just in that instant the boat caught against some obstacle, turned slowly around before the push of the current, swung loose with a jerk and floated on, the water bubbling through the flooring. A hole had been torn in the canvas, and the cockle-shell was foundering.

"Sound!" shouted Thurstane to Sweeny; then, turning to Glover, "Haul up the Grizzly!"

The tub-boat of bearskin was dragged alongside, and Thurstane instantly threw the provisions and arms into it.

"Three foot," squealed Sweeny.

"Jump overboard," ordered the lieutenant.

By the time they were on their feet in the water the Buchanan was half full, and the swift current was pulling at it like a giant, while the Grizzly, floating deep, was almost equally unmanageable. The situation had in one minute changed from tranquil voyaging to deadly peril. Sweeny, unable to swim, and staggering in the rapid, made a plunge at the bearskin boat, probably with an idea of getting into it. But Thurstane, all himself from the first, shouted in that brazen voice of military command which is so secure of obedience, "Steady, man! Don't climb in. Cut the lariat close up to the Buchanan, and then hold on to the Grizzly."

Restored to his self-possession, Sweeny laboriously wound the straining lariat around his left arm and sawed it in two with his jagged pocket-knife. Then came a doubtful fight between him and the Colorado for the possession of the heavy and clumsy tub.

Meantime Thurstane and Glover, the former at the bow and the latter at the stern of the Buchanan, were engaged in a similar tussle, just barely holding on and no more.

"We can't stand this," said the officer. "We must empty her."

"Jest so," panted Glover. "You're up stream. Can you raise your eend? We mustn't capsize her; we might lose the flooring."

Thurstane stooped slowly and cautiously until he had got his shoulder under the bow.

"Easy!" called Glover. "Awful easy! Don't break her back. Don't upset *me*."

Gently, deliberately, with the utmost care, Thurstane straightened himself until he had lifted the bow of the boat clear of the current.

"Now I'll hoist," said the skipper. "You turn her slowly—jest the least mite. Don't capsize her."

It was a Herculean struggle. There was still a ponderous weight of water in the boat. The slight frame sagged and the flexible siding bulged. Glover with difficulty kept his feet, and he could only lift the stern very slightly.

"You can't do it," decided Thurstane. "Don't wear yourself out trying it. Hold steady where you are, while I let down."

When the boat was restored to its level it floated higher than before, for some of the water had drained out.

"Now lift slowly," directed Thurstane. "Slow and sure. She'll clear little by little."

A quiet, steady lift, lasting perhaps two or three minutes, brought the floor of the boat to the surface of the current.

"It's wearing," said the lieutenant, cheering his worried fellow-laborer with a smile. "Stand steady for a minute and try to rest. You, Sweeny, move in toward the bank. Hold on to your boat like the devil. If the water deepens, sing out."

Sweeny, gripping his lariat desperately, commenced a staggering march over the cobble-stone bottom, his anxious nose pointed toward a beach of bowlders beneath the southern precipice.

"Now then," said Thurstane to Glover, "we must get her on our heads and follow Sweeny. Are you ready? Up with her!"

A long, reeling hoist set the Buchanan on the heads of the two men, one standing under the bow and one under the stern, their arms extended and their hands clutching the sides. The beach was forty yards away; the current was swift and as opaque as chocolate; they could not see what depths might gape before them; but they must do the distance without falling, or perish.

"Left foot first," shouted the officer. "Forward—march!"

CHAPTER XXIX.

When the adventurers commenced their tottering march toward the shore of the Colorado, Sweeny, dragging the clumsy bearskin boat, was a few yards in advance of Thurstane and Glover, bearing the canvas boat.

Every one of the three had as much as he could handle. The Grizzly, pulled at by the furious current, bobbed up and down and hither and thither, nearly capsizing Sweeny at every other step. The Buchanan, weighing one hundred and fifty pounds when dry, and now somewhat heavier because of its thorough wetting, made a heavy load for two men who were hip deep in swift water.

"Slow and sure," repeated Thurstane. "It's a five minutes job. Keep your courage and your feet for five minutes. Then we'll live a hundred years."

"Liftinant, is this soldierin'?" squealed Sweeny.

"Yes, my man, this is soldiering."

"Thin I'll do me dooty if I pull me arrms off."

But there was not much talking. Pretty nearly all their breath was needed for the fight with the river. Glover, a slender and narrow-shouldered creature, was particularly distressed; and his only remark during the pilgrimage shoreward was, "I'd like to change hosses."

Sweeny, leading the way, got up to his waist once and yelled, "I'll drown."

Then he backed a little, took a new direction, found shallower water, and tottled onward to victory. The moment he reached the shore he gave a shrill hoot of exultation, went at his bearskin craft with both hands, dragged it clean out of the water, and gave it a couple of furious kicks.

"Take that!" he yelped. "Ye're wickeder nor both yer fathers. But I've bate ye. Oh, ye blatherin', jerkin', bogglin' baste, ye!"

Then he splashed into the river, joined his hard-pressed comrades, got his head under the centre of the Buchanan, and lifted sturdily. In another minute the precious burden was safe on a large flat rock, and the three men were stretched out panting beside it. Glover was used up; he was trembling from head to foot with fatigue; he had reached shore just in time to fall on it instead of into the river.

"Ye'd make a purty soldier," scoffed Sweeny, a habitual chaffer, like most Irishmen.

"It was the histin' that busted me," gasped the skipper. "I can't handle a ton o' water."

"Godamighty made ye already busted, I'm a thinkin'," retorted Sweeny.

As soon as Glover could rise he examined the Buchanan. There was a ragged rent in the bottom four inches long, and the canvas in other places had been badly rubbed. The voyagers looked at the hole, looked at the horrible chasm which locked them in, and thought with a sudden despair of the great environment of desert.

The situation could hardly be more gloomy. Having voyaged for five days in the Great Cañon, they were entangled in the very centre of the folds of that monstrous anaconda. Their footing was a lap of level not more than thirty yards in length by ten in breadth, strewn with pebbles and bowlders, and showing not one spire of vegetation. Above them rose a precipice, the summit of which they could not see, but which was undoubtedly a mile in height. Had there been armies or cities over their heads, they could not have discovered it by either eye or ear.

At their feet was the Colorado, a broad rush of liquid porphyry, swift and pitiless. By its color and its air of stoical cruelty it put one in mind of the red race of America, from whose desert mountains it came and through whose wildernesses it hurried. On the other side of this grim current rose precipices five thousand feet high, stretching to right and left as far as the eye could pierce. Certainly never before did shipwrecked men gaze upon such imprisoning immensity and inhospitable sterility.

Directly opposite them was horrible magnificence. The face of the fronting rampart was gashed a mile deep by the gorge of a subsidiary cañon. The fissure was not a clean one, with even sides. The strata had been torn, ground, and tattered by the river, which had first raged over them and then through them. It was a Petra of ruins, painted with all stony colors, and sculptured into a million outlines. On one of the boldest abutments of the ravine perched an enchanted castle with towers and spires hundreds of feet in height. Opposite, but further up the gap, rose a rounded mountain-head of solid sandstone and limestone. Still higher and more retired, towering as if to look into the distant cañon of the Colorado, ran the enormous terrace of one of the loftier plateaus, its broad, bald forehead wrinkled with furrows that had once held cataracts. But language has no charm which can master these sublimities and horrors. It stammers; it repeats the same words over and over; it can only *begin* to tell the monstrous truth.

"Looks like we was in our grave," sighed Glover.

"Liftinant," jerked out Sweeny, "I'm thinkin' we're dead. We ain't livin', Liftinant. We've been buried. We've no business trying to *walk*."

Thurstane had the same sense of profound depression; but he called up his courage and sought to cheer his comrades.

"We must do our best to come to life," he said. "Mr. Glover, can nothing be done with the boat?"

"Can't fix it," replied the skipper, fingering the ragged hole. "Nothin' to patch it with."

"There are the bearskins," suggested Thurstane.

Glover slapped his thigh, got up, danced a double-shuffle, and sat down again to consider his job. After a full minute Sweeny caught the idea also and set up a haw-haw of exultant laughter, which brought back echoes from the other side of the cañon, as if a thousand Paddies were holding revel there.

"Oh! yees may laugh," retorted Sweeny, "but yees can't laugh us out av it."

"I'll sheath the whole-bottom with bearskin," said Glover. "Then we can let her grind. It'll be an all day's chore, Capm—perhaps two days."

They passed thirty-six hours in this miserable bivouac. Glover worked during every moment of daylight. No one else could do anything. A green hand might break a needle, and a needle broken was a step toward death. From dawn to dusk he planned, cut, punctured, and sewed with the patience of an old sailor, until he had covered the rent with a patch of bearskin which fitted as if it had grown there. Finally the whole bottom was doubled with hide, the long, coarse fur still on it, and the grain running from stem to stern so as to aid in sliding over the sand and pebbles of the shallows.

While Glover worked the others slept, lounged, cooked, waited. There was no food, by the way, but the hard, leathery, tasteless jerked meat of the grizzly bears, which had begun to pall upon them so they could hardly swallow it. Eating was merely a duty, and a disagreeable one.

When Glover announced that the boat was ready for launching, Sweeny uttered a yelp of joy, like a dog who sees a prospect of hunting.

"Ah, you paddywhack!" growled the skipper. "All this work for you. Punch another hole, 'n' I'll take yer own hide to patch it."

"I'll give ye lave," returned Sweeny. "Wan bare skin 's good as another. Only I might want me own back agin for dress-parade."

Once more on the Colorado. Although the boat floated deeper than before, navigation in it was undoubtedly safer, so that they made bolder ventures and swifter progress. Such portages, however, as they were still obliged to traverse, were very severe, inasmuch as the Buchanan was now much above its original weight. Several times they had to carry one half of their materials for a mile or more, through a labyrinth of rocks, and then trudge back to get the other half.

Meantime their power of endurance was diminishing. The frequent wettings, the shivering nights, the great changes of temperature, the stale and wretched food, the constant anxiety, were sapping their health and strength. On the tenth day of their wanderings in the Great Cañon Glover began to complain of rheumatism.

"These cussed draughts!" he groaned. "It's jest like travellin' in a bellows nozzle."

"Wid the divil himself at the bellys," added Sweeny. "Faix, an' I wish he'd blow us clane out intirely. I'm gittin' tired o' this same, I am. I didn't lisht to sarve undher ground."

"Patience, Sweeny," smiled Thurstane. "We must be nearly through the cañon."

"An' where will we come out, Liftinant? Is it in Ameriky? Bedad, we ought to be close to the Chaynees by this time. Liftinant, what sort o' paple lives up atop of us, annyway?"

"I don't suppose anybody lives up there," replied the officer, raising his eyes to the dizzy precipices above. "This whole region is said to be a desert."

"Be gorry, an' it 'll stay a desert till the ind o' the worrld afore I'll poppylate it. It wasn't made for Sweenys. I haven't seen sile enough in tin days to raise wan pataty. As for livin' on dried grizzly, I'd like betther for the grizzlies to live on me. Liftinant, I niver see sich harrd atin'. It tires the top av me head off to chew it."

About noon of the twelfth day in the Great Cañon this perilous and sublime navigation came to a close. The walls of the chasm suddenly spread out into a considerable opening, which absolutely seemed level ground to the voyagers, although it was encumbered with mounds or buttes of granite and sandstone. This opening was produced by the entrance into the main channel of a subsidiary one, coming from the south. At first they did not observe further particulars, for they were in extreme danger of shipwreck, the river being studded with rocks and running like a mill-race. But on reaching the quieter water below the rapid, they saw that the branch cañon contained a rivulet, and that where the two streams united there was a triangular basin, offering a safe harbor.

"Paddle!" shouted Thurstane, pointing to the creek. "Don't let her go by. This is our place."

A desperate struggle dragged the boat out of the rushing Colorado into the tranquillity of the basin. Everything was landed; the boat itself was hoisted on to the rocks; the voyage was over.

"Think ye know yer way, Capm?" queried Glover, squinting doubtfully up the arid recesses of the smaller cañon.

"Of course I may be mistaken. But even if it is not Diamond Creek, it will take us in our direction. We have made westing enough to have the Cactus Pass very nearly south of us."

As there was still a chance of returning to the river, the boat was taken to pieces, rolled up, and hidden under a pile of stones and driftwood. The small remnant of jerked meat was divided into three portions. Glover, on account of his inferior muscle and his rheumatism, was relieved of his gun, which was given to Sweeny. Canteens were filled, blankets slung, ammunition belts buckled, and the march commenced.

Arrived at a rocky knoll which looked up both waterways, the three men halted to take a last glance at the Great Cañon, the scene of a pilgrimage that had been a poem, though a terrible one. The Colorado here was not more than fifty yards wide, and only a few hundred yards of its course were visible either way, for the confluence was at the apex of a bend. The dark, sullen, hopeless, cruel current rushed out of one mountain-built mystery into another. The walls of the abyss rose straight from the water into dizzy abutments, conical peaks, and rounded masses, beyond and above which gleamed the distant sunlit walls of a higher terrace of the plateau.

"Come along wid ye," said Sweeny to Glover, "It's enough to give ye the rheumatiz in the oyes to luk at the nasty black hole. I'm thinkin' it's the divil's own place, wid the fires out."

The Diamond Creek Cañon, although far inferior to its giant neighbor, was nevertheless a wonderful excavation, striking audaciously into sombre mountain recesses, sublime with precipices, peaks, and grotesque masses. The footing was of the ruggedest, a *débris* of confused and eroded rocks, the pathway of an extinct river. One thing was beautiful: the creek was a perfect contrast to the turbid Colorado; its waters were as clear and bright as crystal. Sweeny halted over and over to look at it, his mouth open and eyes twinkling like a pleased dog.

"An' there's nothing nagurish about that, now," he chuckled. "A pataty ud laugh to be biled in it."

After slowly ascending for a quarter of a mile, they turned a bend and came upon a scene which seemed to them like a garden. They were in a broad opening, made by the confluence of two cañons. Into this gigantic rocky nest had been dropped an oasis of turf and of thickets of green willows. Through the centre of the verdure the Diamond Creek flowed dimpling over a pebbly bed, or shot in sparkles between barring bowlders, or plunged over shelves in toy cascades. The travellers had seen nothing so hospitable in nature since leaving the country of the Moquis weeks before.

Sweeny screamed like a delighted child. "Oh! an' that's just like ould Oirland. Oh, luk at the turrf! D'ye iver see the loikes o' that, now? The blessed turrf! Here ye be, right in the divil's own garden. Liftinant, if ye'll let me build a fort here, I'll garrison it. I'll stay here me whole term of sarvice."

"Halt," said Thurstane. "We'll eat, refill canteens, and inspect arms. If this is Diamond Cañon, and I think there is no doubt of it, we may expect to find Indians soon."

"I'll fight 'em," declared Sweeny. "An' if they've got anythin' betther nor dried grizzly, I'll have it."

"Wait for orders," cautioned Thurstane. "No firing without orders."

After cleaning their guns and chewing their tough and stale rations, they resumed their march, leaving the rivulet and following the cañon, which led toward the southwest.. As they were now regaining the level of the plateau, their advance was a constant and difficult ascent, sometimes struggling through labyrinths of detached rocks, and sometimes climbing steep shelves which had once been the leaping-places of cataracts. The sides of the chasm were two thousand feet high, and it was entered by branch ravines of equal grandeur.

The sun had set for them, although he was still high above the horizon of upper earth, when Thurstane halted and whispered, "Wigwams!"

Perched among the rocks, some under projecting strata and others in shadowy niches between huge buttresses, they discovered at first three or four, then a dozen, and finally twenty wretched cabins. They scarcely saw before they were seen; a hideous old squaw dropped a bundle of fuel and ran off screeching; in a moment the whole den was in an uproar. Startling yells burst from lofty nooks in the mountain flanks, and scarecrow figures dodged from ambush to ambush of the sombre gully. It was as if they had invaded the haunts of the brownies.

The Hualpais, a species of Digger Indians, dwarfish, miserable, and degraded, living mostly on roots, lizards, and the like, were nevertheless conscious of scalps to save. In five minutes from the discovery of the strangers they had formed a straggling line of battle, squatting along a ledge which crossed the cañon. There were not twenty warriors, and they were no doubt wretchedly armed, but their position was formidable.

Sweeny, looking like an angry rat, his nose twitching and eyes sparkling with rage, offered to storm the rampart alone, shouting, "Oh, the nasty, lousy nagurs! Let 'em get out of our way."

"Guess we'd better talk to the cusses," observed Glover. "Tain't the handiest place I ever see for fightin'; an' I don't keer 'bout havin' my ears 'n' nose bored any more at present."

"Stay where you are," said Thurstane. "I'll go forward and parley with them."

CHAPTER XXX.

THURSTANE had no great difficulty in making a sort of let-me-alone-and-I'll-let-you-alone treaty with the embattled Hualpais.

After some minutes of dumb show they came down from their stronghold and dispersed to their dwellings. They seemed to be utterly without curiosity; the warriors put aside their bows and lay down to sleep; the old squaw hurried off to pick up her bundle of fuel; even the papooses were silent and stupid. It was a race lower than the Hottentots or the Australians. Short, meagre, badly built, excessively ugly, they were nearly naked, and their slight clothing was rags of skins. Thurstane tried to buy food of them, but either they had none to spare or his buttons seemed to them of no value. Nor could he induce any one to accompany him as a guide.

"Do ye think Godamighty made thim paple?" inquired Sweeny.

"Reckon so," replied Glover.

"I don't belave it," said Sweeny. "He'd be in more rispactable bizniss. It's me opinyin the divil made um for a joke on the rest av us. An' it's me opinyin he made this whole counthry for the same rayson."

"The priest 'll tell ye God made all men, Sweeny."

"They ain't min at all. Thim crachurs ain't min. They're nagurs, an' a mighty poor kind at that. I hate um. I wish they was all dead. I've kilt some av um, an' I'm goin' to kill slathers more, God willin'. I belave it's part av the bizniss av white min to finish off the nagurs."

Profound and potent sentiment of race antipathy! The contempt and hatred of white men for yellow, red, brown, and black men has worked all over earth, is working yet, and will work for ages. It is a motive of that tremendous tragedy which Spencer has entitled "the survival of the fittest," and Darwin, "natural selection."

The party continued to ascend the cañon. At short intervals branch cañons exhibited arid and precipitous gorges, more and more gloomy with twilight. It was impossible to choose between one and another. The travellers could never see three hundred yards in advance. To right and left they were hemmed in by walls fifteen hundred feet in height. Only one thing was certain: these altitudes were gradually diminishing; and hence they knew that they were mounting the plateau. At last, four hours after leaving Diamond Creek, wearied to the marrow with incessant toil, they halted by a little spring, stretched themselves on a scrap of starveling grass, and chewed their meagre, musty supper.

The scenery here was unearthly. Barring the bit of turf and a few willows which had got lost in the desert, there was not a tint of verdure. To right and left rose two huge and steep slopes of eroded and ragged rocks, tortured into every conceivable form of jag, spire, pinnacle, and imagery. In general the figures were grotesque; it seemed as if the misshapen gods of India and of China and of barbarous lands had gathered there; as if this were a place of banishment and punishment for the fallen idols of all idolatries. Above this coliseum of monstrosities rose a long line of sharp, jagged needles, like a vast *chevaux-de-frise*, forbidding escape. Still higher, lighted even yet by the setting sun, towered five cones of vast proportions. Then came cliffs capped by shatters of tableland, and then the long, even, gleaming ledge of the final plateau.

Locked in this bedlam of crazed strata, unable to see or guess a way out of it, the wanderers fell asleep. There was no setting of guards; they trusted to the desert as a sentinel.

At daylight the blind and wearisome climbing recommenced. Occasionally they found patches of thin turf and clumps of dwarf cedars struggling with the rocky waste. These bits of greenery were not the harbingers of a new empire of vegetation, but the remnants of one whose glory had vanished ages ago, swept away by a vandalism of waters. Gradually the cañon dwindled to a ravine, narrow, sinuous, walled in by stony steeps or slopes, and interlocking continually with other similar chasms. A creek, which followed the chasm, appeared and disappeared at intervals of a mile or so, as if horrified at the face of nature and anxious to hide from it in subterranean recesses.

The travellers stumbled on until the ravine became a gully and the gully a fissure. They stepped out of it; they were on the rolling surface of the tableland; they were half a mile above the Colorado.

Here they halted, gave three cheers, and then looked back upon the northern desert as men look who have escaped an enemy. A gigantic panorama of the country which they had traversed was unrolled to their vision. In the foreground stretched declining tablelands, intersected by numberless ravines, and beyond these a lofty line of bluffs marked the edge of the Great Cañon of the Colorado. Through one wide gap in these heights came a vision of endless plateaux, their terraces towering one above another until they were thousands of feet in the air, the horizontal azure bands extending hundreds of miles northward, until the deep blue faded into a lighter blue, and that into the sapphire of the heavens.

"It looks a darned sight finer than it is," observed Glover.

"Bedad, ye may say that," added Sweeny. "It's a big hippycrit av a counthry. Ye'd think, to luk at it, ye could ate it wid a spoon."

Now came a rolling region, covered with blue grass and dotted with groves of cedars, the earth generally hard and smooth and the marching easy. Striking southward, they reached a point where the plateau culminated in a low ridge, and saw before them a long gentle slope of ten miles, then a system of rounded hills, and then mountains.

"Halt here," said Thurstane. "We must study our topography and fix on our line of march."

"You'll hev to figger it," replied Glover. "I don't know nothin' in this part o' the world."

"Ye ain't called on to know," put in Sweeny. "The liftinant 'll tell ye."

"I think," hesitated Thurstane, "that we are about fifty miles north of Cactus Pass, where we want to strike the trail."

"And I'm putty nigh played out," groaned Glover.

"Och! *you* howld up yer crazy head," exhorted Sweeny. "It 'll do ye iver so much good."

"It's easy talkin'," sighed the jaded and rheumatic skipper.

"It's as aisy talkin' right as talkin' wrong," retorted Sweeny. "Ye've no call to grunt the curritch out av yer betthers. Wait till the liftinant says die."

Thurstane was studying the landscape. Which of those ranges was the Cerbat, which the Aztec, and which the Pinaleva? He knew that, after leaving Cactus Pass, the overland trail turns southward and runs toward the mouth of the Gila, crossing the Colorado hundreds of miles away. To the west of the pass, therefore, he must not strike, under peril of starving amid untracked plains and ranges. On the whole, it seemed probable that the snow-capped line of summits directly ahead of him was the Cerbat range, and that he must follow it southward along the base of its eastern slope.

"We will move on," he said. "Mr. Glover, we must reach those broken hills before night in order to find water. Can you do it?"

"Reckon I kin jest about do it, 's the feller said when he walked to his own hangin'," returned the suffering skipper.

The failing man marched so slowly and needed so many halts that they were five hours in reaching the hills. It was now nightfall; they found a bright little spring in a grassy ravine; and after a meagre supper, they tried to stifle their hunger with sleep. Thurstane and Sweeny took turns in watching, for smoke of fires had been seen on the mountains, and, poor as they were, they could not afford to be robbed. In the morning Glover seemed refreshed, and started out with some vigor.

"Och! ye'll go round the worrld," said Sweeny, encouragingly. "Bones can march furder than fat anny day. Yer as tough as me rations. Dried grizzly is nothin' to ye."

After threading hills for hours they came out upon a wide, rolling basin, prettily diversified by low spurs of the encircling mountains and bluish green with the long grasses known as *pin* and *grama*. A few deer and antelopes, bounding across the rockier places, were an aggravation to starving men who could not follow them.

"Why don't we catch some o' thim flyin' crachurs?" demanded Sweeny.

"We hain't got no salt to put on their tails," explained Glover, grinning more with pain than with his joke.

"I'd ate 'em widout salt," said Sweeny. "If the tails was feathers, I'd ate 'em."

"We must camp early, and try our luck at hunting," observed Thurstane.

"I go for campin' airly," groaned the limping and tottering Glover.

"Och! yees ud like to shlape an shnore an' grunt and rowl over an' shnore agin the whole blissid time," snapped Sweeny, always angered by a word of discouragement. "Yees ought to have a dozen o' thim nagurs wid their long poles to make a fither bed for yees an' tuck up the blankets an' spat the pilly. Why didn't ye shlape all ye wanted to whin yees was in the boat?"

"Quietly, Sweeny," remonstrated Thurstane. "Mr. Glover marches with great pain."

"I've no objiction to his marchin' wid great pain or annyway Godamighty lets him, if he won't grunt about it."

"But you must be civil, my man."

"I ax yer pardon, Liftinant. I don't mane no harrum by blatherin'. It's a way we have in th' ould counthry. Mebbe it's no good in th' arrmy."

"Let him yawp, Capm," interposed Glover. "It's a way they hev, as he says. Never see two Paddies together but what they got to fightin' or pokin' fun at each other. Me an' Sweeny won't quarrel. I take his clickatyclack for what it's worth by the cart-load. 'Twon't hurt me. Dunno but what it's good for me."

"Bedad, it's betther for ye nor yer own gruntin'," added the irrepressible Irishman.

By two in the afternoon they had made perhaps fifteen miles, and reached the foot of the mountain which they proposed to skirt. As Glover was now fagged out, Thurstane decided to halt for the night and try deer-stalking. A muddy water-hole, surrounded by thickets of willows, indicated their camping ground. The sick man was *cached* in the dense foliage; his canteen was filled for him and placed by his side; there could be no other nursing.

"If the nagurs kill ye, I'll revenge ye," was Sweeny's parting encouragement. "I'll git ye back yer scallup, if I have to cut it out of um."

Late in the evening the two hunters returned empty. Sweeny, in spite of his hunger and fatigue, boiled over with stories of the hairbreadth escapes of the "antyloops" that he had fired at. Thurstane also had seen game, but not near enough for a shot.

"I didn't look for such bad luck," said the weary and half-starved young fellow, soberly. "No supper for any of us. We must save our last ration to make to-morrow's march on."

"It's a poor way of atin' two males in wan," remarked Sweeny. "I niver thought I'd come to wish I had me haversack full o' dried bear."

The next day was a terrible one. Already half famished, their only food for the twenty-four hours was about four ounces apiece of bear meat, tough, ill-scented, and innutritious. Glover was so weak with hunger and his ailments that he had to be supported most of the way by his two comrades. His temper, and Sweeny's also, gave out, and they snarled at each other in good earnest, as men are apt to do under protracted hardships. Thurstane stalked on in silence, sustained by his youth and health, and not less by his sense of responsibility. These men were here through his doing; he must support them and save them if possible; if not, he must show them how to die bravely; for it had come to be a problem of life and death. They could not expect to travel two days longer without food. The time was approaching when they would fall down with faintness, not to rise again in this world.

In the morning their only provision was one small bit of meat which Thurstane had saved from his ration of the day before. This he handed to Glover, saying with a firm eye and a cheerful smile, "My dear fellow, here is your breakfast."

The starving invalid looked at it wistfully, and stammered, with a voice full of tears, "I can't eat when the rest of ye don't."

Sweeny, who had stared at the morsel with hungry eyes, now broke out, "I tell ye, ate it. The liftinant wants ye to."

"Divide it fair," answered Glover, who could hardly restrain himself from sobbing.

"I won't touch a bit av it," declared Sweeny. "It's the liftinant's own grub."

"We won't divide it," said Thurstane. "I'll put it in your pocket, Glover. When you can't take another step without it, you must go at it."

"Bedad, if ye don't, we'll lave yees," added Sweeny, digging his fists into his empty stomach to relieve its gnawing.

Very slowly, the well men sustaining the sick one, they marched over rolling hills until about noon, accomplishing perhaps ten miles. They were now on a slope looking southward; above them the wind sighed through a large grove of cedars; a little below was a copious spring of clear, sweet water. There they halted, drinking and filling their canteens, but not eating. The square inch of bear meat was still in Glover's pocket, but he could not be got to taste it unless the others would share.

"Capm, I feel 's though Heaven 'd strike me if I should eat your victuals," he whispered, his voice having failed him. "I feel a sort o' superstitious 'bout it. I want to die with a clear conscience."

But when they rose his strength gave out entirely, and he dropped down fainting.

"Now ate yer mate," said Sweeny, in a passion of pity and anxiety. "Ate yer mate an' stand up to yer marchin'."

Glover, however, could not eat, for the fever of hunger had at last produced nausea, and he pushed away the unsavory morsel when it was put to his lips.

"Go ahead," he whispered. "No use all dyin'. Go ahead." And then he fainted outright.

"I think the trail can't be more than fifteen miles off," said Thurstane, when he had found that his comrade still breathed. "One of us must push on to it and the other stay with Glover. Sweeny, I can track the country best. You must stay."

For the first time in this long and suffering and perilous journey Sweeny's courage failed him, and he looked as if he would like to shirk his duty.

"My lad, it is necessary," continued the officer. "We can't leave this man so. You have your gun. You can try to hunt. When he comes to, you must get him along, following the course you see me take. If I find help, I'll save you. If not, I'll come back and die with you."

Sitting down by the side of the insensible Glover, Sweeny covered his face with two grimy hands which trembled a little. It was not till his officer had got some thirty feet away that he raised his head and looked after him. Then he called, in his usual quick, sharp, chattering way, "Liftinant, is this soldierin'?"

"Yes, my lad," replied Thurstane with a sad, weary smile, thinking meantime of hardships past, "this is soldiering."

"Thin I'll do me dooty if I rot jest here," declared the simple hero.

Thurstane came back, grasped Sweeny's hand in silence, turned away to hide his shaken face, and commenced his anxious journey.

There were both terrible and beautiful thoughts in his soul as he pushed on into the desert. Would he find the trail? Would he encounter the rare chance of traders or emigrants? Would there be food and rest for him and rescue for his comrades? Would he meet Clara? This last idea gave him great courage; he struggled to keep it constantly in his mind; he needed to lean upon it.

By the time that he had marched ten miles he found that he was weaker than he had supposed. Weeks of wretched food and three days of almost complete starvation had taken the strength pretty much out of his stalwart frame. His breath was short; he stumbled over the slightest obstacles; occasionally he could not see clear. From time to time it struck him that he had been dreaming or else that his mind was beginning to wander. Things that he remembered and things that he hoped for seemed strangely present. He spoke to people who were hundreds of miles away; and, for the most part, he spoke to them pettishly or with downright anger; for in the main he felt more like a wretched, baited animal than a human being.

It was only when he called Clara to mind that this evil spirit was exorcised, and he ceased for a moment to resemble a hungry, jaded wolf. Then he would be for a while all sweetness, because he was for the while perfectly happy. In the next instant, by some hateful and irresistible magic, happiness and sweetness would be gone, and he could not even remember them nor remember *her*.

Meantime he struggled to command himself and pay attention to his route. He must do this, because his starving comrades lay behind him, and he must know how to lead men back to their rescue. Well, here he was; there were hills to the left; there was a mountain to the right; he would stop and fix it all in his memory.

He sat down beside a rock, leaned his back against it to steady his dizzy head, had a sensation of struggling with something invincible, and was gone.

CHAPTER XXXI.

LEAVING Thurstane in the desert, we return to Clara in the desert. It will be remembered that she stood on the roof of the Casa Grande when her lover was swept oarless down the San Juan.

She was watching him; of course she was watching him; at the moment of the catastrophe she saw him; she felt sure also that he was looking at her. The boat began to fly down the current; then the two oarsmen fell to paddling violently; what did it mean? Far from guessing that the towline had snapped, she was not aware that there was one.

On went the boat; presently it whirled around helplessly; it was nearing the rocks of the rapid; there was evidently danger. Running to the edge of the roof, Clara saw a Mexican cattle-driver standing on the wall of the enclosure, and called to him, "What is the matter?"

"The lariats have broken," he replied. "They are drifting."

Clara uttered a little gasp of a shriek, and then did not seem to breathe again for a minute. She saw Thurstane led away in captivity by the savage torrent; she saw him rise up in the boat and wave her a farewell; she could not lift her hand to respond; she could only stand and stare. She had a look, and there was within her a sensation, as if her soul were starting out of her eyes. The whole calamity revealed itself to her at once and without mercy. There was no saving him and no going after him; he was being taken out of her sight; he was disappearing; he was gone. She leaned forward, trying to look around the bend of the river, and was balked by a monstrous, cruel advance of precipices. Then, when she realized that he had vanished, there was a long scream ending in unconsciousness.

When she came to herself everybody was talking of the calamity. Coronado, Aunt Maria, and others overflowed with babblings of regret, astonishment, explanations, and consolation. The lariats had broken. How could it have happened! How dreadful! etc.

"But he will land," cried Clara, looking eagerly from face to face.

"Oh, certainly," said Coronado. "Landings can be made. There are none visible, but doubtless they exist."

"And then he will march back here?" she demanded.

"Not easily. I am afraid, my dear cousin, not very easily. There would be cañons to turn, and long ones. Probably he would strike for the Moqui country."

"Across the desert? No water!"

Coronado shrugged his shoulders as if to say that he could not help it.

"If we go back to-morrow," she began again, "do you think we shall overtake them?"

"I think it very probable," lied Coronado.

"And if we don't overtake them, will they join us at the Moqui pueblos?"

"Yes, yes. I have little doubt of it."

"When do you think we ought to start?"

"To-morrow morning."

"Won't that be too early?"

"Day after to-morrow then."

"Won't that be too late?"

Coronado nearly boiled over with rage. This girl was going to demand impossibilities of him, and impossibilities that he would not perform if he could. He must be here and he must be there; he must be quick enough and not a minute too quick; and all to save his rival from the pit which he had just dug for him. Turning his back on Clara, he paced the roof of the Casa in an excitement which he could not conceal, muttering, "I will do the best I can—the best I can."

Presently the remembrance that he had at least gained one great triumph enabled him to recover his self-possession and his foxy cunning.

"My dear cousin," he said gently, "you must not suppose that I am not greatly afflicted by this accident. I appreciate the high merit of Lieutenant Thurstane, and I grieve sincerely at his misfortune. What can I do? I will do the best I can for all. Trusting to your good sense, I will do whatever you say. But if you want my advice, here it is. We ought for our own sakes to leave here to-morrow; but for his sake we will wait a day. In that time he may rejoin us, or he may regain the Moqui trail. So we will set out, if you have no objection, on the morning of day after to-morrow, and push for the pueblos. When we do start, we must march, as you know, at our best speed."

"Thank you, Coronado," said Clara. "It is the best you can do."

There were not five minutes during that day and the next that the girl did not look across the plain to the gorge of the dry cañon, in the hope that she might see Thurstane approaching. At other times she gazed eagerly down the San Juan, although she knew that he could not stem the current. Her love and her sorrow were ready to believe in miracles. How is it possible, she often thought, that such a brief sweep of water should carry him so utterly away? In spite of her fear of vexing Coronado, she questioned him over and over as to the course of the stream and the nature of its banks, only to find that he knew next to nothing.

"It will be hard for him to return to us," the man finally suggested, with an air of being driven unwillingly to admit it. "He may have to go on a long way down the river."

The truth is that, not knowing whether the lost men could return easily or not, he was anxious to get away from their neighborhood.

Before the second day of this suspense was over, Aunt Maria had begun to make herself obnoxious. She hinted that Thurstane knew what he was about; that the river was his easiest road to his station; that, in short, he had deserted. Clara flamed up indignantly and replied, "I know him better."

"Why, what has he got to do with us?" reasoned Aunt Maria. "He doesn't belong to our party."

"He has his men here. He wouldn't leave his soldiers."

"His men! They can take care of themselves. If they can't, I should like to know what they are good for. I think it highly probable he went off of his own choice."

"I think it highly probable you know nothing about it," snapped Clara. "You are incapable of judging him."

The girl was not just now herself. Her whole soul was concentrated in justifying, loving, and saving Thurstane; and her manner, instead of being serenely and almost lazily gentle, was unpleasantly excited. It was as if some charming alluvial valley should suddenly give forth the steam and lava of a volcano.

Finding no sympathy in Aunt Maria, and having little confidence in the good-will of Coronado, she looked about her for help. There was Sergeant Meyer; he had been Thurstane's right-hand man; moreover, he looked trustworthy. She seized the first opportunity to beckon him up to her eerie on the roof of the Casa.

"Sergeant, I must speak with you privately," she said at once, with the frankness of necessity.

The sergeant, a well-bred soldier, respectful to ladies, and especially to ladies who were the friends of officers, raised his forefinger to his cap and stood at attention.

"How came Lieutenant Thurstane to go down the river?" she asked.

"It was the lariat proke," replied Meyer, in a whispering, flute-like voice which he had when addressing his superiors.

"Did it break, or was it cut?"

The sergeant raised his small, narrow, and rather piggish gray eyes to hers with a momentary expression of anxiety.

"I must pe gareful what I zay," he answered, sinking his voice still lower. "We must poth pe gareful. I examined the lariat. I fear it was sawed. But we must not zay this."

"Who sawed it?" demanded Clara with a gasp.

"It was no one in the poat," replied Meyer diplomatically.

"Was it that man—that hunter—Smith?"

Another furtive glance between the sandy eyelashes expressed an uneasy astonishment; the sergeant evidently had a secret on his mind which he must not run any risk of disclosing.

"I do not zee how it was Schmidt" he fluted almost inaudibly. "He was watching the peasts at their basture."

"Then who did saw it?"

"I do not know. I do not feel sure that it was sawed."

Perceiving that, either from ignorance or caution, he would not say more on this point, Clara changed the subject and asked, "Can Lieutenant Thurstane go down the river safely?"

"I would like noting petter than to make the exbedition myself," replied Meyer, once more diplomatic.

Now came a silence, the soldier waiting respectfully, the girl not knowing how much she might dare to say. Not that she doubted Meyer; on the contrary, she had a perfect confidence in him; how could she fail to trust one who had been trusted by Thurstane?

"Sergeant," she at last whispered, "we must find him."

"Yes, miss," touching his cap as if he were taking an oath by it.

"And you," she hesitated, "must protect *me*."

"Yes, miss," and the sergeant repeated his gesture of solemn affirmation.

"Perhaps I will say more some time."

He saluted again, and seeing that she had nothing to add, retired quietly.

For two nights there was little sleep for Clara. She passed them in pondering Thurstane's chances, or in listening for his returning footsteps. Yet when the train set out for the Moqui pueblos, she seemed as vigorous and more vivacious than usual. What supported her now and for days afterward was what is called the strength of fever.

The return across the desert was even more terrible than the advance, for the two scant water-holes had been nearly exhausted by the Apaches, so that both beasts and human beings suffered horribly with thirst. There was just this one good thing about the parched and famished wilderness, that it relieved the emigrants from all fear of ambushing enemies. Supernatural beings alone could have bushwhacked here. The Apaches had gone.

Meanwhile Sergeant Meyer had a sore conscience. From the moment the boat went down the San Juan he had more or less lain awake with the idea that, according to the spirit of his instructions from Thurstane, he ought to have Texas Smith tied up and shot. Orders were orders; there was no question about that, as a general principle; the sergeant had never heard the statement disputed. But when he came to consider the case now before him, he was outgeneralled by a doubt. This drifting of a boat down a strange river, was it murder in the sense intended by Thurstane? And, supposing it to be murder, could it be charged in any way upon Smith? In the whole course of his military experience Sergeant Meyer had never been more perplexed. On the evening of the first day's march he could bear his sense of responslbility no longer, and decided to call a council of war. Beckoning his sole remaining comrade aside from the bivouac, he entered upon business.

"Kelly, we are unter insdructions," he began in his flute-like tone.

"I know it, sergeant," replied Kelly, decorously squirting his tobacco-juice out of the corner of his mouth furthest from his superior.

"The question is, Kelly, whether Schmidt should pe shot."

"The responsibility lies upon you, sergeant. I will shoot him if so be such is orders."

"Kelly, the insdructions were to shoot him if murder should habben in this barty. The instructions were loose."

"They were so, sergeant—not defining murder."

"The question is, Kelly, whether what has habbened to the leftenant is murder. If it is murder, then Schmidt must go."

The two men were sitting on a bowlder side by side, their hands on their knees and their muskets leaning against their shoulders. They did not look at each other at all, but kept their grave eyes on the ground. Kelly squirted his tobacco-juice sidelong two or three times before he replied.

"Sergeant," he finally said, "my opinion is we can't set this down for murder until we know somebody is dead."

"Shust so, Kelly. That is my obinion myself."

"Consequently it follows, sergeant, if you don't see to the contrary, that until we know that to be a fact, it would be uncalled for to shoot Smith."

"What you zay, Kelly, is shust what I zay."

"Furthermore, however, sergeant, it might be right and in the way of duty, to call up Smith and make him testify as to what he knows of this business, whether it be murder, or meant for murder."

"Cock your beece, Kelly."

Both men cocked their pieces.

"Now I will gall Schmidt out and question him," continued Meyer. "You will stand on one side and pe ready to opey my orders."

"Very good, sergeant," said Kelly, and dropped back a little into the nearly complete darkness.

Meyer sang out sharply, "Schmidt! Texas Schmidt!"

The desperado heard the summons, hesitated a moment, cocked the revolver in his belt, loosened his knife in its sheath, rose from his blanket, and walked slowly in the direction of the voice. Passing Kelly without seeing him, he confronted Meyer, his hand on his pistol. There was not the slightest tremor in the hoarse, low croak with which he asked, "What's the game, sergeant?"

"Schmidt, stand berfectly still," said Meyer in his softest fluting. "Kelly has his beece aimed at your head. If you stir hant or foot, you are a kawn koose."

CHAPTER XXXII.

TEXAS SMITH was too old a borderer to attempt to draw his weapons wnile such a man as Kelly was sighting him at ten feet distance.

"Play yer hand, sergeant," he said; "you've got the keerds."

"You know, Schmidt, that our leftenant has been garried down the river," continued Meyer.

The bushwhacker responded with a grunt which expressed neither pleasure nor sorrow, but merely assent.

"You know," went on the sergeant, "that such things cannot habben to officers without investigations."

"He war a squar man, an' a white man," said Texas. "I didn't have nothin' to do with cuttin' him loose, if he war cut loose."

"You didn't saw the lariat yourself, Schmidt, I know that. But do you know who did saw it?"

"I dunno the first thing about it."

"Bray to pe struck tead if you do."

"I dunno how to pray."

"Then holt up your hants and gurse yourself to hell if you do."

Lifting his hands over his head, the ignorant savage blasphemed copiously.

"Do you think you can guess how it was pusted?" persisted the soldier.

"Look a hyer!" remonstrated Smith, "ain't you pannin' me out a leetle too fine? It mought 'a' been this way, an' it mought 'a' been that. But I've no business to point if I can't find. When a man's got to the bottom of his pile, you can't fo'ce him to borrow. 'Sposin' I set you barkin' up the wrong tree; what good's that gwine to do?"

"Vell, Schmidt, I don't zay but what you zay right. You mustn't zay anyting you don't know someting apout."

After another silence, during which Texas continued to hold his hands above his head, Meyer added, "Kelly, you may come to an order. Schmidt, you may put down your hants. Will you haf a jew of topacco?"

The three men now approached each other, took alternate bites of the sergeant's last plug of pigtail, and masticated amicably.

"You army fellers run me pootty close," said Texas, after a while, in a tone of complaint and humiliation. "I don't want to fight brass buttons. They're too many for me. The Capm he lassoed me, an' choked me some; an' now you're on it."

"When things habben to officers, they must pe looked into," replied Meyer.

"I dunno how in thunder the lariat got busted," repeated Texas. "An' if I should go for to guess, I mought guess wrong."

"All right, Schmidt; I pelieve you. If there is no more drubble, you will not pe called up again."

"Ask him what he thinks of the leftenant's chances," suggested Kelly to his superior.

"Reckon he'll hev to run the river a spell," returned the borderer. "Reckon he'll hev to run it a hell of a ways befo' he'll be able to git across the darn country."

"Ask him what the chances be of running the river safely," added Kelly.

"Dam slim," answered Texas; and there the talk ended. There was some meditative chewing, after which the three returned to the bivouac, and either lay down to sleep or took their tours at guard duty.

At dawn the party recommenced its flight toward the Moqui country. There were sixty hours more of hard riding, insufficient sleep, short rations, thirst, and anxiety. Once the suffering animals stampeded after water, and ran for several miles over plateaux of rock, dashing off burdens and riders, and only halting when they were plunged knee-deep in the water-hole which they had scented. One of the wounded rancheros expired on the mule to which he was strapped, and was carried dead for several hours, his ashy-brown face swinging to and fro, until Coronado had him thrown into a crevice.

Amid these hardships and horrors Clara showed no sign of flagging or flinching. She was very thin; bad food, excessive fatigue, and anxiety had reduced her; her face was pinched, narrowed, and somewhat lined; her expression was painfully set and eager. But she never asked for repose, and never complained. Her mind was solely fixed upon finding Thurstane, and her feverish bright eyes continually searched the horizon for him. She seemed to have lost her power of sympathizing with any other creature. To Mrs. Stanley's groanings and murmurings she vouchsafed rare and brief condolences. The dead muleteer and the tortured, bellowing animals attracted little of her notice. She was not hard-hearted; she was simply almost insane. In this state of abnormal exaltation she continued until the party reached the quiet and safety of the Moqui pueblos.

Then there was a change; exhausted nature required either apathy or death; and for two days she lay in a sort of stupor, sleeping a great deal, and crying often when awake. The only person capable of rousing her was Sergeant Meyer, who made expeditions to the other pueblos for news of Thurstane, and brought her news of his hopes and his failures.

After a three days' rest Coronado decided to resume his journey by moving southward toward the Bernalillo trail. Freed from Thurstane, he no longer contemplated losing Clara in the desert, but meant to marry her, and trusted that he could do it. Two of his wagons he presented to the Moquis, who were, of course, delighted with the acquisition, although they had no more use for wheeled vehicles than for gunboats. With only four wagons, his animals were more than sufficient, and the train made tolerably rapid progress, in spite of the roughness of the country.

The land was still a wonder. The water wizards of old had done their grotesque utmost here. What with sculpturing and frescoing, they had made that most fantastic wilderness the Painted Desert. It looked like a mirage. The travellers had an impression that here was some atmospheric illusion. It seemed as if it could not last five minutes if the sun should shine upon it. There were crowding hills so variegated and gay as to put one in mind of masses of soap-bubbles. But the coloring was laid on fifteen hundred feet deep. It consisted of sandstone marls, red, blue, green, orange, purple, white, brown, lilac, and yellow, interstratified with magnesian limestone in bands of purple, bluish-white, and mottled, with here and there shining flecks or great glares of gypsum.

Among the more delicate wonders of the scene were the petrified trunks which had once been pines and cedars, but which were now flint or jasper. The washings of geologic æons have exposed to view immense quantities of these enchanted forests. Fragments of silicified trees are not only strewn over the lowlands, but are piled by the hundred cords at the bases of slopes, seeming like so much drift-wood from wonder-lands far up the stream of time. Generally they are in short bits, broken square across the grain, as if sawed. Some are jasper, and look like masses of red sealing-wax ; others are agate, or opalescent chalcedony, beautifully lined and variegated ; many retain the graining, layers, knots, and other details of their woody structure.

In places where the marls had been washed away gently, the emigrants found trunks complete, from root to summit, fifty feet in length and three in diameter. All the branches, however, were gone ; the tree had been uprooted, transported, whirled and worn by deluges ; then to commemorate the victory of the water sprites, it had been changed into stone. The sight of these remnants of antediluvian woodlands made history seem the reminiscence of a child. They were already petrifactions when the human race was born.

The Painted Desert has other marvels. Throughout vast stretches you pass between tinted *mesas*, or tables, which face each other across flat valleys like painted palaces across the streets of Genova la Superba. They are giant splendors, hundreds of feet in height, built of blood-red sandstone capped with variegated marls. The torrents, which scooped out the intersecting levels, amused their monstrous leisure with carving the points and abutments of the *mesa* into fantastic forms, so that the traveller sees towers, minarets, and spires loftier than the pinnacles of cathedrals.

The emigrants were often deceived by these freaks of nature. Beheld from a distance, it seemed impossible that they should not be ruins, the monuments of some Cyclopean race. Aunt Maria, in particular, discovered casas grandes and casas de Montezuma very frequently.

"There is another casa," she would say, staring through her spectacles (broken) at a butte three hundred feet high. "What a people it must have been which raised such edifices!"

And she would stick to it, too, until she was close up to the solid rock, and then would renew the transforming miracle five or ten miles further on.

During this long and marvellous journey Coronado renewed his courtship. He was cautious, however ; he made a confidant of his friend Aunt Maria ; begged her favorable intercession.

"Clara," said Mrs. Stanley, as the two women jolted along in one of the lumbering wagons, "there is one thing in your life which perhaps you don't suspect."

The girl, who wanted to hear about Thurstane all the time, and expected to hear about him, asked eagerly, "What is it?"

"You have made Mr. Coronado fa'l in love with you," said Aunt Maria, thinking it wise to be clear and straightforward, as men are reputed to be.

The young lady, instantly revolting from the subject, made no reply.

"I think, Clara, that if you take a husband—and most women do—he would be just the person for you."

Clara, once the gentlest of the gentle, was perfectly angelic no longer. She gave her relative a stare which was partly intense misery, but which had much the look of pure anger, as indeed it was in a measure.

The expressions of violent emotion are alarming to most people. Aunt Maria, beholding this tortured soul glaring at her out of its prison windows, recoiled in surprise and awe. There was not another word spoken at the time concerning the obnoxious match-making. A single stare of Marius had put to flight the executioner.

In one way and another Clara continued to baffle her suitor and her advocate. The days dragged on; the expedition steadily traversed the desert; the Santa Anna region was crossed, and the Bernalillo trail reached; one hundred, two hundred, three hundred miles and more were left behind; and still Coronado, though without a rival, was not accepted.

Then came an adventure which partly helped and partly hindered his plans. The train was overtaken by a detachment of the Fifth United States Cavalry, commanded by Major John Robinson, pushing for California. Of course Sergeant Meyer reported himself and Kelly to the Major, and of course the Major ordered them to join his party as far as Fort Yuma. This deprived Clara of her trusted protectors; but on the other hand, she threatened to take advantage of the escort of Robinson for the rest of her journey; and the mere mention of this at once brought Coronado on his soul's marrow-bones. He swore by the heaven above, by all the saints and angels, by the throne of the Virgin Mary, by every sacred object he could think of, that not another word of love should pass his lips during the journey, that he would live the life of a dead man, etc. Overcome by his pleadings, and by the remonstrances of Aunt Maria, who did not want to have her favorite driven to commit suicide, Clara agreed to continue with the train.

After this scene followed days of hot travelling over hard, gravelly plains, thinly coated with grass and dotted with cacti, mezquit trees, the leafless palo verde, and the greasewood bush. Here and there towered that giant cactus, the saguarra, a fluted shaft, thirty, forty, and even sixty feet high, with a coronet of richly-colored flowers, the whole fabric as splendid as a Corinthian column. Prickly pears, each one large enough to make a thicket, abounded. Through the scorching sunshine ran scorpions and lizards, pursued by enormous rattlesnakes. During the days the heat ranged from 100 to 115 deg. in the shade, while the nights were swept by winds as parching as the breath of an oven. The distant mountains glared at the eye like metals brought to a white heat. Not seldom they passed horses, mules, cattle, and sheep, which had perished in this terrible transit and been turned to mummies by the dry air and baking sun. Some of these carcasses, having been set on their legs by passing travellers, stood upright, staring with blind eyeballs, grinning through dried lips, mockeries of life, statues of death.

In spite of these hardships and horrors, Clara kept up her courage and was almost cheerful; for in the first place Coronado had ceased his terrifying attentions, and in the second place they were nearing Cactus Pass, where she hoped to meet Thurstane. When love has not a foot of certainty to stand upon, it can take wing and soar through the incredible. The idea that they two, divided hundreds of miles back, should come together at a given point by pure accident, was obviously absurd. Yet Clara could trust to the chance and live for it.

The scenery changed to mountains. There were barren, sublime, awful peaks to the right and left. To the girl's eyes they were beautiful, for she trusted that Thurstane beheld them. She was always on horseback now, scanning every feature of the landscape, searching of course for him. She did not pass a cactus, or a thicket of mezquit, or a bowlder without anxious examination. She imagined herself finding him helpless with hunger, or passing him unseen and leaving him to die. She was so pale and thin with constant anxiety that you might have thought her half starved, or recovering from some acute malady.

About five one afternoon, as the train was approaching its halting-place at a spring on the western side of the pass, Clara's feverish mind fixed on a group of rocks half a mile from the trail as the spot where she would find Thurstane. In obedience to similar impressions she had already made many expeditions of this nature. Constant failure, and a consciousness that all this searching was folly, could not shake her wild hopes. She set off at a canter alone; but after going some four hundred yards she heard a gallop behind her, and, looking over her shoulder, she saw Coronado. She did not want to be away from the train with him; but she must at all hazards reach that group of rocks; something within impelled her. Better mounted than she, he was soon by her side, and after a while struck out in advance, saying, "I will look out for an ambush."

When Coronado reached the rocks he was fifty yards ahead of Clara. He made the circuit of them at a slow canter; in so doing he discovered the starving and fainted Thurstane lying in the high grass beneath a low shelf of stone; he saw him, he recognized him, and in an instant he trembled from head to foot. But such was his power of self-control that he did not check his horse, nor cast a second look to see whether the man was alive or dead. He turned the last stone in the group, met Clara with a forced smile, and said gently, "There is nothing."

She reined up, drew a long sigh, thought that here was another foolish hope crushed, and turned her horse's head toward the train.

CHAPTER XXXIII.

THE tread of Coronado's horse passing within fifteen feet of Thurstane roused him from the troubled sleep into which he had sunk after his long fainting fit.

Slowly he opened his eyes, to see nothing but long grasses close to his face, and through them a haze of mountains and sky. His first moments of wakening were so far from being a full consciousness that he did not comprehend where he was. He felt very, very weak, and he continued to lie still.

But presently he became aware of sounds; there was a trampling, and then there were words; the voices of life summoned him to live. Instantly he remembered two things: the starving comrades whom it was his duty to save, and the loved girl whom he longed to find. Slowly and with effort, grasping at the rock to aid his trembling knees, he rose to his feet just as Clara turned her horse's head toward the plain.

Coronado threw a last anxious glance in the direction of the wretch whom he meant to abandon to the desert. To his horror he saw a lean, smirched, ghostly face looking at him in a dazed way, as if out of the blinding shades of death. The quickness of this villain was so wonderful that one is almost tempted to call it praiseworthy. He perceived at once that Thurstane would be discovered, and that he, Coronado, must make the discovery, or he might be charged with attempting to leave him to die.

"Good heavens!" he exclaimed loudly, "there he is!"

Clara turned: there was a scream of joy: she was on the ground, running: she was in Thurstane's arms. During that unearthly moment there was no thought in those two of Coronado, or of any being but each other. It is impossible fully to describe such a meeting; its exterior signs are beyond language; its emotion is a lifetime. If words are feeble in presence of the heights and depths of the Colorado, they are impotent in presence of the altitudes and abysses of great passion. Human speech has never yet completely expressed human intellect, and it certainly never will completely express human sentiments. These lovers, who had been wandering in chasms impenetrable to hope, were all of a sudden on mountain summits dizzy with joy. What could they say for themselves, or what can another say for them?

Clara only uttered inarticulate murmurs, while her hands crawled up Thurstane's arms, pressing and clutching him to make sure that he was alive. There was an indescribable pathos in this eagerness which could not trust to sight, but must touch also, as if she were blind. Thurstane held her firmly, kissing hair, forehead, and temples, and whispering, "Clara! Clara!" Her face, which had turned white at the first glimpse of him, was now roseate all over and damp with a sweet dew. It became smirched with the dust of his face; but she would only have rejoiced, had she known it; his very squalor was precious to her.

At last she fell back from him, held him at arm's length with ease, and stared at him. "Oh, how sick!" she gasped. "How thin! You are starving."

She ran to her horse, drew from her saddle-bags some remnants of food, and brought them to him. He had sunk down faint upon a stone, and he was too weak to speak aloud; but he gave her a smile of encouragement which was at once pathetic and sublime. It said, "I can bear all alone; you must not suffer for me." But it said this out of such visible exhaustion, that, instead of being comforted, she was terrified.

"Oh, you must not die," she whispered with quivering mouth. "If you die, I will die."

Then she checked her emotion and added, "There! Don't mind me. I am silly. Eat."

Meanwhile Coronado looked on with such a face as Iago might have worn had he felt the jealousy of Othello. For the first time he positively knew that the woman he loved was violently in love with another. He suffered so horribly that we should be bound to pity him, only that he suffered after the fashion of devils, his malignity equalling his agony. While he was in such pain that his heart ceased beating, his fingers curled like snakes around the handle of his revolver. Nothing kept him from shooting that man, yes, and that woman also, but the certainty that the deed would make him a fugitive for life, subject everywhere to the summons of the hangman.

Once, almost overcome by the temptation, he looked around for the train. It was within hearing; he thought he saw Mrs. Stanley watching him; two of his Mexicans were approaching at full speed. He dismounted, sat down upon a stone, partially covered his face with his hand, and tried to bring himself to look at the two lovers. At last, when he perceived that Thurstane was eating and Clara merely kneeling by, he walked tremulously toward them, scarcely conscious of his feet.

"Welcome to life, lieutenant," he said. "I did not wish to interrupt. Now I congratulate."

Thurstane looked at him steadily, seemed to hesitate for a moment, and then put out his hand.

"It was I who discovered you," went on Coronado, as he took the lean, grimy fingers in his buckskin gauntlet.

"I know it," mumbled the young fellow; then with a visible effort he added, "Thanks."

Presently the two Mexicans pulled up with loud exclamations of joy and wonder. One of them took out of his haversack a quantity of provisions and a flask of aguardiente; and Coronado handed them to Thurstane with a smile, hoping that he would surfeit himself and die.

"No," said Clara, seizing the food. "You have eaten enough. You may drink."

"Where are the others?" she presently asked.

"In the hills," he answered. "Starving. I must go and find them."

"No, no!" she cried. "You must go to the train. Some one else will look for them."

One of the rancheros now dismounted and helped Thurstane into his saddle. Then, the Mexican steadying him on one side and Clara riding near him on the other, he was conducted to the train, which was at that moment going into park near a thicket of willows.

In an amazingly short time he was very like himself. Healthy and plucky, he had scarcely swallowed his food and brandy before he began to draw strength from them; and he had scarcely begun to breathe freely before he began to talk of his duties.

"I must go back," he insisted. "Glover and Sweeny are starving. I must look them up."

"Certainly," answered Coronado.

"No!" protèsted Clara. "You are not strong enough."

"Of course not," chimed in Aunt Maria with real feeling, for she was shocked by the youth's haggard and ghastly face.

"Who else can find them?" he argued. "I shall want two spare animals. Glover can't march, and I doubt whether Sweeny can."

"You shall have all you need," declared Coronado.

"He mustn't go," cried Clara. Then, seeing in his face that he *would* go, she added, "I will go with him."

"No, no," answered several voices. "You would only be in the way."

"Give me my horse," continued Thurstane. "Where are Meyer and Kelly?"

He was told how they had gone on to Fort Yuma with Major Robinson, taking his horse, the government mules, stores, etc.

"Ah! unfortunate," he said. "However, that was right. Well, give me a mule for myself, two mounted muleteers, and two spare animals; some provisions also, and a flask of brandy. Let me start as soon as the men and beasts have eaten. It is forty miles there and back."

"But you can't find your way in the night," persisted Clara.

"There is a moon," answered Thurstane, looking at her gratefully; while Coronado added encouragingly, "Twenty miles are easily done."

"Oh yes!" hoped Clara. "You can almost get there before dark. Do start at once."

But Coronado did not mean that Thurstane should set out immediately. He dropped various obstacles in the way: for instance, the animals and men must be thoroughly refreshed; in short, it was dusk before all was ready.

Meantime Clara had found an opportunity of whispering to Thurstane, "*Must* you?" And he had answered, looking at her as the Huguenot looks at his wife in Millais's picture, "My dear love, you know that I must."

"You *will* be careful of yourself?" she begged.

"For your sake."

"But remember that man," she whispered, looking about for Texas Smith.

"He is not going. Come, my own darling, don't frighten yourself. Think of my poor comrades."

"I will pray for them and for you all the time you are gone. But oh, Ralph, there is one thing. I must tell you. I am so afraid. I did wrong to let Coronado see how much I care for you. I am afraid——"

He seemed to understand her. "It isn't possible," he murmured. Then, after eyeing her gravely for a moment, he asked, "I may be always sure of you? Oh yes! I knew it. But Coronado? Well, it isn't possible that he would try to commit a treble murder. Nobody abandons starving men in a desert. Well, I must go. I must save these men. After that we will think of these other things. Good-by, my darling."

The sultry glow of sunset had died out of the west, and the radiance of a full moon was climbing up the heavens in the east when Thurstane set off on his pilgrimage of mercy. Clara watched him as long as the twilight would let her see him, and then sat down with drooped face, like a flower which has lost the sun. If any one spoke to her, she answered tardily and not always to the purpose. She was fulfilling her promise; she was praying for Thurstane and the men whom he had gone to save; that is, she was praying when her mind did not wander into reveries of terror. After a time she started up with the thought, "Where is Texas Smith?" He was not visible, and neither was Coronado. Suspicious of some evil intrigue, she set out in search of them, made the circuit of the fires, and then wandered into the willow thickets. Amid the underwood, hastening toward the wagons, she met Coronado.

"Ah!" he started. "Is that you, my little cousin? You are as terrible in the dark as an Apache."

"Coronado, where is your hunter?" she asked with a beating heart.

"I don't know. I have been looking for him. My dear cousin, what do you want?"

"Coronado, I will tell you the truth. That man is a murderer. I know it."

Coronado just took the time to draw one long breath, and then replied with sublime effrontery, "I fear so. I learn that he has told horrible stories about himself. Well, to tell the truth, I have discharged him."

"Oh, Coronado!" gasped Clara, not knowing whether to believe him or not.

"Shall I confess to you," he continued, "that I suspect him of having weakened that towline so as to send our friend down the San Juan?"

"He never went near the boat," heroically answered Clara, at the same time wishing she could see Coronado's face.

"Of course not. He probably hired some one. I fear our rancheros are none too good to be bribed. I will confess to you, my cousin, that ever since that day I have been watching Smith."

"Oh, Coronado!" repeated Clara. She was beginning to believe this prodigious liar, and to be all the more alarmed because she did believe him. "So you have sent him away? I am so glad. Oh, Coronado, I thank you. But help me look for him now. I want to know if he is in camp."

It is almost impossible to do Coronado justice. While he was pretending to aid Clara in searching for Texas Smith, he knew that the man had gone out to murder Thurstane. We must remember that the man was almost as wretched as he was wicked; if punishment makes amends for crime, his was in part absolved. As he walked about with the girl he thought over and over, Will it kill her? He tried to answer, No. Another voice persisted in saying, Yes. In his desperation he at last replied, Let it!

We must follow Texas Smith. He had not started on his errand until he had received five hundred dollars in gold, and five hundred in a draft on San Francisco. Then he had himself proposed, "I mought quit the train, an' take my own resk acrost the plains." This being agreed to, he had mounted his horse, slipped away through the willows, and ridden into the desert after Thurstane.

He knew the trail; he had been from Cactus Pass to Diamond River and back again; he knew it at least as well as the man whose life he was tracking. He thought he remembered the spring where Glover had broken down, and felt pretty sure that it could not be less than twenty miles from the camp. Mounted as he was, he could put himself ahead of Thurstane and ambush him in some ravine. Of a sudden he laughed. It was not a burst of merriment, but a grim wrinkling of his dark, haggard cheeks, followed by a hissing chuckle. Texas seldom laughed, and with good reason, for it was enough to scare people.

"Mought be done," he muttered. "Mought git the better of 'em all that way. Shute, 'an then yell. The greasers 'ud think it was Injuns, an' they'd travel for camp. Then I'd stop the spare mules an' start for Californy."

For Texas this plan was a stroke of inspiration. He was not an intelligent scoundrel. All his acumen, though bent to the one point of roguery, had barely sufficed hitherto to commit murders and escape hanging. He had never prospered financially, because he lacked financial ability. He was a beast, with all a tiger's ferocity, but with hardly more than a tiger's intelligence. He was a savage numskull. An Apache Tonto would have been more than his match in the arts of murder, and very nearly his match in the arts of civilization.

Instead of following Thurstane directly, he made a circuit of several miles through a ravine, galloped across a wide grassy plain, and pulled up among some rounded hillocks. Here, as he calculated, he was fifteen miles from camp, and five from the spot where lay Glover and Sweeny. The moon had already gone down and left the desert to the starlight. Posting himself behind a thicket, he waited for half an hour or more, listening with indefatigable attention.

He had no scruples, but he had some fears. If he should miss, the lieutenant would fire back, and he was cool enough to fire with effect. Well, he wouldn't miss; what should he miss for? As for the greasers, they would run at the first shot. Nevertheless, he did occasionally muddle over the idea of going off to California with his gold, and without doing this particular job. What kept him to his agreement was the hope of stealing the spare mules, and the fear that the draft might not be paid if he shirked his work.

"I s'pose I must show his skelp," thought Texas, "or they won't hand over the dust."

At last there was a sound; he had set his ambush just right; there were voices in the distance; then hoofs in the grass. Next he saw something; it was a man on a mule; yes, and it was the right man.

He raised his cocked rifle and aimed, sighting the head, three rods away. Suddenly his horse whinnied, and then the mule of the other reared; but the bullet had already sped. Down went Thurstane in the darkness, while, with an Apache yell, Texas Smith burst from his ambush and charged upon the greasers.

CHAPTER XXXIV.

THE chase after the spare mules carried Texas Smith several miles from the scene of the ambush, so that when he at last caught the frightened beasts, he decided not to go back and cut Thurstane's throat, but to set off at once westward and put himself by morning well on the road to California.

Meanwhile, the two muleteers continued their flight at full gallop, and eventually plunged into camp with a breathless story to the effect that Apaches had attacked them, captured the spare mules, and killed the lieutenant. Coronado, no more able to sleep than Satan, was the first to hear their tale.

"Apaches!" he said, surprised and incredulous. Then, guessing at what had happened, he immediately added, "Those devils again! We must push on, the moment we can see."

Apaches! It was a capital idea. He had an excuse now for hurrying away from a spot which he had stained with murder. If any one demanded that Thurstane's body should be sought for, or that those incumbrances Glover and Sweeny should be rescued, he could respond, Apaches! Apaches! He gave orders to commence preparations for moving at the first dawn.

He expected and feared that Clara would oppose the advance in some trying way. But one of the fugitives relieved him by blurting out the death of Thurstane, and sending her into spasms of alternate hysterics and fainting which lasted for hours. Lying in a wagon, her head in the lap of Mrs. Stanley, a sick, very sick, dangerously sick girl, she was jolted along as easily as a corpse.

Coronado rode almost constantly beside her wagon, inquiring about her every few minutes, his face changing with contradictory emotions, wishing she would die and hoping she would live, loving and hating her in the same breath. Whenever she came to herself and recognized him, she put out her hands and implored, "Oh, Coronado, take me back there!"

"Apaches!" growled Coronado, and spurred away repeating his lie to himself, "Apaches! Apaches!"

Then he checked his horse and rode anew to her side, hoping that he might be able to reason with her.

"Oh, take me back!" was all the response he could obtain. "Take me back and let me die there."

"Would you have us all die?" he shouted—"like Pepita!"

"Don't scold her," begged Aunt Maria, who was sobbing like a child. "She doesn't know what she is asking."

But Clara knew too much; at the word *Pepita* she guessed the torture scene; and then it came into her mind that Thurstane might be even now at the stake. She immediately broke into screams, which ended in convulsions and a long fit of insensibility.

"It is killing her," wailed Aunt Maria. "Oh, my child! my child!"

Coronado spurred at full speed for a mile, muttering to the desert, "Let it kill her! let it!"

At last he halted for the train to overtake him, glanced anxiously at Clara's wagon, saw that Mrs. Stanley was still bending over her, guessed that she was still alive, drew a sigh of relief, and rode on alone.

"Oh, this love-making!" sighed Aunt Maria scores of times, for she had at last learned of the engagement. "When will my sex get over the weakness? It kills them, and they like it."

That night Clara could not sleep, and kept Coronado awake with her moanings. All the next day she lay in a semi-unconsciousness which was partly lethargy and partly fever. It was well; at all events he could bear it so—bear it better than when she was crying and praying for death. The next night she fell into such a long silence of slumber that he came repeatedly to her wagon to hearken if she still breathed. Youth and a strong constitution were waging a doubtful battle to rescue her from the despair which threatened to rob her of either life or reason.

So the journey continued. Henceforward the trail followed Bill Williams's river to the Colorado, tracked that stream northward to the Mohave valley, and, crossing there, took the line of the Mohave river toward California. It was a prodigious pilgrimage still, and far from being a safe one. The Mohaves, one of the tallest and bravest races known, from six feet to six and a half in height, fighting hand to hand with short clubs, were not perfectly sure to be friendly. Coronado felt that, if ever he got his wife and his fortune, he should have earned them. He was resolute, however; there was no flinching yet in this versatile, yet obstinate nature; he was as wicked and as enduring as a Pizarro.

We will not make the journey; we must suppose it. Weeks after the desert had for a second time engulfed Thurstane, a coasting schooner from Santa Barbara entered the Bay of San Francisco, having on board Clara, Mrs. Stanley, and Coronado.

The latter is on deck now, smoking his eternal cigarito without knowing it, and looking at the superb scenery without seeing it. A landscape mirrored in the eye of a horse has about as much effect on the brain within as a landscape mirrored in the eye of Coronado. He is a Latin; he has a fine ear for music, and he would delight in museums of painting and sculpture; but he has none of the passion of the sad, grave, imaginative Anglican race for nature. Mountains, deserts, seas, and storms are to him obstacles and hardships. He has no more taste for them than had Ulysses.

He has agonized with sea-sickness during the voyage, and this is the first day that he has found tolerable. Once more he is able to eat and stand up; able to think, devise, resolve, and execute; able, in short, to be Coronado. Look at the little, sunburnt, sinewy, earnest, enduring man; study his diplomatic countenance, serious and yet courteous, full of gravity and yet ready for gayety; notice his ready smile and gracious wave of the hand as he salutes the skipper. He has been through horrors; he has fought a tremendous fight of passion, crime, and peril; yet he scarcely shows a sign of it. There is some such lasting stuff in him as goes to make the Bolivars, Francias, and Lopez, the restless and indefatigable agitators of the Spanish-American communities. You cannot help sympathizing with him somewhat, because of his energy and bottom. You are tempted to say that he deserves to win.

He has made some progress in his conspiracy to entrap love and a fortune. It must be understood that the two muleteers persisted in their story concerning Apaches, and that consequently Clara has come to think of Thurstane as dead. Meantime Coronado, after the first two days of wild excitement, has conducted himself with rare intelligence, never alarming her with talk of love, always courteous, kind, and useful. Little by little he has worn away her suspicions that he planned murder, and her only remaining anger against him is because he did not attempt to search for Thurstane; but even for that she is obliged to see some excuse in the terrible word "Apaches."

"I have had no thought but for *her* safety," Coronado often said to Mrs. Stanley, who as often repeated the words to Clara. "I have made mistakes," he would go on. "The San Juan journey was one. I will not even plead Garcia's instructions to excuse it. But our circumstances have been terrible. Who could always take the right step amid such trials? All I ask is charity. If humility deserves mercy, I deserve it."

Coronado even schooled himself into expressing sympathy with Clara for the loss of Thurstane. He spoke of him as her affianced, eulogized his character, admitted that he had not formerly done him justice, hinting that this blindness had sprung from jealousy, and so alluded to his own affection. These things he said at first to Aunt Maria, and she, his steady partisan, repeated them to Clara, until at last the girl could bear to hear them from Coronado. Sympathy! the bleeding heart must have it; it will accept this balm from almost any hand, and it will pay for it in gratitude and trust.

Thus in two months from the disappearance of Thurstane his rival had begun to hope that he was supplanting him. Of course he had given up all thought of carrying out the horrible plan with which he had started from Santa Fé. Indeed, he began to have a horror of Garcia, as a man who had set him on a wrong track and nearly brought him into folly and ruin. One might say that Satan was in a state of mind to rebuke sin.

Let us now glance at Clara. She is seated beside Aunt Maria on the quarter-deck of the schooner. Her troubles have changed her; only eighteen years old, she has the air of twenty-four; her once rounded face is thin, and her child-like sweetness has become tender gravity. When she entered on this journey she resembled the girl faces of Greuze; now she is sometimes a *mater amabilis*, and sometimes a *mater dolorosa;* for her grief has been to her as a maternity. The great change, so far from diminishing her beauty, has made her seem more fascinating and nobler. Her countenance has had a new birth, and exhibits a more perfect soul.

We have hitherto had little more than a superficial view of the characters of our people. Events, incidents, adventures, and even landscapes have been the leading personages of the story, and have been to its human individualities what the Olympian gods are to Greek and Trojan heroes in the Iliad. Just as Jove or Neptune rules or thwarts Agamemnon and Achilles, so the monstrous circumstances of the desert have overborne, dwarfed, and blurred these travellers. It is only now, when they have escaped from the *dii majores*, and have become for a brief period tranquil free agents, that we can see them as they are. Even yet they are not altogether untrammelled. Man is never quite himself; he is always under some external influence, past or present; he is always being governed, if not being created.

Clara, born anew of trouble, is admirable. There is a sweet, sedate, and almost solemn womanliness about her, which even overawes Mrs. Stanley, conscious of aunthood and strongmindedness, and insisting upon it that her niece is "a mere child." It is a great victory to gain over a lady who has that sort of self-confidence that if she had been a sunflower and obliged to turn toward the sun for life, she would yet have believed that it was she who made him shine.

When Clara decides a matter Mrs. Stanley, while still mentally saying "Young thing," feels nevertheless that her own decision has been uttered. And in every successive resistance she is overcome the easier, for habit is a conqueror.

They have just had a discussion. Aunt Maria wants Clara to stand on her dignity in a hotel until old Muñoz goes down on his marrow-bones, makes her a handsome allowance, and agrees to leave her at least half his fortune. Clara's reply is substantially, "He is my grandfather and the proper head of my family. I think I ought to go straight to him and say, Grandfather, here I am."

Beaten by this gentle conscientiousness, Aunt Maria endeavored to appeal the matter to Coronado.

"I am so glad to see you enjoying your cigarito once more," she called to him with as sweet a smile as if she didn't hate tobacco.

He left his smoking retreat amidships, took off his hat with a sort of airy gravity, and approached them.

"Mr. Coronado, where do you propose to take us when we reach land?" asked Aunt Maria.

"We will, if you please, go direct to my excellent relative's," was the reply.

Aunt Maria held her head straight up, as if stiff-neckedly refusing to go there, but made no opposition.

Coronado had meditated everything and decided everything. It would not do to go to a hotel, because that might lead to a suspicion that he knew all the while about the death of Muñoz. His plan was to drive at once to the old man's place, demand him as if he expected to see him, express proper surprise and grief over the funereal response, put the estate as soon as possible into Clara's hands, become her man of affairs and trusted friend, and so climb to be her husband. He was anxious; during all his perils in the desert he had never been more so; but he bore the situation heroically, as he could bear; his face revealed nothing but its outside—a smile.

"My dear cousin," he presently said, "when I once fairly set you down in your home, you will owe me, in spite of all my blunders, a word of thanks."

"Coronado, I shall owe you more than I ever can repay," she replied frankly, without remembering that he wanted to marry her. The next instant she remembered it, and her face showed the first blush that had tinted it for two months. He saw the significant color, and turned away to conceal a joy which might have been perilous had she observed it.

Immediately on landing he proceeded to carry out his programme. He took a hack, drove the ladies direct to the house of Muñoz, and there went decorously through the form of learning that the old man was dead. Then, consoling the sorrowful and anxious Clara, he hurried to the best hotel in the city and made arrangements for what he meant should be an impressive scene, the announcement of her fortune. He secured fine rooms for the ladies, and ordered them a handsome lunch, with wine, etc., all without regard to expense. The girl must be perfectly comfortable and under a sense of all sorts of obligations to him when she received his *coup de théâtre.*

He was not so preoccupied but that he quarrelled with his coachman about the hack hire and dismissed him with some disagreeable epithets in Spanish. Next he took a saddle-horse, as being the cheapest conveyance attainable, and cantered off to find the executors of Muñoz, enjoying heartily such stares of admiration as he got for his splendid riding. In an hour he returned, found the ladies in their freshest dresses, and complimented them suitably. At this very moment his anguish of anxiety and suspense was terrible. When Clara should earn that she was a millionaire, what would she do? Would she throw off the air of friendliness which she had lately worn, and scout him as one whom she had long known as a scoundrel? Would all his plots, his labors, his perils, and his love prove in one moment to have been in vain? As he stood there smiling and flattering, he was on the cross.

"But I am talking trifles," he said at last, fairly catching his breath. "Can you guess why I do it? I am prolonging a moment of intense pleasure."

Such was his control over himself that he looked really benign and noble as he drew from his pocket a copy of the will and held it out toward Clara.

"My dear cousin," he murmured, his dark eyes searching her face with intense anxiety, "you cannot imagine my joy in announcing to you that you are the sole heir of the good Pedro Muñoz."

CHAPTER XXXV.

AT the announcement that she was a millionaire Clara turned pale, took the proffered paper mechanically with trembling fingers, and then, without looking at it, said, "Oh, Coronado!"

It was a tone of astonishment, of perplexity, of regret, of protest; it seemed to declare, Here is a terrible injustice, and I will none of it. Coronado was delighted; in a breath he recovered all his presence of mind; he recovered his voice, too, and spoke out cheerfully:

"Ah, you are surprised, my cousin. Well, it is your grandfather's will. You, as well as all others, must submit to it."

Aunt Maria jumped up and walked or rather pranced about the room, saying loudly, "He must have been the best man in the whole world." After repeating this two or three times, she halted and added with even more emphasis, "Except *you*, Mr. Coronado!"

The Mexican bowed in silence; it was almost too much to be praised in that way, feeling as he did; he bowed twice and waved his hand, deprecating the compliment. The interview was a very painful one to him, although he knew that he was gaining admiration with every breath that he drew, and admiration just where it was absolutely necessary to him. Turning to Clara now, he begged, "Read it, if you please, my cousin."

The girl, by this time flushed from chin to forehead, glanced over the paper, and immediately said, "This should not be so. It must not be."

Coronado was overjoyed; she evidently thought that she owed him and Garcia a part of this fortune; even if she kept it, she would feel bound to consider his interests, and the result of her conscientiousness might be marriage.

"Let us have no contest with the dead," he replied grandly. "Their wishes are sacred."

"But Garcia and you are wronged, and I cannot have it so," persisted Clara.

"How wronged?" demanded Aunt Maria. "I don't see it. Mr. Garcia was only a cousin, and he is rich enough already."

Coronado, remembering that he and Garcia were bankrupt, wished he could throw the old lady out of a window.

"Wait," said Clara in a tone of vehement resolution. "Give me time. You shall see that I am not unjust or ungrateful."

"I beg that you will not bestow a thought upon me," implored the sublime hypocrite. "Garcia, it is true, may have had claims. I have none."

Aunt Maria walked up to him, squeezed both his hands, and came near hugging him. Once out of this trial, Coronado could bear no more, but kissed his fingers to the ladies, hastened to his own room, locked the door, and swore all the oaths that there are in Spanish, which is no small multitude.

In a few days after this terrible interview things were going swimmingly well with him. To keep Clara out of the hands of fortune-hunters, but ostensibly to enable her to pass her first mourning in decent retirement, he had induced her to settle in one of Muñoz's haciendas, a few miles from the city, where he of course had her much to himself. He was her adviser; he was closeted frequently with the executors; he foresaw the time when he would be the sole manager of the estate; he began to trust that he would some day possess it. What woman could help leaning upon and confiding in a man who was so useful, so necessary as Coronado, and who had shown such unselfish, such magnanimous sentiments?

Meantime the girl was as admirable in reality as the man was in appearance. Unexpected inheritance of large wealth is almost sure to alter, at least for a time, and generally for the worse, the manner and morale of a young person, whether male or female. Conceit or haughtiness or extravagance or greediness, or some other vice, pretty surely enters into either deportment or conduct. If this girl was changed at all by her great good fortune, she was changed for the better. She had never been more modest, gentle, affable, and sensible than she was now. The fact shows a clearness of mind and a nobleness of heart which place her very high among the wise and good. Such behavior under such circumstances is equal to heroism. We are conscious that in saying these things of Clara we are drawing largely upon the reader's faith. But either her present trial of character was peculiarly fitted to her, or she was one of those select spirits who are purified by temptation.

She remembered Garcia's claims upon her grandfather, and her own supposed obligations to Coronado. She informed the executors that she wished to make over half her property to the old man, trusteeing it so that it should descend to his nephew. Their reply, translated from roundabout and complimentary Spanish into plain English, was this: "Yon can't do it. The estate is not settled, and will not be for a year. Moreover, you have no power to part with it until you are of age, which will not be for three years. Finally, your proposition defies your grandfather's wishes, and it is altogether too generous."

Clara's simple and firm reply was, "Well, I must wait. But it would seem better if I could do it now."

There was one reason why Clara should be so calm and unselfish in her elevation; her sorrows served her as ballast. Why should she let riches turn her head when she found that they could not lighten her heart? There was a certain night in her past which gold could not illuminate; there had once been a precious life near her, which was gone now beyond the power of ransom. Thurstane! How she would have lavished this wealth upon him. He would have refused it; but she would have prayed and forced him to accept it; she would have been the meeker to him because of it. How noble he had been! not now to be brought back! gone forever! And his going had been like the going away of the sun, leaving no beautiful color in all nature, no guiding light for wandering footsteps. She exaggerated him, as love will exaggerate the lost.

Of course she did not always believe that he could be dead, and in her hours of hope she wrote letters inquiring about his fate. In other days he had told her much of himself, stories of his childhood and his battles, the number of his old regiment and his new one, titles of his superiors, names of comrades, etc. To which among all these unknown ones should she address herself? She fixed on the commander of his present regiment, and that awfully mysterious personage the Adjutant-General of the army, a title which seemed to represent omniscience and omnipotence. To each of these gentlemen she sent an epistle recounting where, when, and how Lieutenant Ralph Thurstane had been ambushed by unknown Indians, supposed to be Apaches.

These letters she wrote and mailed without the knowledge of Coronado. This was not caution, but pity; she did not suspect that he would try to intercept them; only that it would pain him to learn how much she yet thought of his rival. Indeed, it would have been cruel to show them to him, for he would have seen that they were blurred with tears. You perceive that she had come to be tender of the feelings of this earnest and scoundrelly lover, believing in his sincerity and not in his villany.

"Surely some of those people will know," thought Clara, with a trust in men and dignitaries which makes one say *sancta simplicitas*. "If they do not know," she added, with a prayer in her heart, "God will discover it to them."

But no answers came for months. The colonel was not with his regiment, but on detached service at New York, whither Clara's letter travelled to find him, being addressed to his name and not marked "Official business." What he did of course was to forward it to the Adjutant-General of the army at Washington. The Adjutant-General successively filed both communications, and sent a copy of each to headquarters at Santa Fé and San Francisco, with an endorsement advising inquiries and suitable search. The mails were slow and circuitous, and the official routine was also slow and circuitous, so that it was long before headquarters got the papers and went to work.

Does any one marvel that Clara did not go directly to the military authorities in the city? It must be remembered that man has his own world, as woman has hers, and that each sex is very ignorant of the spheres and missions of the other, the retired sex being especially limited in its information. The girl had never been told that there was such a thing as district headquarters, or that soldiers in San Francisco had anything to do with soldiers at Fort Yuma. Nor was she in the way of learning such facts, being miles away from a uniform, and even from an American.

One day, when she was fuller of hope than usual, she dared to write to that ghost, Thurstane. Where should the letter be addressed? It cost her much reflection to decide that it ought to go to the station of his company, Fort Yuma. This gave her an idea, and she at once penned two other letters, one directed "To the Captain of Company I," and one to Sergeant Meyer. But unfortunately those three epistles were not sent off before it occurred to Coronado that he ought to overlook the packages that were sent from the hacienda to the city. By the way, he had from the first assumed a secret censorship over the mails which arrived.

Meantime he also had his anxiety and his correspondence. He feared lest Garcia should learn how things had been managed, and should hasten to San Francisco to act henceforward as his own special providence. In that case there would be awkward explanations, there would be complicated and perilous plottings, there might be stabbings or poisonings. Already, as soon as he reached the Mohave valley, he had written one cajoling letter to his uncle. Scattered through six pages on various affairs were underscored phrases and words, which, taken in sequence, read as follows:

"Things have gone well and ill. What was most desirable has not been fully accomplished. There have been perils and deaths, but not the one required. The wisest plans have been foiled by unforeseen circumstances. The future rests upon slow poison. A few weeks more will suffice. Do not come here. It would rouse suspicion. Trust all to me."

He now sent other letters, reporting the progress of the malady caused by the poison, urging Garcia to remain at a distance, assuring him that all would be well, etc.

"There will be no will," declared one of these lying messengers. "If there is a will, you will be the inheritor. In all events, you will be safe. Rely upon my judgment and fidelity."

It is curious, by the way, that such men as Coronado and Garcia, knowing themselves and each other to be liars, should nevertheless expect to be believed, and should frequently believe each other. One is inclined to admit the seeming paradox that rogues are more easily imposed upon than honest men.

No responses came from Garcia. But, by way of consolation, Coronado had Clara's correspondence to read. One day this hidalgo, securely locked in his room, held in his delicate dark fingers a letter addressed to Miss Clara Van Diemen, and postmarked in writing "Fort Yuma." Hot as the day was, there was a brazier by his side, and a kettle of water bubbling on the coals. He held the letter in the steam, softened the wafer to a pulp, opened the envelope carefully, threw himself on a sofa, scowled at the beating of his heart, and began to read.

Before he had glanced through the first line he uttered an exclamation, turned hastily to the signature, and then burst into a stream of whispered curses. After he had blasphemed himself into a certain degree of calmness, he read the letter twice through carefully, and learned it by heart. Then he thrust it deep into the coals of the brazier, watched it steadily until its slight flame had flickered away, lighted a cigarito, and meditated.

This epistle was not the only one that troubled him. He already knew that Clara was inquiring about this man of whom she never spoke, and conducting her inquiries with an intelligence and energy which showed that her heart was in the business. If things went on so, there might be trouble some day, and there might be punishment. For a time he was so disturbed that he felt somewhat as if he had a conscience, and might yet know what it is to be haunted by remorse.

As for Clara, he was furious with her, notwithstanding his love for her, and indeed because of it. It was outrageous that a woman whom he adored should seek to ferret out facts which might send him to State's Prison. It was abominable that she would not cease to care for that stupid officer after he had been so carefully put out of her way. Coronado felt that he was persecuted.

Well, what should be done? He must put a stop to Clara's inquiries, and he would do it by inquiring himself. Yes, he would write to people about Thurstane, show the letters to the girl (but never send them), and so gradually get this sort of correspondence into his own hands, when he would drop it. She would be led thereby to trust him the more, to be grateful to him, perhaps to love him. It was a hateful mode of carrying on a courtship, but it seemed to be the best that he had in his power. Having so decided, this master hypocrite, "full of all subtlety and wiles of the devil," turned his attention to his siesta.

For twenty minutes he slept the sleep of the just; then he was awakened by a timid knock at his door. Guessing from the shyness of the demand for entrance that it came from a servant, he called pettishly, "What do you want? Go away."

"I must see you," answered a voice which, feeble and indistinct as it was, took Coronado to the door in an instant, trembling in every nerve with rage and alarm.

CHAPTER XXXVI.

OPENING the door softly and with tremulous fingers, Coronado looked out upon an old gray-headed man, short and paunchy in build, with small, tottering, uneasy legs, skin mottled like that of a toad, cheeks drooping and shaking, chin retiring, nose bulbous, one eye a black hollow, the other filmy and yet shining, expression both dull and cunning, both eager and cowardly.

The uncle seemed to be even more agitated at the sight of the nephew than the nephew at the sight of the uncle. For an instant each stared at the other with a strange expression of anxiety and mistrust. Then Coronado spoke. The words which he had in his heart were, What are you here for, you scoundrelly old marplot? The words which he actually uttered were, "My dear uncle, my benefactor, my more than parent! How delighted I am to see you! Welcome, welcome!"

The two men grasped each other's arms, and stuck their heads over each other's shoulders in a pretence of embracing. Perhaps there never was anything of the kind more curious than the contrast between their affectionate attitude and the suspicion and aversion painted on their faces.

"Have you been seen?" asked Coronado as soon as he had closed and locked the door. "I must contrive to get you away unperceived. Why have you come? My dear uncle, it was the height of imprudence. It will expose you to suspicion. Did you not get my letters?"

"Only one," answered Garcia, looking both frightened and obstinate, as if he were afraid to stay and yet determined not to go. "One from the Mohave valley."

"But I urged you in that to remain at a distance, until all had been arranged."

"I know, my son, I know. I thought like you at first. But presently I became anxious."

"Not suspicious of my good faith!" exclaimed Coronado in a horrified whisper. "Oh, *that* is surely impossible."

"No, no—not suspicious—no, no, my son," chattered Garcia eagerly. "But I began to fear that you needed my help. Things seemed to move so slowly. Madre de Dios! All across the continent, and nothing done yet."

"Yes, much has been done. I had obstacles. I had people to get rid of. There was a person who undertook to be lover and protector."

"Is he gone?" inquired the old man anxiously.

"Ask no questions. The less told, the better. I wish to spare you all responsibility."

"Carlos, you are my son and heir. You deserve everything that I can give. All shall be yours, my son."

"That Texas Smith of yours is a humbug," broke out Coronado, his mind reverting to the letter which he had just burned. "I put work on him which he swore to do and did not do. He is a coward and a traitor."

"Oh, the pig! Did you pay him?"

"I had to pay him in advance—and then nothing done right," confessed Coronado.

"Oh, the pig, the dog, the toad, the villanous toad, the pig of hell!" chattered Garcia in a rage. "How much did you pay him? Five hundred dollars! Oh, the pig and the dog and the toad!"

"Well, I have been frank with you," said Coronado. (He had diminished by one half the sum paid to Texas Smith.) "I will continue to be frank. You must not stay here. The question is how to get you away unseen."

"It is useless; I have been recognized," lied Garcia, who was determined not to go.

"All is lost!" exclaimed Coronado. "The presence of us two—both possible heirs—will rouse suspicion. Nothing can be done."

But no intimidations could move the old man; he was resolved to stay and oversee matters personally; perhaps he suspected Coronado's plan of marrying Clara.

"No, my son," he declared. "I know better than you. I am older and know the world better. Let me stay and take care of this. What if I am suspected and denounced and hung? The property will be yours."

"My more than father!" cried Coronado. "You shall never sacrifice yourself for me. God forbid that I should permit such an infamy!"

"Let the old perish for the young!" returned Garcia, in a tone of meek obstinacy which settled the controversy.

It was a wonderful scene; it was prodigious acting. Each of these men, while endeavoring to circumvent the other, was making believe offer his life as a sacrifice for the other's prosperity. It was amazing that neither should lose patience; that neither should say, You are trying to deceive me, and I know it. We may question whether two men of northern race could have carried on such a dialogue without bursting out in open anger, or at least glaring with eyes full of suspicion and defiance.

"You will find her changed," continued Coronado, when he had submitted to the old man's persistence. "She has grown thinner and sadder. You must not notice it, however; you must compliment her on her health."

"What is she taking?" whispered Garcia.

"The less said, the better. My dear uncle, you must know nothing. Do not talk of it. The walls have ears."

"I know something that would be both safe and sure," persisted the old man in a still lower whisper.

"Leave all with me," answered Coronado, waving his hand authoritatively. "Too many cooks spoil the broth. What has begun well will end well."

After a time the two men went down to a shady veranda which half encircled the house, and found Mrs. Stanley taking an accidental siesta on a sort of lounge or sofa. Being a light sleeper, like many other active-minded people, she awoke at their approach and sat up to give reception.

"Mrs. Stanley, this is my uncle Garcia, my more than father," bowed Coronado.

"I have not forgotten him," replied Aunt Maria, who indeed was not likely to forget that mottled face, dyed blue with nitrate of silver.

Warmly shaking the puffy hand of the old toad, and doing her very best to smile upon him, she said, "How do you do, Mr. Gracia? I hope you are well. Mr. Coronado, do tell him that, and that I am rejoiced to see him."

Garcia's snaky glance just rose to the honest woman's face, and then crawled hurriedly all about the veranda, as if trying to hide in corners. Thanks to Coronado's fluency and invention, there was a mutually satisfactory conversation between the couple. He amplified the lady's compliments and then amplified the Mexican's compliments, until each looked upon the other as a person of unusual intelligence and a fast friend, Aunt Maria, however, being much the more thoroughly humbugged of the two.

"My uncle has come on urgent mercantile business, and he crowds in a few days with us," Coronado presently explained. "I have told him of my little cousin's good fortune, and he is delighted."

"I am so glad to hear it," said Mrs. Stanley. "What an excellent old man he is, to be sure! And you are just like him, Mr. Coronado—just as good and unselfish."

"You overestimate me," answered Coronado, with a smile which was almost ironical.

Before long Clara appeared. Garcia's eye darted a look at her which was like the spring of an adder, dwelling for just a second on the girl's face, and then scuttling off in an uncleanly, poisonous way for hiding corners. He saw that she was thin, and believed to a certain extent in Coronado's hints of poison, so that his glance was more cowardly than ordinary.

Liking the man not overmuch, but pleased to see a face which had been familiar to her childhood, and believing that she owed him large reparation for her grandfather's will, Clara advanced cordially to the old sinner.

"Welcome, Señor Garcia," she said, wondering that he did not kiss her cheek. "Welcome to your own house. It is all yours. Whatever you choose is yours."

"I rejoice in your good fortune," sighed Garcia.

"It is our common fortune," returned Clara, winding her arm in his and walking him up and down the veranda.

"May God give you long life to enjoy it," prayed Garcia.

"And you also," said Clara.

Coronado translated this conversation as fast as it was uttered to Mrs. Stanley.

"This is the golden age," cried that enthusiastic woman. "You Spaniards are the best people I ever saw. Your men absolutely emulate women in unselfishness."

"We would do it if it were possible," bowed Coronado.

"You do it," magnanimously insisted Aunt Maria, who felt that the baser sex ought to be encouraged.

"Señor Garcia, I ask a favor of you," continued Clara. "You must charge all the costs of the journey overland to me."

"It is unjust," replied the old man. "Madre de Dios! I can never permit it."

"If you need the money now, I will request my guardians, the executors, to advance it," persisted Clara, seeing that he refused with a faint heart.

"I might borrow it," conceded Garcia. "I shall have need of money presently. That journey was a great cost—a terribly bad speculation," he went on, shaking his mottled, bluish head wofully. "Not a piaster of profit."

"We will see to that," said Clara. "And then, when I am of age—but wait."

She shook her rosy forefinger gayly, radiant with the joy of generosity, and added, "You shall see. Wait!"

Coronado, in a rapid whisper, translated this conversation phrase by phrase to Mrs. Stanley, his object being to make Clara's promises public and thus engage her to their fulfilment.

"Of course!" exclaimed the impulsive Aunt Maria, who was amazingly generous with other people's money, and with her own when she had any to spare. "Of course Clara ought to pay. It is quite a different thing from giving up her rights. Certainly she must pay. That train did nothing but bring us two women. I really believe Mr. Garcia sent it for that purpose alone. Besides, the expense won't be much, I suppose."

"No," said Coronado, and he spoke the exact truth; that is, supposing an honest balance. The expedition proper had cost seven or eight thousand dollars, and about two thousand more had been sunk in assassination fees and other "extras." On the other hand, he had sold his wagons and beasts at the high prices of California, making a profit of two thousand dollars. In short, even deducting all that Coronado meant to appropriate to himself, Garcia would obtain a small profit from the affair.

Now ensued a strange underhanded drama. Garcia stayed week after week, riding often to the city on business or pretence of business, but passing most of his time at the hacienda, where he wandered about a great deal in a ghost-like manner, glancing slyly at Clara a hundred times a day without ever looking her in the eyes, and haunting her steps without overtaking or addressing her. Every time that she returned from a ride he shambled to the door to see if the saddle were empty. During the night he hearkened in the passages for outcries of sudden illness. And while he thus watched the girl, he was himself incessantly watched by his nephew.

"She gets no worse," the old man at last complained to the younger one. "I think she is growing fat."

"It is one of the symptoms," replied Coronado. "By the way, there is one thing which we ought to consider. If she gives you half of this estate——?"

"Madre de Dios! I would take it and go. But she cannot give until she is of age. And meantime she may marry."

He glanced suspiciously at his nephew, but Coronado kept his bland composure, merely saying, "No present danger of that. She sees no one but us."

He thought of adding, "Why not marry her yourself, my dear uncle?" But Garcia might retort, "And you?" which would be confusing.

"Suppose she should make a will in your favor?" the nephew preferred to suggest.

"I cannot wait. I must have money now. Make a will? Madre de Dios! She would outlive me. Besides, he who makes a will can break a will."

After a minute of anxious thought, he asked, "How much do you think she will give me?"

"I will ask her."

"Not *her*," returned Garcia petulantly. "Are you a pig, an ass, a fool? Ask the old one—the duenna. It ought to be a great deal; it ought to be half—and more."

To satisfy the old man as well as himself, Coronado sounded Mrs. Stanley as to the proposed division.

"Yes, indeed!" said the lady emphatically. "Clara must do something for Garcia, who has been such an excellent friend, and who ought to have been named in the will. But you know she has her duties toward herself as well as toward others. Now the property is not a million; it may be some day or other, but it isn't now. The executors say it might bring three hundred thousand dollars in ready money."

The executors, by the way, had been sedulously depreciating the value of the estate to Clara, in order to bring down her vast notions of generosity.

"Well," continued Aunt Maria, "my niece, who is a true woman and magnanimous, wanted to give up half. But that is too much, Mr. Coronado. You see money" (here she commenced on something which she had read)—"money is not the same thing in our hands that it is in yours. When a man has a hundred and fifty thousand dollars, he puts it into business and doubles it, trebles it, and so on. But a woman can't do that; she is trammelled and hampered by the prejudices of this male world; she has to leave her money at small interest. If it doubles once in her life, she is lucky. So, you see, one half given to Garcia would be, practically speaking, much more than half," concluded Aunt Maria, looking triumphantly through her argument at Coronado.

The Mexican assented; he always assented to whatever she advanced; he did so because he considered her a fool and incapable of reasoning. Moreover, he was not anxious to see half of this estate drop into the hands of Garcia, believing that whatever Clara kept for herself would shortly be his own by right of marriage.

"You are the greatest woman of our times," he said, stepping backward a pace or two and surveying her as if she were a cathedral. "I should never have thought of those ideas. You ought to be a legislator and reform our laws."

"I never had a doubt that you would agree with me, Mr. Coronado," returned the gratified Aunt Maria. "Well, so does Clara; at least I trust so," she hesitated. "Now as to the sum which our good Garcia should receive. I have settled upon thirty thousand dollars. In his hands, you know, it would soon be a hundred and fifty thousand; that is to say, practically speaking, it would be half the estate."

"Certainly," bowed Coronado, meanwhile thinking, "You old ass!" "And my little cousin is of your opinion, I trust?" he added.

"Well—not quite—as yet," candidly admitted Aunt Maria. "But she is coming to it. I have no sort of doubt that she will end there."

So Coronado had learned nothing as yet of Clara's opinions. As he sauntered away to find Garcia, he queried whether he had best torment him with this unauthorized babble of Mrs. Stanley. On the whole, yes; it might bring him down to reasonable terms; the rapacious old man was expecting too large a slice of the dead Muñoz. So he told his tale, giving it out as something which could be depended on, but increasing the thirty thousand dollars to fifty thousand, on his own responsibility. To his alarm Garcia broke out in a venomous rage, calling everybody pigs, dogs, toads, etc.; and crying and cursing alternately.

"Fifty thousand piasters!" he squeaked, tottering about the room on his short weak legs and wringing his hands, so that he looked like a fat dog walking on his hind feet. "Fifty thousand piasters! O Madre de Dios! It is nothing. It is nothing. It will not save me from ruin. It will not cover my debts. I shall be sold out. I am ruined. Fifty thousand piasters! O Madre de Dios!"

Fifty thousand dollars would have left him more than solvent; but ten times that sum would not have satisfied his grasping soul.

Coronado saw that he had made a blunder, and sought to rectify it by lying copiously. He averred that he had been merely trying his uncle; he begged his pardon for this absurd and ill-timed joke; he admitted that he was a pig and a dog and everything else ignoble; he should not have trifled with the feelings of his benefactor, his more than father; those feelings were to him sacred, and should be held so henceforward and forever

But he was not believed. He could fool the old man sometimes, but not on this occasion. Garcia, greedy and anxious, apt by nature to see the dark side of things, judged that the fifty-thousand-dollar story was the true one. Although he pretended at last to accept Coronado's explanation for fact, he remained at bottom unconvinced, and showed it in his swollen and trembling visage.

Thenceforward the nephew watched the uncle incessantly; during his absence he stole into his room, opened his baggage, and examined his drawers. and if he saw him near Clara at table, or when refreshments were handed around, he never took his eyes off him.

But he could not be always at hand. One day the two men rode to the city in company. Garcia dodged Coronado, hastened back to the hacienda, asked to have some chocolate prepared, poured out a cup for Clara, looked at her eagerly while she drank it, and then fell down in a fit.

An hour later Coronado returned at a full run, to find the old man just recovering his senses and Clara alarmingly ill.

CHAPTER XXXVII.

CLARA had been taken ill while waiting on the unconcious Garcia, and the attack had been so violent as to drive her at once to her room and bed.

The first person whom Coronado met when he reached the house was Aunt Maria, oscillating from one invalid to the other in such fright and confusion that she did not know whether she was strong-minded or not; but thus far chiefly troubled about Garcia, who seemed to her to be in a dying state.

"Your uncle!" she exclaimed, beckoning wildly to Coronado as he rushed in at the door.

"I know," he answered hastily. "A servant told me. How is Clara?"

He was as pale as a man of his dark complexion could be. Aunt Maria caught his alarm, and, forgetting at once all about Garcia, ran on with him to Clara's room. The girl was just then in one of her spasms, her features contracted and white, and her forehead covered with a cold sweat.

"What is it?" whispered Mrs. Stanley, clutching Coronado by the arm and staring eagerly at his anxious eyes.

"It is—fever," he returned, making a great effort to control his rage and terror. "Give her warm water to drink. My God! give her something."

He sent three servants in succession to search for three different physicians swearing at them violently while they made their preparations, telling them to ride like the devil, to kill their horses, etc. When he returned to Clara's room she had come out of her paroxysm, and was feebly trying to smile away Aunt Maria's terrors.

"My cousin!" he whispered in unmistakable anguish of spirit.

"I am better," she replied. "Thank you, Coronado. How is Garcia?"

Coronado looked as if he were devoting some one to the infernal furies; but he suppressed his emotion and replied in a smothered voice, "I will go and see."

Hurrying to his uncle's room, he motioned out the attendants, closed the door, locked it, and then, with a scowl of rage and alarm, advanced upon the invalid, who by this time was perfectly conscious.

"What have you given her?" demanded Coronado, in a hoarse mutter.

"I don't know what you mean," stammered the old man. He shut his one eye, not because he could not keep it open, but to evade the conflict which was coming upon him.

Taking quick advantage of the closed eye, Coronado turned to a dressing-table, pulled out a drawer, seized a key, and opened Garcia's trunk. Before the old man could interfere, the younger one held in his hand a paper containing two ounces or so of white powder.

"Did you give her this?" demanded Coronado.

Garcia stared at the paper with such a scared and guilty face, that it was equivalent to a confession.

Coronado turned away to hide his face. There was a strange smile upon it; at first it was a joy which made him half angelic; then it became amusement. He tottered to a chair, threw himself into it with the air of a thoroughly wearied man who finds rest delicious, put a grain of the powder on his tongue, and then drew a long sigh, a sigh of entire relief.

We must explain. The inner history of this scene is not a tragedy, but a farce. For two weeks or more Coronado had been watching his uncle day and night, and at last had found in his trunk a paper of powder which he suspected to be arsenic. A blunderer would have destroyed or hidden it, thereby warning Garcia that he was being looked after, and causing him to be more careful about his hiding places. Coronado emptied the paper, snapped off every grain of the powder with his finger, wiped it clean with his handkerchief, and refilled it with another powder. The selection of this second powder was another piece of cleverness. He had at hand both flour and finely pulverized sugar; but he wanted to learn whether Garcia would really dose the girl, and he wanted a chance to frighten him; so he chose a substance which would be harmless, and yet would cause illness.

"You will be hung," said Coronado, staring sternly at his uncle.

"I don't know what you mean," mumbled the old man, trembling all over.

"What a fool you were to use a poison so easily detected as arsenic! I have sent for doctors. They will recognize her symptoms. You prepared the chocolate. Here is the arsenic in your trunk. You will be hung."

"Give me that paper," whimpered Garcia, rising from his bed and staggering toward Coronado. "Give it to me. It is mine."

Coronado put the package behind him with one hand and held off his uncle with the other.

"You must go," he persisted. "She won't live two hours. Be off before you are arrested. Take horse for San Francisco. If there is a steamer, get aboard of it. Never mind where it sails to."

"Give me the paper," implored Garcia, going down on his knees. "O Madre de Dios! My head, my head! Oh, what extremities! Give me the paper. Carlos, it was all for your sake."

"Are you going?" demanded Coronado.

"Oh yes. Madre de Dios! I am going."

"Come along. By the back way. Do you want to pass *her* room? Do you want to see your work? I will send your trunk to the bankers. Quit California at the first chance. Quit it at once, if you go to China."

As Coronado looked after the flying old man he heard himself called by Mrs. Stanley, who was by this time in great terror about Clara, trotting hither and thither after help and counsel.

"Oh, Mr. Coronado, do come!" she urged. Then, catching sight of the galloping Garcia, "But what does that mean? Has he gone mad?"

"Nearly," said Coronado. "I brought him news of pressing business. How is my cousin?"

"Oh dear! I am terribly alarmed. Do look at her. Will those doctors never come!"

Coronado, who had been a little in advance of Mrs. Stanley as they hurried toward Clara's room, suddenly stopped, wheeled about with a smile, seized her hands, and shook them heartily.

"I have it," he exclaimed with a fine imitation of joyful astonishment. "There is no danger. I can explain the whole trouble. My poor uncle has these attacks, and he is extravagantly fond of chocolate. To relieve the attacks he always carries a paper of medicine in one of his vest pockets. To sweeten his chocolate he carries a paper of sugar in the companion pocket. You may be sure that he has made a mistake between the two. He has dosed Clara with his physic. There is no danger."

He laughed in the most natural manner conceivable; then he checked himself and said: "My poor little cousin! It is no joke for her."

"Certainly not," snapped Aunt Maria, relieved and yet angry. "How excessively stupid! Here is Clara as sick as can be, and I frightened out of my senses. Men ought not to meddle with cookery. They are such botches, even in their own business!"

But presently, after she had given Coronado's explanation to Clara, and the girl had laughed heartily over it and declared herself much better, Aunt Maria recovered her good humor and began to pity that poor, sick, driven Garcia.

"The brave old creature!" she said. "Out of his fits and off on his business. I must say he is a wonder. Let us hope he will come out all right, and soon return to us. But really he ought to be seen to. He may fall off his horse in a fit, or he may dose somebody dreadfully with his chocolate and get taken up for poisoning. Mr. Coronado, you ought to ride into town to-morrow and look after him."

"Certainly," replied Coronado. He did so, and returned with the news that Garcia had sailed to San Diego, having been summoned back to Santa Fé by the state of his affairs. That day and the night following he slept fourteen hours, making up the arrears of rest which he had lost in watching his uncle. Henceforward he was easier; he had a pretty clear field before him; there was no one present to poison Clara; no one but himself to court her. And the courtship went forward with a better prospect of success than is quite agreeable to contemplate.

Coronado and Clara were Adam and Eve; they were the only man and woman in this paradise. People thus situated are claimed by a being whom most call a goddess, and some a demon. She is protean; she is at once an invariable formula and an individual caprice; she is a law governing the universal multitude, and a passion swaying the unit. She seems to be under an impression that, where a couple are left alone together, they are the last relics of the human race, and that if they do not marry the type will perish. Indifferent to all considerations but one, she pushes them toward each other.

There is comparative safety from her in a crowd. Bachelors and maidens who mingle by hundreds may remain bachelors and maidens. But pair them off in lonely places and see if the result is not amazingly hymeneal. A fellow who has run the gauntlet of seven years of parties in New York will marry the first agreeable girl whom he meets in Alaska. There is such a thing as leaving the haunts of men and repairing to waste places to find a husband. We are told that English girls have reduced this to a system, and that fair archers who have failed at Brighton go out to hunt successfully in India.

Well, Coronado had the favoring chances of solitude, propinquity, and daily opportunity. Seldom away from Clara for a day together, he was in condition to take advantage of any of those moods which lay woman open to courtship, such as gratitude for attentions, a disgust with loneliness, a desire for something to love. It was a great thing for him that there was work about the hacienda which no woman could easily do; that there were men servants to govern, horses to be herded, valued, and sold, and lands to be cultivated. All these male mysteries were soon handed over to Coronado, subject to the advice of Aunt Maria and the final judgment of Clara. The result was that *he* and *she* got into a way of frequently discussing many things which threatened to habituate her to the idea of being at one with him through life.

Have you ever watched two specks floating in a vessel of water? For a long time they approach each other so slowly that the movement is imperceptible; but at last they are within range of each other's magnetism; there is a start, a swift rush, and they are together. Thus it was that Clara was gently, very gently, and unconsciously to herself, approaching Coronado. A mote on the wave of life, she was subject to attraction, as all of us motes are, and this man was the only tractor at hand. Aunt Maria did not count, for woman cnnnot absorb woman. As to Thurstane, he not only was not there, but he was not anywhere, as she at last believed.

Not a word from him or about him, except one letter from the Adjutant-General, which somehow evaded Coronado's brazier, gave her a moment of choking hope and fear, opened its white, official lips, acknowledged her "communication," and stopped there. The unseen tragedies in which souls suffer are numberless. Here was one. The girl had written with tears and heart-beats, and then with tears and heart-beats had waited. At last came the words, "I have the honor to acknowledge, etc., very respectfully, etc." It was one of the business-like facts of life unknowingly trampling upon a bleeding sentiment.

Imagine Clara's agitations during this long suspense; her plans and hopes and despairs would furnish matter for a library. There was not a day, if indeed there was an hour, during which her mind was not the theatre of a dozen dramas whereof Thurstane was the hero, either triumphant or perishing. They were horribly fragmentary; they broke off and pieced on to each other like nightmares; one moment he was rescued, and the next tomahawked. And this last fancy, despite all her struggles to hope, was for the most part victorious. Meantime Coronado, guessing her sufferings, and suffering horribly himself with jealousy, talked much and sympathetically to her of Thurstane. So much did this man bear, and with such outward sweetness did he bear it, that one half longs to consider him a martyr and saint. Pity that his goodness should not bear dissection; that it should have no more life in it than a stuffed mannikin; that it should be just fit to scare crows with.

But hypocrite as Coronado was, he was clever enough to win every day more of Clara's confidence; and perhaps she might have walked into this whited sepulchre in due time had it not been for an accident. Cantering into San Francisco to hold a consultation with her lawyer, she was saluted in the street by a United States officer, also on horseback. She instinctively drew rein, her pulse throbbing at sight of the uniform, and wild hopes beating at her heart.

"Miss Van Diemen, I believe," said the officer, a dark, stout, bold-looking trooper. "I am glad to see that you reached here in safety. You have forgotten me. I am Major Robinson."

"I remember," said Clara, who had not recollected him at first because she was looking solely for Thurstane. "You passed us in the desert."

"Yes, I took your soldiers away from you, and you declined my escort. I was anxious about you afterwards. Well, it has ended right in spite of me. Of course you have heard of Thurstane's escape."

"Escape!" exclaimed Clara, her face turning scarlet and then pale. "Oh! tell me!"

The major stared. He had guessed a love affair between these two; he had inferred it in the desert from the girl's anxiety about the young man. How came it that she knew nothing of the escape?

"So I have heard," he went on. "I think there can be no mistake about it. I learned it from a civilian who left Fort Yuma some weeks ago. I don't think he could have been mistaken. He told me that the lieutenant was there then. Not well, I am sorry to say; rather broken down by his hardships. Oh, nothing serious, you know. But he was a trifle under the weather, which may account for his not letting his friends hear from him."

At the story that Thurstane was alive, all Clara's love had arisen as if from a grave, and the mightier because of its resurrection. She was full of self-reproaches. It seemed to her that she had neglected him; that she had cruelly left him to die. Why had she not guessed that he was sick there, and flown to nurse him to health? What had he thought of her conduct? She must go to him at once.

"I am sorry to say that I can tell you no more," continued the major in response to her eager gaze.

"I am so obliged to you!" gasped Clara. "If you hear anything more, will you please let me know? Will you please come and see me?"

The major promised and took down her address, but added that he was just starting on an inspecting tour, and that for a fortnight to come he should be able to give her no further information.

They had scarcely parted ere Clara had resolved to go at once to Fort Yuma. The moment was favorable, for she had with her an intelligent and trustworthy servant, and Coronado had been summoned to a distance by business, so that he could make no opposition. She hastened to her lawyer's, finished her affairs there, drew what money she needed for her journey, learned that a brig was about to start for the Gulf, and sent her man to secure a passage. When he returned with news that the Lolotte would sail next day at noon, she decided not to go back to the hacienda, and took rooms at a hotel.

What would people say? She did not care; she was going. She had been womanish and timorous too long; this was the great crisis which would decide her future; she must be worthy of it and of *him*. But remembering Aunt Maria, she sent a letter by messenger to the hacienda, explaining that pressing business called her to be absent for some weeks, and confessing in a postscript that her business referred to Lieutenant Thurstane. This letter brought Coronado down upon her next morning. Returning home unexpectedly, he learned the news from his friend Mrs. Stanley, and was hammering at Clara's door not more than an hour later, all in a tremble with anxiety and rage.

"This must not be," he stormed. "Such a journey! Twenty-five hundred miles! And for a man who has not deigned to write to you! It is degrading. I will not have it. I forbid it."

"Coronado, stop!" ordered Clara; and it is to be feared that she stamped her little foot at him; at all events she quelled him instantly.

He sat down, glared like a mad dog, sprang up and rushed to the door, halted there to stare at her imploringly, and finally muttered in a hoarse voice, "Well—let it be so—since you are crazed. But I shall go with you."

"You can go," replied Clara haughtily, after meditating for some seconds, during which he looked the picture of despair. "You can go, if you wish it."

An hour later she said, in her usually gentle tone, "Coronado, pardon me for having spoken to you angrily. You are kinder than I deserve."

The reader can infer from this speech how humble, helpful, and courteous the man had been in the mean time. Coronado was no half-way character; if he did not like you, he was the fellow to murder you; if he decided to be sweet, he was all honey. Perhaps we ought to ask excuse for Clara's tartness by explaining that she was in a state of extreme anxiety, remembering that Robinson had hesitated when he said Thurstane was not so very ill, and fearing lest he knew worse things than he had told.

Meanwhile, let no one suppose that the Mexican meant to let his lady love go to Fort Yuma. He had his plan for stopping her, and we may put confidence enough in him to believe that it was a good one; only at the last moment circumstances turned up which decided him to drop it. Yes, at the last moment, just as he was about to pull his leading strings, he saw good reason for wishing her far away from San Francisco.

A face appeared to him; at the first glimpse of it Coronado slipped into the nearest doorway, and from that moment his chief anxiety was to cause the girl to vanish. Yes, he must get her started on her voyage, even at the risk of her continuing it.

"What the devil is he here for?" he muttered. "Has he found out that she is living?"

CHAPTER XXXVIII.

At noon the Lolotte, a broad-beamed, flat-floored brig of light draught and good sailing qualities, hove up her anchor and began beating out of the Bay of San Francisco, with Coronado and Clara on her quarter-deck.

"You have no other passengers, I understood you to say, captain," observed Coronado, who was anxious on that point, preferring there should be none.

The master, a Dane by birth named Jansen, who had grown up in the American mercantile service, was a middle-sized, broad-shouldered man, with a red complexion, red whiskers, and a look which was at once grave and fiery. He paused in his heavy lurching to and fro, looked at the Mexican with an air which was civil but very stiff, and answered in that discouraging tone with which skippers are apt to smother conversation when they have business on hand, "Yes, sir, one other."

Coronado presently slipped down the companionway, found the colored steward, chinked five dollars into his horny palm, and said, "My good fellow, you must look out for me; I shall want a good deal of help during the passage."

"Yes, sah, very good, sah," was the answer, uttered in a greasy chuckle, as though it were the speech of a slab of bacon fat. "Make you up any little thing, sah. Have a sup now, sah? Little gruel? Little brof?"

"No, thank you," returned Coronado, turning half sick at the mention of those delicacies. "Nothing at present. By the way, one of the staterooms is occupied I see. Who is the other passenger?"

"Dunno, sah; keeps hisself shut up, an' says nothin' to nobody. 'Pears like he is sailin' under secret orders. Cur'ous' lookin' old gent; got only one eye."

One eye! Coronado thought of the face which had frightened him out of San Francisco, and wondered whether he were shut up in the Lolotte with it.

"One eye?" he asked. "Short, stout, dark old gentleman? Indeed! I think I know him."

Stepping to the door of a stateroom which he had already noticed as being kept closed, he tapped lightly. There was a muttering inside, a shuffling as of some one getting out of a berth, and then a low inquiry in Spanish, "Who is there?"

"Me, sah," returned Coronado, imitating, and imitating perfectly, the accent of the steward, who meantime had gone forward, talking and sniggering to himself, after an idiotic way that he had.

The door opened a trifle, and Coronado instantly slipped the toe of his little boot into the crack, at the same time saying in his natural tone, "My dear uncle!"

Seeing that he was discovered, Garcia gave his nephew entrance, closed the door after him, locked it, and sat down trembling on the edge of the lower berth, groaning and almost whimpering, "Ah, my son! Ah, my dear Carlos! Oh, what a life I have to lead! Madre de Dios, what a life! I thought you were one of my creditors. I did indeed, my dear Carlos, my son."

"I thought you went back to Santa Fé," was Coronado's reply.

"No, I did not go; I started, but I came back," mumbled Garcia. Then, plucking up a little spirit, he turned his one eye for a moment on his nephew's face, and added, "Why should I go to Santa Fé? I had no business there. My business is here."

"But after your attempt at the hacienda?"

"My attempt! I made no attempt. All that was a mistake. Because I was sick, I was frightened and did not know what to do. I ran away because you told me to run. I had given her nothing. Yes, I did put something in her chocolate, but it was my medicine. I meant to put in sugar, but I made a mistake and went to the wrong pocket, the pocket of my medicine. That was it, Carlos. I give you my word, word of a hidalgo, word of a Christian."

It was the same explanation which Coronado had invented to forestall suspicions at the hacienda. It was surely a wonderful coincidence of lying, and shows how great minds work alike. Vexed and angry as the nephew was, he could scarcely help smiling.

"My dear uncle!" he exclaimed, grasping Garcia's pudgy hand melodramatically. "The very thing that occurred to me! I told them so."

"Did you?" replied the old man, not much believing it. "Then all is well."

He wanted to ask how it was that Clara had survived her dose; but of course curiosity on that subject must not find vent; it would be equivalent to a confession.

"Where is she going?" were his next words.

"To Fort Yuma."

"To Fort Yuma! What for?"

"I may as well tell it," burst out Coronado angrily. "She is going there to nurse that officer. He escaped, but he has been sick, and she *will* go."

"She must not go," whispered Garcia. "Oh, the——." And here he called Clara a string of names which cannot be repeated. "She shall not go there," he continued. "She will marry him. Then the property is gone, and we are ruined. Oh, the——." And then came another assortment of violent and vile epithets, such as are not found in dictionaries.

Coronado was anxious to divert and dissipate a rage which might make trouble; and as soon as he could get in a word, he asked, "But what have you been doing, my uncle?"

By dint of questioning and guessing he made out the story of the old man's adventures since leaving the hacienda. Garcia, in extreme terror of hanging, had gone straight to San Francisco and taken passage for San Diego, with the intention of not stopping until he should be at least as far away as Santa Fé. But after a few hours at sea, he had recovered his wits and his courage, and asked himself, why should he fly? If Clara died, the property would be his, and if she survived, he ought to be near her; while as for Carlos, he would surely never expose and hang a man who could cut him off with a shilling. So he landed at Monterey, took the first coaster back to San Francisco, lurked about the city until he learned that the girl was still living, and was just about to put a bold front on the matter by going to see her at the hacienda, when he learned accidentally that she was on the point of voyaging southward. Puzzled and alarmed by this, he resolved to accompany her in her wanderings, and succeeded in getting himself quietly on board the Lolotte.

"Well, let us go on deck," said Coronado, when the old man had regained his tranquillity. "But let us be gentle, my uncle. We know how to govern ourselves, I hope. You will of course behave like a mother to our little cousin. Congratulate her on her recovery; apologize for your awkward mistake. It was caused by the coming on of the fit, you remember. A man who is about to have an attack of epilepsy can't of course tell one pocket from another. But such a man is all the more bound to be unctuous."

Clara received the old man cordially, although she would have preferred not to see him there, fearing lest he should oppose her nursing project. But as nothing was said on this matter, and as Garcia put his least cloven foot foremost, the trio not only got on amicably together, but seemed to enjoy one another's society. This was no common feat by the way; each of the three had a great load of anxiety; it was wonderful that they should not show it. Coronado, for instance, while talking like a bird song, was planning how he could get rid of Garcia, and carry Clara back to San Francisco. The idea of pushing the old man overboard was inadmissible; but could he not scare him ashore at the next port by stories of a leak? As for Clara, he could not imagine how to manage her, she was so potent with her wealth and with her beauty. He was still thinking of these things, and prattling mellifluously of quite other things, when the Lolotte luffed up under the lee of the little island of Alcatraz.

"What does this mean?" he asked, looking suspiciously at the fortifications, with the American flag waving over them.

"Stop here to take in commissary stores for Fort Yuma," explained the thin, sallow, grave, meek-looking, and yet resolute Yankee mate.

The chain cable rattled through the hawse hole, and in no loug while the loading commenced, lasting until nightfall. During this time Coronado chanced to learn that an officer was expected on board who would sail as far as San Diego; and, as all uniforms were bugbears to him, he watched for the new passenger with a certain amount of anxiety; taking care, by the way, to say nothing of him to Clara. About eight in the evening, as the girl was playing some trivial game of cards with Garcia in the cabin, a splashing of oars alongside called Coronado on deck. It was already dark; a sailor was standing by the manropes with a lantern; the captain was saying in a grumbling tone, "Very late, sir."

"Had to wait for orders, captain," returned a healthy, ringing young voice which struck Coronado like a shot.

"Orders!" muttered the skipper. "Why couldn't they have had them ready? Here we are going to have a southeaster."

There was anxiety as well as impatience in his voice; but Coronado just now could not think of tempests; his whole soul was in his eyes. The next instant he beheld in the ruddy light of the lantern the face of the man who was his evil genius, the man whose death he had so long plotted for and for a time believed in, the man who, as he feared, would yet punish him for his misdeeds. He was so thoroughly beaten and cowed by the sight that he made a step or two toward the companionway, with the purpose of hiding in the cabin. Then desperation gave him courage, and he walked straight up to Thurstane.

"My dear Lieutenant!" he cried, trying to seize the young fellow's hand. "Once more welcome to life! What a wonder! Another escape. You are a second Orlando—almost a Don Quixote. And where are your two Sancho Panzas?"

"You here!" was Thurstane's grim response, and he did not take the proffered hand.

"Come!" implored Coronado, stepping toward the waist of the vessel and away from the cabin. "This way, if you please," he urged, beckoning earnestly. "I have a word to say to you in private."

Not a tone of this conversation had been heard below. Before the boat had touched the side the crew were laboring at the noisy windlass with their shouts of "Yo heave ho! heave and pawl! heave hearty ho!" while the mate was screaming from the knight-heads, "Heave hearty, men—heave hearty. Heave and raise the dead. Heave and away."

Amid this uproar Coronado continued: "You won't shake hands with me, Lieutenant Thurstane. As a gentleman, speaking to another gentleman, I ask an explanation."

Thurstane hesitated; he had ugly suspicions enough, but no proofs; and if he could not prove guilt, he must not charge it.

"Is it because we abandoned you?" demanded Coronado. "We had reason. We heard that you were dead. The muleteers reported Apaches. I feared for the safety of the ladies. I pushed on. You, a gentleman and an officer—what else would you have advised?"

"Let it go," growled Thurstane. "Let that pass. I won't talk of it—nor of other things. But," and here he seemed to shake with emotion, "I want nothing more to do with you—you nor your family. I have had suffering enough."

"Ah, it is with *her* that you quarrel rather than with me," inferred Coronado impudently, for he had recovered his self-possession. "Certainly, my poor Lieutenant! You have reason. But remember, so has she. She is enormously rich and can have any one. That is the way these women understand life."

"You will oblige me by saying not another word on that subject," broke in Thurstane savagely. "I got her letter dismissing me, and I accepted my fate without a word, and I mean never to see her again. I hope that satisfies you."

"My dear Lieutenant," protested Coronado, "you seem to intimate that I influenced her decision. I beg you to believe, on my word of honor as a gentleman, that I never urged her in any way to write that letter."

"Well—no matter—I don't care," replied the young fellow in a voice like one long sob. "I don't care whether you did or not. The moment she could write it, no matter how or why, that was enough. All I ask is to be left alone—to hear no more of her."

"I am obliged to speak to you of her," said Coronado. "She is aboard.

"Aboard!" exclaimed Thurstane, and he made a step as if to reach the shore or to plunge into the sea.

"I am sorry for you," said Coronado, with a simplicity which seemed like sincerity. "I thought it my duty to warn you."

"I cannot go back," groaned the young fellow. "I must go to San Diego. I am under orders."

"You must avoid her. Go to bed late. Get up early. Keep out of her way."

Turning his back, Thurstane walked away from this cruel and hated counsellor, not thinking at all of him however, but rather of the deep beneath, a refuge from trouble.

We must slip back to his last adventure with Texas Smith, and learn a little of what happened to him then and up to the present time.

It will be remembered how the bushwhacker sat in ambush; how, just as he was about to fire at his proposed victim, his horse whinnied; and how this whinny caused Thurstane's mule to rear suddenly and violently. The rearing saved the rider's life, for the bullet which was meant for the man buried itself in the forehead of the beast, and in the darkness the assassin did not discover his error. But so severe was the fall and so great Thurstane's weakness that he lost his senses and did not come to himself until daybreak.

There he was, once more abandoned to the desert, but rich in a full haversack and a dead mule. Having breakfasted, and thereby given head and hand a little strength, he set to work to provide for the future by cutting slices from the carcass and spreading them out to dry, well knowing that this land of desolation could furnish neither wolf nor bird of prey to rob his larder. This work done, he pushed on at his best speed, found and fed his companions, and led them back to the mule, their storehouse. After a day of rest and feasting came a march to the Cactus Pass, where the three were presently picked up by a caravan bound to Santa Fé, which carried them on for a number of days until they met a train of emigrants going west. Thus it was that Glover reached California, and Thurstane and Sweeny Fort Yuma.

Once in quiet, the young fellow broke down, and for weeks was too sick to write to Clara, or to any one. As soon as he could sit up he sent off letter after letter, but after two months of anxious suspense no answer had come, and he began to fear that she had never reached San Francisco. At last, when he was half sick again with worrying, arrived a horrible epistle in Clara's hand and signed by her name, informing him of her monstrous windfall of wealth and terminating the engagement. The cruelest thing in this cruel forgery was the sentence, "Do you not think that in paying courtship to me in the desert you took unfair advantage of my loneliness?"

She had trampled on his heart and flouted his honor; and while he writhed with grief he writhed also with rage. He could not understand it; so different from what she had seemed; so unworthy of what he had believed her to be! Well, her head had been turned by riches; it was just like a woman; they were all thus. Thus said Thurstane, a fellow as ignorant of the female kind as any man in the army, and scarcely less ignorant than the average man of the navy. He declared to himself that he would never have anything more to do with her, nor with any of her false sex. At twenty-three he turned woman-hater, just as Mrs. Stanley at forty-five had turned man-hater, and perhaps for much the same sort of reason.

Shortly after Thurstane had received what he called his cashiering, his company was ordered from Fort Yuma to San Francisco. It had garrisoned the Alcatraz fort only two days, and he had not yet had a chance to visit the city, when he was sent on this expedition to San Diego to hunt down a deserting quartermaster-sergeant. The result was that he found himself shipped for a three days' voyage with the woman who had made him first the happiest man in the army and then the most miserable.

How should he endure it? He would not see her; the truth is that he could not endure the trial; but what he said to himself was that he *would* not. In the darkness tears forced their way out of his eyes and mingled with the spray which the wind was already flinging over the bows. Crying! Three months ago, if any man had told him that he was capable of it, he would have considered himself insulted and would have felt like fighting. Now he was not even ashamed of it, and would hardly have been ashamed if it had been daylight. He was so thoroughly and hopelessly miserable that he did not care what figure he cut.

But, once more, what should he do? Oh, well, he would follow Coronado's advice; yes, damn him! follow the scoundrel's advice; he could think of nothing for himself. He would stay out until late; then he would steal below and go to bed; after that he would keep his stateroom. However, it was unpleasant to remain where he was, for the spray was beginning to drench the waist as well as the forecastle; and, the quarter-deck being clear of passengers, he staggered thither, dropped under the starboard bulwark, rolled himself in his cloak, and lay brooding.

Meanwhile Coronado had amused Clara below until he felt seasick and had to take to his berth. Escaping thus from his duennaship, she wanted to see a storm, as she called the half-gale which was blowing, and clambered bravely alone to the quarter-deck, where the skipper took her in charge, showed her the compass, walked her up and down a little, and finally gave her a post at the foot of the shrouds. Thurstane had recognized her by the light of the binnacle, and once more he thought, as weakly as a scared child, "What shall I do?" After hiding his face for a moment he uncovered it desperately, resolving to see whether she would speak. She did look at him; she even looked steadily and sharply, as if in recognition; but after a while she turned tranquilly away to gaze at the sea.

Forgetting that no lamp was shining upon him, and that she probably had no cause for expecting to find him here, Thurstane believed that she had discovered who he was and that her mute gesture confirmed his rejection. Under this throttling of his last hope he made no protest, but silently wished himself on the battle-field, falling with his face to the foe. For several minutes they remained thus side by side.

The Lolotte was now well at sea, the wind and waves rising rapidly, the motion already considerable. Presently there was an order of "Lay aloft and furl the skysails," and then short shouts resounded from the darkness, showing that the work was being done. But in spite of this easing the vessel labored a good deal, and heavy spurts of spray began to fly over the quarter-deck rail.

"I think, Miss, you had better go below unless you want to get wet," observed the skipper, coming up to Clara. "We shall have a splashing night of it."

Taking the nautical arm, Clara slid and tottered away, leaving Thurstane lying on the sloppy deck.

CHAPTER XXXIX.

HAD Clara recognized Thurstane, she would have thrown herself into his arms, and he would hardly have slept that night for joy.

As it was, he could not sleep for misery; festering at heart because of that letter of rejection; almost maddened by his supposed discovery that she would not speak to him, yet declaring to himself that he never would have married her, because of her money; at the same time worshipping and desiring her with passion ; longing to die, but longing to die for her ; half enraged, and altogether wretched.

Meantime the southeaster, dead ahead and blowing harder every minute, was sending its seas further and further aft. He left his wet berth on the deck, reeled, or rather was flung, to the stern of the vessel, lodged himself between the little wheel-house and the taffrail, and watched a scene in consonance with his feelings. Innumerable twinklings of stars faintly illuminated a cloudless, serene heaven, and a foaming, plunging ocean. The slender, dark outlines of the sailless upper masts were leaning sharply over to leeward, and describing what seemed like mystic circles and figures against the lighter sky. The crests of seas showed with ghostly whiteness as they howled themselves to death near by, or dashed with a jar and a hoarse whistle over the bulwarks, slapping against the sails and pounding upon the decks. The waves which struck the bows every few seconds gave forth sounds like the strokes of Thor's hammer, and made everything tremble from cathead to sternpost.

Every now and then there were hoarse orders from the captain on the quarter-deck, echoed instantly by sharp yells from the mate in the waist. Now it was, "Lay aloft and furl the fore royal;" and ten minutes later, "Lay aloft and furl the main royal." Scarcely was this work done before the shout came, "Lay aloft and reef the fore-t'gallant-s'l;" followed almost immediately by "Lay aloft and reef the main-t'gallant-s'l." Next came, "Lay out forrard and furl the flying jib." Each command was succeeded by a silent, dark darting of men into the rigging, and presently a trampling on deck and a short, sharp singing out at the ropes, with cries from aloft of "Haul out to leeward; taut hand; knot away."

Under the reduced sail the brig went easier for a while ; but the half gale had made up its mind to be a hurricane. It was blowing more savagely every second. One after another the topgallant sails were double-reefed, close-reefed, and at last furled. The watch on deck had its hands full to accomplish this work, so powerfully did the wind drag on the canvas. Presently, far away forward—it seemed on board some other craft, so faint was the sound—there came a bang, bang, bang! on the scuttle of the forecastle, and a hollow shout of "All hands reef tops'ls ahoy!"

Up tumbled the "starbowlines," or starboard watch, and joined the "larbowlines" in the struggle with the elements. No more sleep that night for man, boy. mate, or master. Reef after reef was taken in the topsails, until they were two long, narrow shingles of canvas, and still the wind brought the vessel well down on her beam ends, as if it would squeeze her by main force under water. The men were scarcely on deck from their last reefing job, when boom! went the jib, bursting out as if shot from a cannon, and then whipping itself to tatters.

"Lay out forrard!" screamed the mate. "Lay out and furl it."

After a desperate struggle, half the time more or less under water, two men dragged in and fastened the fragments of the jib, while others set the foretopmast staysail in its place. But the wind was full of mischief; it seemed to be playing with the ship's company; it furnished one piece of work after another with dizzying rapidity. Hardly was the jib secured before the great mainsail ripped open from top to bottom, and in the same puff the close-reefed foretopsail split in two with a bang, from earing to earing. Now came the orders fast and loud: "Down yards! Haul out reef tackle! Lay out and furl! Lay out and reef!"

It was a perfect mess; a score of ropes flying at once; the men rolling about and holding on ; the sails slapping like mad, and ends of rigging streaming off to leeward. After an exhausting fight the mainsail was furled, the upper half of the topsail set close-reefed, and everything hauled taut again. Now came an hour or so without accident, but not without incessant and fatiguing labor, for the two royal yards were successively sent down to relieve the upper masts, and the foretopgallant sail, which had begun to blow loose, was frapped with long pieces of sinnet.

During this period of comparative quiet Thurstane ventured an attempt to reach his stateroom. The little gloomy cabin was going hither and thither in a style which reminded him of the tossings of Gulliver's cage after it had been dropped into the sea by the Brobdingnag eagle. The steward was seizing up mutinous trunks and chairs to the table legs with rope-yarns.. The lamp was swinging and the captain's compass see-sawing like monkeys who had gone crazy in bedlams of tree-tops. From two of the staterooms came sounds which plainly confessed that the occupants were having a bad night of it.

" How is the lady passenger ? " Thurstane could not help whispering.

"Guess she's asleep, sah," returned the negro. "Fus-rate sailor, sah. But them greasers is having tough times," he grinned. "Can't abide the sea, greasers can't, sah."

Smiling with a grim satisfaction at this last statement, Thurstane gave the man a five-dollar piece, muttered, "Call me if anything goes wrong," and slipped into his narrow dormitory. Without undressing, he lay down and tried to sleep; but, although it was past midnight, he stayed broad awake for an hour or more ; he was too full of thoughts and emotions to find easy quiet in a pillow. Near him—yes, in the very next stateroom—lay the being who had made his life first a heaven and then a hell. The present and the past struggled in him, and tossed him with their tormenting contest. After a while, too, as the plunging of the brig increased, and he heard renewed sounds of disaster on deck, he began to fear for Clara's safety. It was a strange feeling. and yet a most natural one. He had not ceased to love ; he seemed indeed to love her more than ever; to think of her struggling in the billows was horrible; he knew even then that he would willingly die to save her. But after a time the incessant motion affected him, and he dozed gradually into a sound slumber.

Hours later the jerking and pitching became so furious that it awakened him, and when he rose on his elbow he was thrown out of his berth by a tremendous lurch. Sitting up with his feet braced, he listened for a little to the roar of the tempest, the trampling feet on deck, and the screaming orders. Evidently things were going hardly above ; the storm was little less than a tornado. Seriously anxious at last for Clara—or, as he tried to call her to himself, Miss Van Diemen—he stole out of his room, clambered or fell up the companionway, opened the door after a struggle with a sea which had just come inboard, got on to the quarter-deck, and, holding by the shrouds, quailed before a spectacle as sublime and more terrible than the Great Cañon of the Colorado.

It was daylight. The sun was just rising from behind a waste of waters ; it revealed nothing but a waste of waters. All around the brig, as far as the eye could reach, the Pacific was one vast tumble of huge blue-gray, mottled masses, breaking incessantly in long, curling ridges, or lofty, tossing steeps of foam. Each wave was composed of scores of ordinary waves, just as the greater mountains are composed of ranges and peaks. They seemed moving volcanoes, changing form with every minute of their agony, and spouting lavas of froth. All over this immense riot of tormented deeps rolled beaten and terrified armies of clouds. The wind reigned supreme, driving with a relentless spite, a steady and obdurate pressure, as if it were a current of water. It pinned the sailors to the yards, and nearly blew Thurstane from the deck.

The Lolotte was down to close-reefed topsails, close-reefed spencer and spanker, and storm-jib. Even upon this small and stout spread of canvas the wind was working destruction, for just as Thurstane reached the deck the jib parted and went to leeward in ribbons. Sailors were seen now on the bowsprit fighting at once with sea and air, now buried in water, and now holding on against the storm, and slowly gathering in the flapping, snapping fragments. Next a new jib (a third one) was bent on, hoisted half-way, and blown out like a piece of wet paper. Almost at the same moment the captain saw threatening mouths grimace in the mainsail, and screamed "Never mind there forrard. Lay up on the maintawps'l yard. Lay up and furl."

After half an hour's fight, the sail bagging and slatting furiously, it was lashed anyway around the yard, and the men crawled slowly down again, jammed and bruised against the shrouds by the wind. Every jib and forestaysail on board having now been torn out, the brig remained under close-reefed foretopsail, spencer, and spanker, and did little but drift to leeward. The gale was at its height, blowing as if it were shot out of the mouths of cannon, and chasing the ocean before it in mountains of foam. One thing after another went; the top-gallants shook loose and had to be sent down; the chain bobstays parted and the martingale slued out of place; one of the anchors broke its fastenings and hammered at the side; the galley gave way and went slopping into the lee scuppers. No food that morning except dry crackers and cold beef; all hands laboring exhaustingly to repair damages and make things taut. For more than half an hour three men were out on the guys and backropes endeavoring to reset the martingale, deluged over and over by seas, and at last driven in beaten. Others were relashing the galley, hauling the loose anchor and all the anchors up on the rail, and resetting the loose lee rigging, which threatened at every lurch to let the masts go by the board.

Thurstane presently learned that the wind had changed during the night, at first dropping away for a couple of hours, then reopening with fresh rage from the west, and finally hauling around into the northwest, whence it now came in a steady tempest. The vessel too had altered her course; she was no longer beating in long tacks toward the southeast; she was heading westward and struggling to get away from the land. Thurstane asked few questions; he was a soldier and had learned to meet fate in silence; he knew too that men weighted with responsibilities do not like to be catechised. But he guessed from the frequent anxious looks of the captain eastward that the California coast was perilously near, and that the brig was more likely to be drifting toward it than making headway from it. Surveying through his closed hands the stormy windward horizon, he gave up all thoughts of getting away from Clara by reaching San Diego, and turned toward the idea of saving her from shipwreck.

None of the other passengers came on deck this morning. Garcia, horribly seasick and frightened, held on desperately to his berth, and passed the time in screaming for the "stewrt," cursing his evil surroundings, calling everybody he could think of pigs, dogs, etc., and praying to saints and angels. Coronado, not less sick and blasphemous, had more command over his fears, and kept his prayers for the last pinch. Clara, a much better sailor, and indeed an uncommonly good one, was so far beaten by the motion that she did not get up, but lay as quiet as the brig would let her, patiently awaiting results, now and then smiling at Garcia's shouts, but more frequently thinking of Thurstane, and sometimes praying that she might find him alive at Fort Yuma.

The steward carried cold beef, hard bread, brandy, coffee, and gruel (made in his pantry) from stateroom to stateroom. The girl ate heartily, inquired about the storm, and asked, "When shall we get there?" Garcia and Coronado tried a little of the gruel and a good deal of the brandy and water, and found, as people usually do under such circumstances, that nothing did them any good. The old man wanted to ask the steward a hundred questions, and yelled for his nephew to come and translate for him. Coronado, lying on his back, made no answer to these cries of despair, except in muttered curses and sniffs of angry laughter. So passed the morning in the cabin.

Thurstane remained on deck, eating in soldierly fashion, his pockets full of cold beef and crackers, and his canteen (for every infantry officer learns to carry one) charged with hot coffee. He was pretty wet, inasmuch as the spray showered incessantly athwart ships, while every few minutes heavy seas came over the quarter bulwarks, slamming upon the deck like the tail of a shark in his agonies. During the morning several great combers had surmounted the port bow and rushed aft, carrying along everything loose or that could be loosened, and banging against the companion door with the force of a runaway horse. And these deluges grew more frequent, for the gale was steadily increasing in violence, howling and shrieking out of the gilded eastern horizon as if Lucifer and his angels had been hurled anew from heaven.

About noon the close-reefed foretopsail burst open from earing to earing, and then ripped up to the yard, the corners stretching out before the wind and cracking like musket shots. To set it again was impossible; the orders came, "Down yard—haul out reef tackle;" then half a dozen men laid out on the spar and began furling. Scarcely was this terrible job well under way when a whack of the slatting sail struck a Kanaka boy from his hold, and he was carried to leeward by the gale as if he had been a bag of old clothes, dropping forty feet from the side into the face of a monstrous billow. He swam for a moment, but the next wave combed over him and he disappeared. Then he was seen further astern, still swimming and with his face toward the brig; then another vast breaker rushed upon him with a lion-like roar, and he was gone. Nothing could be done; no boat might live in such a sea; it would have been perilous to change course. The captain glanced at the unfortunate, clenched his fists desperately, and turned to his rigging. Another man took the vacant place on the yard, and the hard, dizzy, frightful labor there went on unflaggingly, with the usual cries of "Haul out, knot away," etc. It was one of the forms of a sailor's funeral.

No time for comments or emotions; the gale filled every mind every minute. It was soon found that the spanker, a pretty large sail, well aft and not balanced by any canvas at the bow, drew too heavily on the stern and made steering almost impossible. A couple of Kanakas were ordered to reef it, but could do nothing with it; the skipper cursed them for "sojers" (our infantryman smiling at the epithet) and sent two first-class hands to replace them; but these also were completely beaten by the hurricane. It was not till a whole watch was put at the job that the big, bellying sheet could be hauled in and made fast in the reef knots. The brig now had not a rag out but her spencer and reduced spanker, both strong, small, and low sails, eased a good deal by their slant, shielded by the elevated port-rail, and thus likely to hold. But it was not sailing; it was simply lying to. The vessel rose and fell on the monstrous waves, but made scarcely more headway than would a tub, and drifted fast toward the still unseen California coast.

All might still have gone well had the northwester continued as it was. But about noon this tempest, which already seemed as furious as it could possibly be, suddenly increased to an absolute hurricane, the wind fairly shoving the brig sidelong over the water. Bang went the spanker, and then bang the spencer, both sails at once flying out to leeward in streamers, and flapping to tatters before the men could spring on the booms to secure them. The destruction was almost as instant and complete as if it had been effected by the broadside of a seventy-four fired at short range.

"Bend on the new spencer," shouted the captain. "Out with it and up with it before she rolls the sticks out of her."

But the rolling commenced instantly, giving the sailors no time for their work. No longer steadied by the wind, the vessel was entirely at the mercy of the sea, and went twice on her beam ends for every billow, first to lee and then to windward. Presently a great, white, hissing comber rose above her larboard bulwark, hung there for a moment as if gloating on its prey, and fell with the force of an avalanche, shaking every spar and timber into an ague, deluging the main deck breast high, and swashing knee-deep over the quarter-deck. The galley, with the cook in it, was torn from its lashings and slung overboard as if it had been a hencoop. The companion doors were stove in as if by a battering ram, and the cabin was flooded in an instant with two feet of water, slopping and lapping among the baggage, and stealing under the doors of the staterooms. The sailors in the waist only saved themselves by rushing into the rigging during the moment in which the breaker hung suspended.

Nothing could be done; the vessel must lift herself from this state of submergence; and so she did, slowly and tremulously, like a sick man rising from his bed. But while the ocean within was still running out of her scuppers, the ocean without assaulted her anew. Successive billows rolled under her, careening her dead weight this way and that, and keeping her constantly wallowing. No rigging could bear such jerking long, and presently the dreaded catastrophe came.

The larboard stays of the foremast snapped first; then the shrouds on the same side doubled in a great bight and parted; next the mast, with a loud, shrieking crash, splintered and went by the board. It fell slowly and with an air of dignified, solemn resignation, like Cæsar under the daggers of the conspirators. The cross stays flew apart like cobwebs, but the lee shrouds unfortunately held good; and scarcely was the stick overboard before there was an ominous thumping at the sides, the drum-beat of death. It was like guns turned on their own columns; like Pyrrhus's elephants breaking the phalanx of Pyrrhus.

"Axes!" roared the captain at the first crack. "Axes!" yelled the mate as the spar reeled into the water. "Lay forward and clear the wreck," were the next orders; "cut away with your knives."

Two axes were got up from below; the sailors worked like beavers, waist-deep in water; one, who had lost his knife, tore at the ropes with his teeth. After some minutes of reeling, splashing, chopping, and cutting, the fallen mast, the friend who had become an enemy, the angel who had become a demon, was sent drifting through the creamy foam to leeward. Meantime the mate had sounded the pumps, and brought out of them a clear stream of water, the fresh invasion of ocean.

Directly on this cruel discovery, and as if to heighten its horror to the utmost, the captain, clinging high up the mainmast shrouds, shouted, "Landalee! Get ready the boats."

Without a word Thurstane hurried down into the cabin to save Clara from this twofold threatening of death.

CHAPTER XL.

WHEN Thurstane got into the cabin, he found it pretty nearly clear of water, the steward having opened doors and trap-doors and drawn off the deluge into the hold.

The first object that he saw, or could see, was Clara, curled up in a chair which was lashed to the mast, and secured in it by a lanyard. As he paused at the foot of the stairway to steady himself against a sickening lurch, she uttered a cry of joy and astonishment, and held out her hand. The cry was not speech; her gladness was far beyond words; it was simply the first utterance of nature; it was the primal inarticulate language.

He had expected to stand at a distance and ask her leave to save her life. Instead of that, he hurried toward her, caught her in his arms, kissed her hand over and over, called her pet names, uttered a pathetic moan of grief and affection, and shook with inward sobbing. He did not understand her; he still believed that she had rejected him—believed that she only reached out to him for help. But he never thought of charging her with being false or hard-hearted or selfish. At the mere sight of her asking rescue of him he devoted himself to her. He dared to kiss her and call her dearest, because it seemed to him that in this awful moment of perhaps mortal separation he might show his love. If they were to be torn apart by death, and sepulchred possibly in different caves of the ocean, surely his last farewell might be a kiss.

If she talked to him, he scarcely heard her words, and did not realize their meaning. If it was indeed true that she kissed his cheek, he thought it was because she wanted rescue and would thank any one for it. She was, as he understood her, like a pet animal, who licks the face of any friend in need, though a stranger. Never mind; he loved her just the same as if she were not selfish; he would serve her just the same as if she were still his. He unloosed her arms from his shoulders, wondering that they should be there, and crawling with difficulty to the cabin locker, groped in it for life-preservers. There was only one in the vessel; that one he buckled around Clara.

"Oh, my darling!" she exclaimed; "what do you mean?"

"My darling!" he echoed, "bear it bravely. There is great danger; but don't be afraid—I will save you."

He had no doubts in making this promise; it seemed to him that he could overcome the billows for her sake—that he could make himself stronger than the powers of nature.

"Where did you come from? from another vessel?" she asked, stretching out her arms to him again.

"I was here," he said, taking and kissing her hands; "I was here, watching over you. But there is no time to lose. Let me carry you."

"They must be saved," returned Clara, pointing to the staterooms. "Garcia and Coronado are there."

Should he try to deliver those enemies from death? He did not hesitate a moment about it, but bursting open the doors of the two rooms he shouted, "On deck with you! Into the boats! We are sinking!"

Next he set Clara down, passed his left arm around her waist, clung to things with his right hand, dragged her up the companionway to the quarter-deck, and lashed her to the weather shrouds, with her feet on the wooden leader. Not a word was spoken during the five minutes occupied by this short journey. Even while Clara was crossing the deck a frothing comber deluged her to her waist, and Thurstane had all he could do to keep her from being flung into the lee scuppers. But once he had her fast and temporarily safe, he made a great effort to smile cheerfully, and said, "Never fear; I won't leave you."

"Oh! to meet to die!" she sobbed, for the strength of the water and the rage of the surrounding sea had frightened her. "Oh, it is cruel!"

Presently she smothered her crying, and implored, "Come up here and tie yourself by my side; I want to hold your hand."

He wondered whether she loved him again, now that she saw him; and in spite of the chilling seas and the death at hand, he thrilled warm at the thought. He was about to obey her when Coronado and Garcia appeared, pale as two ghosts, clinging to each other, tottering and helpless. Thurstane went to them, got the old man lashed to one of the backstays, and helped Coronado to secure himself to another. Garcia was jabbering prayers and crying aloud like a scared child, his jaws shaking as if in a palsy. Coronado, although seeming resolved to bear himself like an hidalgo and maintain a grim silence, his face was wilted and seamed with anxiety, as if he had become an old man in the night. It was rather a fine sight to see him looking into the face of the storm with an air of defying death and all that it might bring; and perhaps he would have been helpful, and would have shown himself one of the bravest of the brave, had he not been prostrated by sickness. As it was, he took little interest in the fate of others, hardly noticing Thurstane as he resumed his post beside Clara, and only addressing the girl with one word: "Patience!"

Clara and Thurstane, side by side and hand in hand, were also for the most part silent, now looking around them upon their fate, and then at each other for strength to bear it.

Meantime part of the crew had tried the pumps, and been washed away from them twice by seas, floating helplessly about the main deck, and clutching at rigging to save themselves, but nevertheless discovering that the brig was filling but slowly, and would have full time to strike before she could founder.

"'Vast there!" called the captain; "'vast the pumps! All hands stand by to launch the boats!"

"Long boat's stove!" shouted the mate, putting his hands to his mouth so as to be heard through the gale.

"All hands aft!" was the next order. "Stand by to launch the quarter-boats!"

So the entire remaining crew—two mates and eight men, including the steward—splashed and clambered on to the quarter-deck and took station by the boat-falls, hanging on as they could.

"Can I do anything?" asked Thurstane.

"Not yet," answered the captain; "you are doing what's right; take care of the lady."

"What are the chances?" the lieutenant ventured now to inquire.

With fate upon him, and seemingly irresistible, the skipper had dropped his grim air of conflict and become gentle, almost resigned. His voice was friendly, sympathetic, and quite calm, as he stepped up by Thurstane's side and said, "We shall have a tough time of it. The land is only about ten miles away. At this rate we shall strike it inside of three hours. I don't see how it can be helped."

"Where shall we strike?"

"Smack into the Bay of Monterey, between the town and Point Pinos.'

"Can I do anything?"

"Do just what you've got in hand. Take care of the lady. See that she gets into the biggest boat—if we try the boats."

Clara overheard, gave the skipper a kind look, and said, "Thank you, captain."

"You're fit to be capm of a liner, miss," returned the sailor. "You're one of the best sort."

For some time longer, while waiting for the final catastrophe, nothing was done but to hold fast and gaze. The voyagers were like condemned men who are preceded, followed, accompanied, jostled, and hurried to the place of death by a vindictive people. The giants of the sea were coming in multitudes to this execution which they had ordained; all the windward ocean was full of rising and falling billows, which seemed to trample one another down in their savage haste. There was no mercy in the formless faces which grimaced around the doomed ones, nor in the tempestuous voices which deafened them with threatenings and insult. The breakers seemed to signal to each other; they were cruelly eloquent with menacing gestures. There was but one sentence among them, and that sentence was a thousand times repeated, and it was always DEATH.

To paint the shifting sublimity of the tempest is as difficult as it was to paint the steadfast sublimity of the Great Cañon. The waves were in furious movement, continual change, and almost incessant death. They destroyed themselves and each other by their violence. Scarcely did one become eminent before it was torn to pieces by its comrades, or perished of its own rage. They were like barbarous hordes, exterminating one another or falling into dissolution, while devastating everything in their course.

There was a frantic revelry, an indescribable pandemonium of transformations. Lofty plumes of foam fell into hoary, flattened sheets; curling and howling cataracts became suddenly deep hollows. The indigo slopes were marbled with white, but not one of these mottlings retained the same shape for an instant; it was broad, deep, and creamy when the eye first beheld it; in the next breath it was waving, shallow, and narrow; in the next it was gone. A thousand eddies, whirls, and ebullitions of all magnitudes appeared only to disappear. Great and little jets of froth struggled from the agitated centres toward the surface, and never reached it. Every one of the hundred waves which made up each billow rapidly tossed and wallowed itself to death.

Yet there was no diminution in the spectacle, no relaxation in the combat. In the place of what vanished there was immediately something else. Out of the quick grave of one surge rose the white plume of another. Marbling followed marbling, and cataract overstrode cataract. Even to their bases the oceanic ranges and peaks were full of power, activity, and, as it were, explosions. It seemed as if endless multitudes of transformations boiled up through them from their abodes in sea-deep caves. There was no exhausting this reproductiveness of form and power. At every glance a thousand worlds of waters had perished, and a thousand worlds of waters had been created. And all these worlds, the new even more than the old, were full of malignity toward the wreck, and bent on its destruction.

The wind, though invisible, was not less wonderful. It surpassed the ocean in strength, for it chased, gashed, and deformed the ocean. It inflicted upon it countless wounds, slashing fresh ones as fast as others healed. It not only tore off the hoary scalps of the billows and flung them through the air, but it wrenched out and hurled large masses of water, scattering them in rain and mist, the blood of the sea. Now and then it made all the air dense with spray, causing the Pacific to resemble the Sahara in a simoom. At other times it levelled the tops of scores of waves at once, crushing and kneading them by the immense force that lay in its swiftness.

It would not be looked in the face; it blinded the eyes that strove to search it; it seemed to flap and beat them with harsh, churlish wings; it was as full of insult as the billows. Its cry was not multitudinous like that of the sea, but one and incessant and invariable, a long scream that almost hissed. On reaching the wreck, however, this shriek became hoarse with rage, and howled as it shook the rigging. It used the shrouds and stays of the still upright mainmast as an æolian harp from which to draw horrible music. It made the tense ropes tremble and thrill, and tortured the spars until they wailed a death-song. Its force as felt by the shipwrecked ones was astonishing; it beat them about as if it were a sea, and bruised them against the shrouds and bulwarks; it asserted its mastery over them with the long-drawn cruelty of a tiger.

Just around the wreck the tumult of both wind and sea was of course more horrible than anywhere else. These enemies were infuriated by the sluggishness of the disabled hulk; they treated it as Indians treat a captive who cannot keep up with their march; they belabored it with blows and insulted it with howls. The brig, constantly tossed and dropped and shoved, was never still for an instant. It rolled heavily and somewhat slowly, but with perpetual jerks and jars, shuddering at every concussion. Its only regularity of movement lay in this, that the force of the wind and direction of the waves kept it larboard side on, drifting steadily toward the land.

One moment it was on a lofty crest, seeming as if it would be hurled into air. The next it was rolling in the trough of the sea, between a wave which hoarsely threatened to engulf it, and another which rushed seething and hissing from beneath the keel. The deck stood mostly at a steep angle, the weather bulwarks being at a considerable elevation, and the lee ones dipping the surges. Against this helpless and partially water-logged mass the combers rushed incessantly, hiding it every few seconds with sheets of spray, and often sweeping it with deluges. Around the stern and bow the rush of bubbling, roaring whirls was uninterrupted.

The motion was sickly and dismaying, like the throes of one who is dying. It could not be trusted; it dropped away under the feet traitorously; then, by an insolent surprise, it violently stopped or lifted. It was made the more uncertain and distressing by the swaying of the water which had entered the hull. Sometimes, too, the under boiling of a crushed billow caused a great lurch to windward; and after each of these struggles came a reel to leeward which threatened to turn the wreck bottom up; the breakers meantime leaping aboard with loud stampings as if resolved to beat through the deck.

During hours of this tossing and plunging, this tearing of the wind and battering of the sea, no one was lost. The sailors were clustered around the boats, some clinging to the davits and others lashed to belaying pins, exhausted by long labor, want of sleep, and constant soakings, but ready to fight for life to the last. Coronado and Garcia were still fast to the backstays, the former a good deal wilted by his hardships, and the latter whimpering. Thurstane had literally seized up Clara to thc outside of the weather shrouds, so that, although she was terribly jammed by the wind, she could not be carried away by it, while she was above the heaviest pounding of the seas. His own position was alongside of her, secured in like manner by ends of cordage.

Sometimes he held her hand, and sometimes her waist. She could lean her shoulder against his, and she did so nearly all the while. Her eyes were fixed as often on his face as on the breakers which threatened her life. The few words that she spoke were more likely to be confessions of love than of terror. Now and then, when a billow of unusual size had slipped harmlessly by, he gratefully and almost joyously drew her close to him, uttering a few syllables of cheer. She thanked him by sending all her affectionate heart through her eyes into his.

Although there had been no explanations as to the past, they understood each other's present feelings. It could not be, he was sure, that she clung to him thus and looked at him thus merely because she wanted him to save her life. She had been detached from him by others, he said; she had been drawn away from thinking of him during his absence; she had been brought to judge, perhaps wisely, that she ought not to marry a poor man; but now that she saw him again she loved him as of old, and, standing at death's door, she felt at liberty to confess it. Thus did he translate to himself a past that had no existence. He still believed that she had dismissed him, and that she had done it with cruel harshness. But he could not resent her conduct; he believed what he did and forgave her; he believed it, and loved her.

There were moments when it was delightful for them to be as they were. As they held fast to each other, though drenched and exhausted and in mortal peril, they had a sensation as if they were warm. The hearts were beating hotly clean through the wet frames and the dripping clothing.

"Oh, my love!" was a phrase which Clara repeated many times with an air of deep content.

Once she said, "My love, I never thought to die so easily. How horrible it would have been without you!"

Again she murmured, "I have prayed many, many times to have you. I did not know how the answer would come. But this is it."

"My darling, I have had visions about you," was another of these confessions. "When I had been praying for you nearly all one night, there was a great light came into the room. It was some promise for you. I knew it was then; something told me so. Oh, how happy I was!"

Presently she added, "My dear love, we shall be just as happy as that. We shall live in great light together. God will be pleased to see plainly how we love each other."

Her only complaints were a patient "Isn't it hard?" when a new billow had covered her from head to foot, crushed her pitilessly against the shrouds, and nearly smothered her.

The next words would perhaps be, "I am so sorry for you, my darling. I wish for your sake that you had not come. But oh, how you help me!"

"I am glad to be here," firmly and honestly and passionately responded the young man, raising her wet hand and covering it with kisses. "But you shall not die."

He was bearing like a man and she like a woman. He was resolved to fight his battle to the last; she was weak, resigned, gentle, and ready for heaven.

The land, even to its minor features, was now distinctly visible, not more than a mile to leeward. As they rose on the billows they could distinguish the long beach, the grassy slopes, and wooded knolls beyond it, the green lawn on which stood the village of Monterey, the whitewashed walls and red-tiled roofs of the houses, and the groups of people who were watching the oncoming tragedy.

"Are you not going to launch the boats?" shouted Thurstane after a glance at the awful line of frothing breakers which careered back and forth athwart the beach.

"They are both stove," returned the captain calmly. "We must go ashore as we are."

CHAPTER XLI.

WHEN Thurstane heard, or rather guessed from the captain's gestures, that the boats were stove, he called, "Are we to do nothing?"

The captain shouted something in reply, but although he put his hands to his mouth for a speaking trumpet, his words were inaudible, and he would not have been understood had he not pointed aloft.

Thurstane looked upward, and saw for the first time that the main topmast had broken off and been cut clear, probably hours ago when he was in the cabin searching for Clara. The top still remained, however, and twisted through its openings was one end of a hawser, the other end floating off to leeward two hundred yards in advance of the wreck. Fastened to the hawser by a large loop was a sling of cordage, from which a long halyard trailed shoreward, while another connected it with the top. All this had been done behind his back and without his knowledge, so deafening and absorbing was the tempest. He saw at once what was meant and what he would have to do. When the brig struck he must carry Clara into the top, secure her in the sling, and send her ashore. Doubtless the crowd on the beach would know enough to make the hawser fast and pull on the halyard.

The captain shouted again, and this time he could be understood: "When she strikes hold hard."

"Did you hear him?" Thurstane asked, turning to Clara.

"Yes," she nodded, and smiled in his face, though faintly like one dying. He passed one arm around the middle stay of the shrouds and around her waist, passed the other in front of her, covering her chest; and so, with every muscle set, he waited.

Surrounded, pursued, pushed, and hammered by the billows, the wreck drifted, rising and falling, starting and wallowing toward the awful line where the breakers plunged over the undertow and dashed themselves to death on the resounding shore. There was a wide debatable ground between land and water. One moment it belonged to earth, the next lofty curling surges foamed howling over it; then the undertow was flying back in savage torrents. Would the hawser reach across this flux and reflux of death? Would the mast hold against the grounding shock? Would the sling work?

They lurched nearer; the shock was close at hand; every one set teeth and tightened grip. Lifted on a monstrous billow, which was itself lifted by the undertow and the shelving of the beach, the hulk seemed as if it were held aloft by some demon in order that it might be dashed to pieces. But the wave lost its hold, swept under the keel, staggered wildly up the slope, broke in a huge white deafening roll, and rushed backward in torrents. The brig was between two forces; it struck once, but not heavily; then, raised by the incoming surge, it struck again; there was an awful consciousness and uproar of beating and grinding; the next instant it was on its beam ends and covered with cataracts.

Every one aboard was submerged. Thurstane and Clara were overwhelmed by such a mass of water that they thought themselves at the bottom of the sea. Two men who had not mounted the rigging, but tried to cling to the boat davits, were hurled adrift and sent to agonize in the undertow. The brig trembled as if it were on the point of breaking up and dissolving in the horrible, furious yeast of breakers. Even to the people on shore the moment and the spectacle were sublime and tremendous beyond description. The vessel and the people on board disappeared for a time from their sight under jets and cascades of surf. The spray rose in a dense sheet as high as the maintopmast would have been had it stood upright.

When Thurstane came out of his state of temporary drowning, he was conscious of two sailors clambering by him toward the top, and heard a shout in his ears of "Cast loose."

It was the captain. He had sprung alongside of Clara, and was already unwinding her lashings. Thrice before the job was done they were buried in surf, and during the third trial they had to hold on with their hands, the two men clasping the girl desperately and pressing her against the rigging. It was a wonder that she and all of them were not disabled, for the jamming of the water was enough to break bones.

They got her up a few ratlines; then came another surge, during which they gripped hard; then there was a second ascent, and so on. The climbing was the easier and the holding on the more difficult, because the mast was depressed to a low angle, its summit being hardly ten feet higher than its base. Even in the top there was a desperate struggle with the sea, and even after Clara was in the sling she was half drowned by the surf.

Meantime the people on shore had made fast the hawser to a tree and manned the halyard. Not a word was uttered by Clara or Thurstane when they parted, for she was speechless with exhaustion and he with anxiety and terror. The moment he let go of her he had to grip a loop of top-hamper and hold on with all his might to save himself from being pitched into the water by a fresh jerk of the mast and a fresh inundation of flying surge. When he could look at her again she was far out on the hawser, rising and falling in quick, violent, perilous swings, caught at by the toppling breakers and howled at by the undertow. Another deluge blinded him; as soon as he could he gazed shoreward again, and shrieked with joy; she was being carefully lifted from the sling; she was saved—if she was not dead.

When the apparatus was hauled back to the top the captain said to Thurstane, "Your turn now."

The young man hesitated, glanced around for Coronado and Garcia, and replied, "Those first."

It was not merely humanity, and not at all good-will toward these two men, which held him back from saving his life first; it was mainly that motto of nobility, that phrase which has such a mighty influence in the army, "*An officer and a gentleman.*" He believed that he would disgrace his profession and himself if he should quit the wreck while any civilian remained upon it.

Coronado, leaving his uncle to the care of a sailor, had already climbed the shrouds, and was now crawling through the lubber hole into the top. For once his hardihood was beaten; he was pale, tremulous and obviously in extreme terror; he clutched at the sling the moment he was pointed to it. With the utmost care, and without even a look of reproach, Thurstane helped secure him in the loops and launched him on his journey. Next came the turn of Garcia. The old man seemed already dead. He was livid, his lips blue, his hands helpless, his voice gone, his eyes glazed and set. It was necessary to knot him into the sling as tightly as if he were a corpse; and when he reached shore it could be seen that he was borne off like a dead weight.

"Now then," said the captain to Thurstane. "We can't go till you do. Passengers first."

Exhausted by his drenchings, and by a kind of labor to which he was not accustomed, the lieutenant obeyed this order, took his place in the sling, nodded good-by to the brave sailors, and was hurled out of the top by a plunge of surf, as a criminal is pushed from the cart by the hangman.

No idea has been given, and no complete idea can be given, of the difficulties, sufferings, and perils of this transit shoreward. Owing to the rising and falling of the mast, the hawser now tautened with a jerk which flung the voyager up against it or even over it, and now drooped in a large bight which let him down into the seethe of water and foam that had just rushed over the vessel, forcing it down on its beam ends. Thurstane was four or five times tossed and as often submerged. The waves, the wind, and the wreck played with him successively or all together. It was an outrage and a torment which surpassed some of the tortures of the Inquisition. First came a quick and breathless plunge; then he was imbedded in the rushing, swirling waters, drumming in his ears and stifling his breath; then he was dragged swiftly upward, the sling turning him out of it. It seemed to him that the breath would depart from his body before the transit was over. When at last he landed and was detached from the cordage, he was so bruised, so nearly drowned, so every way exhausted, that he could not stand. He lay for quite a while motionless, his head swimming, his legs and arms twitching convulsively, every joint and muscle sore, catching his breath with painful gasps, almost fainting, and feeling much as if he were dying.

He had meant to help save the captain and sailors. But there was no more work in him, and he just had strength to walk up to the village, a citizen holding him by either arm. As soon as he could speak so as to be understood, he asked, first in English and then in Spanish, "How is the lady?"

"She is insensible," was the reply—a reply of unmeant cruelty.

Remembering how he had suffered, Thurstane feared lest Clara had received her death-stroke in the slings, and he tottered forward eagerly, saying, "Take me to her."

Arrived at the house where she lay, he insisted upon seeing her, and had his way. He was led into a room; he did not see and could never remember what sort of a room it was; but there she was in bed, her face pale and her eyes closed; he thought she was dead, and he nearly fell. But a pitying womanly voice murmured to him, "She lives," with other words that he did not understand, or could not afterward recall. Trusting that this unconsciousness was a sleep, he suffered himself to be drawn away by helping hands, and presently was himself in a bed, not knowing how he got there.

Meantime the tragedy of the wreck was being acted out. The sling broke once, the sailor who was in it falling into the undertow, and perishing there in spite of a rush of the townspeople. One of the two men who were washed overboard at the first shock was also drowned. The rest escaped, including the heroic captain, who was the last to come ashore.

When Thurstane was again permitted to see Clara, it was, to his great astonishment, the morning of the following day. He had slept like the dead ; if any one had sought to awaken him, it would have been almost impossible ; there was no strength left in body or spirt but for sleep. Clara's story had been much the same : insensibility, then swoons, then slumber ; twelve hours of utter unconsciousness. On waking the first words of each were to ask for the other. Thurstane put on his scarcely dried uniform and hurried to the girl's room. She received him at the door, for she had heard his step although it was on tiptoe, and she knew his knock although as light as the beating of a bird's wing.

It was another of those interviews which cannot be described, and perhaps should not be. They were uninterrupted, for the ladies of the house had learned from Clara that this was her betrothed, and they had woman's sense of the sacredness of such meetings. Presents came, and were not sent in : Coronado called and was not admitted. The two were alone for two hours, and the two hours passed like two minutes. Of course all the ugly past was explained.

"A letter dismissing you!" exclaimed Clara with tears. "Oh! how could you think that I would write such a letter? Never—never! Oh, I never could. My hand should drop off first. I should die in trying to write such wickedness. What! don't you know me better? Don't you know that I am true to you? Oh, how could you believe it of me? My darling, how could you?"

"Forgive me," begged the humbled young fellow, trembling with joy in his humility. "It was weak and wicked in me. I deserved to be punished as I have been. And, oh, I did not deserve this happiness. But, my little girl, how could I help being deceived? There was your handwriting and your signature."

"Ah! I know who it was," broke out Clara. "It has been he all through. He shall pay for this, and for all," she added, her Spanish blood rising in her cheeks, and her soft eyes sparkling angrily for a minute.

"I have saved his life for the last time," returned Thurstane. "I have spared it for the last time. Hereafter——"

"My darling, my darling!" begged Clara, alarmed by his blackening brow. "Oh, my darling, I don't love to see you angry. Just now, when we have just been spared to each other, don't let us be angry. I spoke angrily first. Forgive me."

"Let him keep out of my way," muttered Thurstane, only in part pacified.

"Yes," answered Clara, thinking that she would herself send Coronado off, so that there might be no duel between him and this dear one.

Presently the lover added one thing which he had felt all the time ought to have been said at first.

"The letter——it was right. Although *he* wrote it, it was right. I have no claim to marry a rich woman, and you have no right to marry a poor man."

He uttered this in profound misery, and yet with a firm resolution. Clara turned pale and stared at him with anxious eyes, her lips parted as though to speak, but saying nothing. Knowing his fastidious sense of honor, she guessed the full force with which this scruple weighed upon him, and she did not know how to drag it off his soul.

"You are worth a million," he went on, in a broken-hearted sort of voice which to us may seem laughable, but which brought the tears into Clara's eyes.

The next instant she brightened; she knew, or thought she knew, that she was not worth a million; so she smiled like a sunburst and caught him gayly by the wrists.

"A million!" she scoffed, laughingly. "Do you believe all Coronado tells you?"

"What! isn't it true?" exclaimed Thurstane, reddening with joy. "Then you are not heir to your grandfather's fortune? It was one of *his* lies? Oh, my little girl, I am forever happy."

She had not meant all this; but how could she undeceive him? The tempting thought came into her mind that she would marry him while he was in this ignorance, and so relieve him of his noble scruples about taking an heiress. It was one of those white lies which, it seems to us, must fade out of themselves from the record book, without even needing to be blotted by the tear of an angel.

"Are you glad?" she smiled, though anxious at heart, for deception alarmed her. "Really glad to find me poor?"

His only response was to cover her hands, and hair, and forehead with kisses.

At last came the question, When? Clara hesitated; her face and neck bloomed with blushes as dewy as flowers; she looked at him once piteously, and then her gaze fell in beautiful shame.

"When would you like?" she at last found breath to whisper.

"Now—here," was the answer, holding both her hands and begging with his blue-black eyes, as soft then as a woman's.

"Yes, at once," he continued to implore. "It is best every way. It will save you from persecutions. My love, is it not best?"

Under the circumstances we cannot wonder that this should be just as she desired.

"Yes—it is—best," she murmured, hiding her face against his shoulder. "What you say is true. It will save me trouble."

After a short heaven of silence he added, "I will go and see what is needed. I must find a priest."

As he was departing she caught him; it seemed to her just then that she could not be a wife so soon; but the result was that after another silence and a faint sobbing, she let him go.

Meantime Coronado, that persevering and audacious but unlucky conspirator, was in treble trouble. He was afraid that he would lose Clara; afraid that his plottings had been brought to light, and that he would be punished; afraid that his uncle would die and thus deprive him of all chance of succeeding to any part of the estate of Muñoz. Garcia had been brought ashore apparently at his last gasp, and he had not yet come out of his insensibility. For a time Coronado hoped that he was in one of his fits; but after eighteen hours he gave up that feeble consolation; he became terribly anxious about the old man; he felt as though he loved him. The people of Monterey universally admitted that they had never before known such an affectionate nephew and tender-hearted Christian as Coronado.

He tried to see Clara, meaning to make the most with her of Garcia's condition, and hoping that thus he could divert her a little from Thurstane. But somehow all his messages failed; the little house which held her repelled him as if it had been a nunnery ; nor could he get a word or even a note from her. The truth is that Clara, fearing lest Coronado should tell more stories about her million to Thurstane, had taken the women of the family into her confidence and easily got them to lay a sly embargo on callers and correspondents.

On the second day Garcia came to himself for a few minutes, and struggled hard to say something to his nephew, but could give forth only a feeble jabber, after which he turned blank again. Coronado, in the extreme of anxiety, now made another effort to get at Clara. Reaching her house, he learned from a bystander that she had gone out to walk with the Americano, and then he thought he discovered them entering the distant church.

He set off at once in pursuit, asking himself with an anxiety which almost made him faint, " Are they to be married ? "

CHAPTER XLII.

IN those days the hymeneal laws of California were as easy as old shoes, and people could espouse each other about as rapidly as they might want to.

The consequence was that, although Ralph Thurstane and Clara Van Diemen had only been two days in Monterey and had gone through no forms of publication, they were actually being married when Coronado reached the village church.

Leaning against the wall, with eyes as fixed and face as livid as if he were a corpse from the neighboring cemetery, he silently witnessed a ceremony which it would have been useless for him to interrupt, and then, stepping softly out of a side door, lurked away.

He walked a quarter of a mile very fast, ran nearly another quarter of a mile, turned into a by-road, sought its thickest underbrush, threw himself on the ground, and growled. For once he had a heavier burden upon him than he could bear in human presence, or bear quietly anywhere. He must be alone ; also he must weep and curse. He was in a state to tear his hair and to beat his head against the earth. Refined as Coronado usually was, admirably as he could imitate the tranquil gentleman of modern civilization, he still had in him enough of the natural man to rave. For a while he was as simple and as violent in his grief as ever was any Celtiberian cave-dweller of the stone age.

Jealousy, disappointed love, disappointed greed, plans balked, labor lost, perils incurred in vain ! All the calamities that he could most dread seemed to have fallen upon him together ; he was like a man sucked by the arms of a polypus, dying in one moment many deaths. We must, however, do him the justice to believe that the wound which tore the sharpest was that which lacerated his heart. At this time, when he realized that he had altogether and forever lost Clara, he found that he loved her as he had never yet believed himself capable of loving. Considering the nobility of this passion, we must grant some sympathy to Coronado.

Unfortunate as he was, another misfortune awaited him. When he returned to the house where Garcia lay, he found that the old man, his sole relative and sole friend, had expired. To Coronado this dead body was the carcass of all remaining hope. The exciting drama of struggle and expectation which had so violently occupied him for the last six months, and which had seemed to promise such great success, was over. Even if he could have resolved to kill Clara, there was no longer anything to be gained by it, for her money would not descend to Coronado. Even if he should kill Thurstane, that would be a harm rather than a benefit, for his widow would hate Coronado. If he did any evil deed now, it must be from jealousy or from vindictiveness. Was murder of any kind worth while? For the time, whether it were worth while or not, he was furious enough to do it.

If he did not act, he must go; for as everything had miscarried, so much had doubtless been discovered, and he might fairly expect chastisement. While he hesitated a glance into the street showed him something which decided him, and sent him far from Monterey before sundown. Half a dozen armed horsemen, three of them obviously Americans, rode by with a pinioned prisoner, in whom Coronado recognized Texas Smith. He did not stop to learn that his old bravo had committed a murder in the village, and that a vigilance committee had sent a deputation after him to wait upon him into the other world. The sight of that haggard, scarred, wicked face, and the thought of what confessions the brute might be led to if he should recognize his former employer, were enough to make Coronado buy a horse and ride to unknown regions.

Under the circumstances it would perhaps be unreasonable to blame him for leaving his uncle to be buried by Clara and Thurstane.

These two, we easily understand, were not much astonished and not at all grieved by his departure.

"He is gone," said Thurstane, when he learned the fact. "No wonder."

"I am so glad!" replied Clara.

"I suspect him now of being at the bottom of all our troubles."

"Don't let us talk of it, my love. It is too ugly. The present is so beautiful!"

"I must hurry back to San Francisco and try to get a leave of absence," said the husband, turning to pleasanter subjects. "I want full leisure to be happy."

"And you won't let them send you to San Diego?" begged the wife. "No more voyages now. If you do go, I shall go with you."

"Oh no, my child. I can't trust the sea with you again. Not after this," and he waved his hand toward the wreck of the brig.

"Then I will beg myself for your leave of absence."

Thurstane laughed; that would never do; no such condescension in *his* wife!

They went by land to San Francisco, and Clara kept the secret of her million during the whole journey, letting her husband pay for everything out of his shallow pocket, precisely as if she had no money. Arrived in the city, he left her in a hotel and hurried to headquarters. Two hours later he returned smiling, with the news that a brother officer had volunteered to take his detail, and that he had obtained a honeymoon leave of absence for thirty days.

"Barclay is a trump," he said. "It is all the prettier in him to go that he has a wife of his own. The commandant made no objection to the exchange. In fact the old fellow behaved like a father to me, shook hands, patted me on the shoulder, congratulated me, and all that sort of thing. Old boy, married himself, and very fond of his family. Upon my word, it seems to better a man's heart to marry him."

"Of course it does," chimed in Clara. "He is so much happier that of course he is better."

"Well, my little princess, where shall we go?"

"Go first to see Aunt Maria. There! don't make a face. She is very good in the long run. She will be sweet enough to you in three days."

"Of course I will go. Where is she?"

"Boarding at a hacienda a few miles from town. We can take horses, canter out there, and pass the night."

She was full of spirits; laughed and chattered all the way; laughed at everything that was said; chattered like a pleased child. Of course she was thinking of the surprise that she would give him, and how she had circumvented his sense of honor about marrying a rich girl, and how hard and fast she had him. Moreover the contrast between her joyous present and her anxious past was alone enough to make her run over with gayety. All her troubles had vanished in a pack; she had gone at one bound from purgatory to paradise.

At the hacienda Thurstane was a little struck by the respect with which the servants received Clara; but as she signed to them to be silent, not a word was uttered which could give him a suspicion of the situation. Mrs. Stanley, moreover, was taking a siesta, and so there was another tell-tale mouth shut.

"Nobody seems to be at home," said Clara, bursting into a merry laugh over her trick as they entered the house. "Where can the master and mistress be?"

They were now in a large and handsomely furnished room, which was the parlor of the hacienda.

"Don't sit down," cried Clara, her eyes sparkling with joy. "Stand just there as you are. Let me look at you a moment. Wait till I tell you something."

She fronted him for a few seconds, watching his wondering face, hesitating, blushing, and laughing. Suddenly she bounded forward, threw her arms around his shoulders and cried excitedly, hysterically, "My love! my husband! all this is yours. Oh, how happy I am!"

The next moment she burst into tears on the shoulder to which she was clinging.

"What is the matter?" demanded Thurstane in some alarm; for he did not know that women can tremble and weep with gladness, and he thought that surely his wife was sick if not deranged.

"What! don't you guess it?" she asked, drawing back with a little more calmness, and looking tenderly into his puzzled eyes.

"You don't mean——?"

"Yes, darling."

"It can't be that——?"

"Yes, darling."

He began to comprehend the trick that had been played upon him, although as yet he could not fully credit it. What mainly bewildered him was that Clara, whom he had always supposed to be as artless as a child—Clara, whom he had cared for as an elder and a father—should have been able to keep a secret and devise a plot and carry out a mystification.

"Great——Scott!" he gasped in his stupefaction, using the name of the then commander-in-chief for an oath, as officers sometimes did in those days.

"Yes, yes, yes," laughed and chattered Clara. "Great Scott and great Thurstane! All yours. Three hundred thousand. Half a million. A million. I don't know how much. All I know is that it is all yours. Oh, my darling! oh, my darling! How I have fooled you! Are you angry with me? Say, are you angry? What will you do to me?"

We must excuse Thurstane for finding no other chastisement than to squeeze her in his arms and choke her with kisses. Next he held her from him, set her down upon a sofa, fell back a pace and stared at her much as if she were a totally new discovery, something in the way of an arrival from the moon. He was in a state of profound amazement at the dexterity with which she had taken his destiny out of his own hands into hers, without his knowledge. He had not supposed that she was a tenth part so clever. For the first time he perceived that she was his match, if indeed she were not the superior nature; and it is a remarkable fact, though not a dark one if one looks well into it, that he respected her the more for being too much for him.

"It beats Hannibal," he said at last. "Who would have expected such generalship in you? I am as much astonished as if you had turned into a knight in armor. Well, how much it has saved me! I should have hesitated and been miserable; and I should have married you all the same; and then been ashamed of marrying money, and had it rankle in me for years. And now—oh, you wise little thing!—all I can say is, I worship you."

"Yes, darling," replied Clara, walking gravely up to him, putting her hands on his shoulders, and looking him thoughtfully in the eyes. "It was the wisest thing I ever did. Don't be afraid of me. I never shall be so clever again. I never shall be so tempted to be clever."

We must pass over a few months. Thurstane soon found that he had the Muñoz estate in his hands, and that, for the while at least, it demanded all his time and industry. Moreover, there being no war and no chance of martial distinction, it seemed absurd to let himself be ordered about from one hot and cramped station to another, when he had money enough to build a palace, and a wife who could make it a paradise. Finally, he had a taste for the natural sciences, and his observations in the Great Cañon and among the other marvels of the desert had quickened this inclination to a passion, so that he craved leisure for the study of geology, mineralogy, and chemistry. He resigned his commission, established himself in San Francisco, bought all the scientific books he could hear of, made expeditions to the California mountains, collected garrets full of specimens, and was as happy as a physicist always is.

Perhaps his happiness was just a little increased when Mrs. Stanley announced her intention of returning to New York. The lady had been amiable on the whole, as she meant always to be; but she could not help daily taking up her parable concerning the tyranny and stupidlty of man and the superior virtue of woman; and sometimes she felt it her duty to put it to Thurstane that he owed everything to his wife; all of which was more or less wearing, even to her niece. At the same time she was such a disinterested, well-intentioned creature that it was impossible not to grant her a certain amount of admiration. For instance, when Clara proposed to make her comfortable for life by settling upon her fifty thousand dollars, she replied peremptorily that it was far too much for an old woman who had decided to turn her back on the frivolities of society, and she could with difficulty be brought to accept twenty thousand.

Furthermore, she was capable, that is, in certain favored moments, of confessing error. "My dear," she said to Clara, some weeks after the marriage, "I have made one great mistake since I came to these countries. I believed that Mr. Coronado was the right man and Mr. Thurstane the wrong one. Oh, that smooth-tongued, shiny-eyed, meeching, bowing, complimenting hypocrite! I see at last what a villain he was. *I* see it," she emphasized, as if nobody else had discovered it. "To think that a person who was so right on the main question [female suffrage] could be so wrong on everything else! The contradiction adds to his guilt. Well, I have had my lesson. Every one must make her mistake. I shall never be so humbugged again."

Some little time after Thurstane had received the acceptance of his resignation and established himself in his handsome city house, Aunt Maria observed abruptly, "My dears, I must go back."

"Go back where? To the desert and turn hermit?" asked Clara, who was accustomed to joke her relative about "spheres and missions."

"To New York," replied Mrs. Stanley. "I can accomplish nothing here. This miserable Legislature will take no notice of my petitions for female suffrage."

"Oh, that is because you sign them alone," laughed the younger lady.

"I can't get anybody else to sign them," said Aunt Maria with some asperity. "And what if I do sign them alone? A house full of men ought to have gallantry enough to grant one lady's request. California is not ripe for any great and noble measure. I can't remain where I find so little sympathy and collaboration. I must go where I can be of use. It is my duty."

And go she did. But before she shook off her dust against the Pacific coast there was an interview with an old acquaintance.

It must be understood that the fatigues and sufferings of that terrible pilgrimage through the desert had bothered the constitution of little Sweeny, and that, after lying in garrison hospital at San Francisco for several months, he had been discharged from the service on "certificate of physical disability." Thurstane, who had kept track of him, immediately took him to his house, first as an invalid hanger-on, and then as a jack of all work.

As the family were sitting at breakfast Sweeny's voice was heard in the veranda outside, "colloguing" with another voice which seemed familiar.

"Listen," whispered Clara. "That is Captain Glover. Let us hear what they say. They are both so queer!"

"An' what" ("fwat" he pronounced it) "the divil have ye been up to?" demanded Sweeny. "Ye're a purty sailor, buttoned up in a long-tail coat, wid a white hankerchy round yer neck. Have ye been foolin' paple wid makin' 'em think ye're a Protestant praste?"

"I've been blowin' glass, Sweeny," replied the sniffling voice of Phineas Glover.

"Blowin' glass! Och, yees was always powerful at blowin'. But I niver heerd ye blow glass. It was big lies mostly whin I was a listing."

"Yes, blowin' glass," returned the Fair Havener in a tone of agreeable reminiscence, as if it had been a not unprofitable occupation. "Found there wasn't a glass-blower in all Californy. Bought 'n old machine, put up to the mines with it, blew all sorts 'f jigmarigs 'n' thingumbobs, 'n' sold 'em to the miners 'n' Injuns. Them critters is jest like sailors ashore; they'll buy anything they set eyes on. Besides, I sounded my horn; advertised big, so to speak; got up a sensation. Used to mount a stump 'n' make a speech; told 'em I'd blow Yankee Doodle in glass, any color they wanted; give 'em that sort 'f gospel, ye know."

"An' could ye do it?" inquired the Paddy, confounded by the idea of blowing a glass tune.

"Lord, Sweeny! you're greener 'n the miners. When ye swaller things that way, don't laugh 'r ye'll choke yerself to death, like the elephant did when he read the comic almanac at breakfast."

"I don't belave that nuther," asseverated Sweeny, anxious to clear himself from the charge of credulity.

"Don't believe that!" exclaimed Glover. "He did it twice."

"Och, go way wid ye. He couldn't choke himself afther he was dead. I wouldn't belave it, not if I see him turn black in the face. It's yerself 'll get choked some day if yees don't quit blatherin'. But what did ye get for yer blowin'? Any more 'n the clothes ye're got to yer back?"

For answer Glover dipped into his pockets, took out two handfuls of gold pieces and chinked them under the Irishman's nose.

"Blazes! ye're lousy wid money," commented Sweeny. "Ye want somebody to scratch yees."

"Twenty thousan' dollars in bank," added Glover. "All by blowin' 'n' tradin'. Goin' hum in the next steamer. Anythin' I can do for ye, old messmate? Say how much."

"It's the liftinant is takin' care av me. He's made a betther livin' nor yees, a thousand times over, by jist marryin' the right leddy. An' he's going to put me in charrge av a farrum that they call the hayshindy, where I'll sell the cattle for myself, wid half to him, an' make slathers o' money."

"Thunder, Sweeny! You'll end by ridin' in a coach. What'll ye take for yer chances? Wal, I'm glad to hear ye're doin' so well. I am so, for old times' sake."

"Come in, Captain Glover," at this moment called Clara through the blinds. "Come in, Sweeny. Let us all have a talk together about the old times and the new ones."

So there was a long talk, miscellaneous and delightful, full of reminiscences and congratulations and good wishes.

"Wal, we're a lucky lot," said Glover at last. "Sh'd like to hear 'f some good news for the sergeant and Mr. Kelly. Sh'd go back hum easier for it."

"Kelly is first sergeant," stated Thurstane, "and Meyer is quartermaster-sergeant, with a good chance of being quartermaster. He is capable of it and deserves it. He ought to have been promoted years ago for his gallantry and services during the war. I hope every day to hear that he has got his commission as lieutenant."

"Wal, God bless 'em, 'n' God bless the hull army!" said Glover, so gratified that he felt pious. "An' now, good-by. Got to be movin'."

"Stay over night with us," urged Thurstane. "Stay a week. Stay as long as you will."

"Do," begged Clara. "You can go geologizing with my husband. You can start Sweeny on his farm."

"Och, he's a thousin' times welkim," put in Sweeny, "though I'm afeard av him. He'd tache the cattle to trade their skins wid ache other, an slather me wid lies till I wouldn't know which was the baste an' which was Sweeny."

Glover grinned with an air of being flattered, but replied, "Like to stay first rate, but can't work it. Passage engaged for to-morrow mornin'."

"Indeed!" exclaimed Aunt Maria, agreeably surprised by an idea.

And the result was that she went to New York under the care of Captain Glover.

As for Clara and Thurstane, they are surely in a state which ought to satisfy their friends, and we will therefore say no more of them.

THE END.

www.ingramcontent.com/pod-product-compliance
Lightning Source LLC
LaVergne TN
LVHW010742120826
845150LV00009B/1407

* 9 7 8 1 4 2 5 5 1 7 7 5 5 *